Historical Problems:
Studies and Documents

Edited by

PROFESSOR G. R. ELTON
University of Cambridge

12

THE AGE OF LLOYD GEORGE

THE AGE OF
LLOYD GEORGE

Kenneth O. Morgan

Fellow of The Queen's College, Oxford
Author *David Lloyd George, Wales in British Politics,*
Keir Hardie, etc.

LONDON: GEORGE ALLEN AND UNWIN LTD
NEW YORK: BARNES AND NOBLE INC

ISBN 0 04 942092 5   CASED
     0 04 942093 3   PAPER

First published in the United States, 1971
by Barnes and Noble, Inc.

Printed in Great Britain
in 10 on 11 point Plantin type
by The Aldine Press, Letchworth

GENERAL INTRODUCTION

The reader and the teacher of history might be forgiven for thinking that there are now too many series of historical documents in existence, all claiming to offer light on particular problems and all able to fulfil their claims. At any rate, the general editor of yet another series feels obliged to explain why he is helping one more collection of such volumes into existence.

One purpose of this series is to put at the disposal of the student original materials illustrating historical problems, but this is no longer anything out of the way. A little less usual is the decision to admit every sort of historical question: there are no barriers of time or place or theme. However, what really distinguishes this enterprise is the fact that it combines generous collections of documents with introductory essays long enough to explore the theme widely and deeply. In the doctrine of educationalists, it is the original documents that should be given to the student; in the experience of teachers, documents thrown naked before the untrained mind turn from pearls to paste. The study of history cannot be confined either to the learning up of results without a consideration of the foundations, or to a review of those foundations without the assistance of the expert mind. The task of teaching involves explanation and instruction, and these volumes recognize this possibly unfashionable fact. Beyond that, they enable the writers to say new and important things about their subject matter: to write history of an exploratory kind, which is the only important historical writing there is.

As a result, each volume will be a historical monograph worth the attention which all such monographs deserve, and each volume will stand on its own. While the format of the series is uniform, the contents will vary according to need. Some problems require the reconsideration which makes the known enlighteningly new; others need the attention of original research; yet others will have to enter controversy because the prevailing notions on many historical questions are demonstrably wrong. The authors of this series are free to treat their subject in whatever manner it seems to them to require. They will present some of their evidence for inspection and help the learner to see how history is written, but they will themselves also write history.

G.R.E.

ACKNOWLEDGEMENTS

The following people and institutions have very kindly granted me permission to quote from documents of which they hold the copyright: Mr A. J. P. Taylor and the First Beaverbrook Foundation (Bonar Law's and J. C. C. Davidson's correspondence; David Lloyd George, *War Memoirs*; *Land and the Nation*; *We Can Conquer Unemployment*; Lloyd George's memorandum in *Life and Letters of Austen Chamberlain*); Mr Mark Bonham-Carter (Asquith's correspondence; Roy Jenkins, *Asquith*; letters by Asquith in Lloyd George, *War Memoirs*); Mrs Mary Bennett (H. A. L. Fisher's correspondence); 5th Marquess of Salisbury (4th Marquess of Salisbury's correspondence); Fladgate & Co (Winston Churchill's correspondence); Lord Kennet (Hilton Young's correspondence); Viscount Addison (Christopher Addison: *Four and a Half Years, 1914–1919*, Hutchinson & Co); Asia Publishing House (Edwin Montagu's correspondence); Constable & Co (F. A. Channing, *Memories of Midland Politics, 1885–1910*); Curtis Brown Ltd (R. J. Campbell, *The New Theology*); Victor Gollancz Ltd (Lord Riddell, *Intimate Diary of the Peace Conference and After, 1918–1923*); London School of Economics (Beatrice Webb, *Our Partnership*); William Heinemann Ltd (Randolph Churchill, *Lord Derby, King of Lancashire*); Macmillan & Co (J. M. Keynes, *Economic Consequences of the Peace*); Oxford University Press (Thomas Jones, *Whitehall Diary*); Stanley Paul & Co Ltd (H. A. Taylor, *Robert Donald*).

PREFACE

This volume is an inquiry into a crucial phase of British party politics. It is not conceived as an addition to the large and growing number of biographical studies of David Lloyd George. Rather it aims to use Lloyd George's career as a means of tracing the revival, triumph, division and decline of his own Liberal Party, in which he himself was the decisive agent for change. It spans the period from 1890, when Lloyd George entered Parliament and when the Liberals were in the early processes of reorganization and recovery, down to the 1929 general election, when Lloyd George's last crusade failed and when the Liberals were shown to be no longer serious challengers for political power.

I am very grateful to The Queen's College for financial and secretarial assistance which has enabled me to complete the research for this book. I am also indebted to Professor G. R. Elton, the editor of this series, for some valuable criticism of my manuscript, to Dr Cameron Hazlehurst for purging the proofs of several errors, and to my father for preparing the Index. And I cannot conclude without mentioning the gratitude felt by all students of Lloyd George's career for the helpfulness of Mr A. J. P. Taylor, Miss Rosemary Brooks and all the staff at the Beaverbrook Library in making so freely available the incomparable archives housed there, and in making research there such an agreeable experience.

The Queen's College, Oxford   K.O.M.
December 1970

CONTENTS

CONTENTS

CONTENTS

PART 1: THE AGE OF LLOYD GEORGE

Introduction:
The Old Liberalism and the New

THE election of a youthful Welsh solicitor, David Lloyd George, as Member of Parliament for the Caernarvon Boroughs in April 1890 attracted scant interest from observers of the political scene. The by-election, it is true, marked a Liberal gain, the seat being wrested from the Conservatives by the narrow margin of eighteen votes. But Liberal successes had been common enough during the past three years as the 'flowing tide' of popular support surged steadily towards the Gladstonians. Their allies, the Irish nationalists, were gaining a new respectability, especially after the triumphant vindication of their leader, Parnell, in a recent libel action against *The Times* newspaper. This latest electoral victory in a remote Welsh constituency, inevitably a difficult terrain for any Conservative to defend, seemed to provide merely further confirmation of a well-established political trend. Even in Wales itself, where Lloyd George's triumph to Westminster naturally aroused much keener interest, there were many, even in the Liberal camp, who questioned its significance. Lloyd George was dismissed by one Welsh critic as 'a second-rate county attorney'; another thought him 'irreconcilable and unpractical'.[1] Even many of his admirers, mindful of his tiny majority, aware of demands imposed upon him during the election campaign that he should declare his independence of the Liberal whips if the party did not immediately sponsor Welsh disestablishment, feared for his future. Caernarvon Boroughs, in fact, was never a safe Liberal seat. Bangor, with a powerful Anglican interest associated with the cathedral, maintained a solid Conservative vote, while the political allegiance of Caernarvon and Conway was unpredictable. Only the three smallest components of the

---

[1] A. C. Humphreys-Owen to Stuart Rendel, 19 August 1888 (N[ational] L[ibrary of] W[ales], Rendel Papers XIV, 496); J. Arthur Price to J. E. Lloyd, 14 October 1892 (Bangor Univ. Library, Lloyd Papers, MS, 314, 449).

constituency, Criccieth, Pwllheli and Nevin, were considered to be safe for Liberalism. During the next two years, the Conservatives, reinforced by a powerful new candidate ('hypocrite and fraud' in Lloyd George's view)[2] were widely expected to regain the seat.

Yet, in reality, this by-election in an obscure Welsh constituency was to inaugurate a new era in British politics. The little-known Welsh attorney was to retain his seat for thirteen further elections and to sit continuously in the House of Commons for over half a century, during which the fortunes of the political parties, and especially of his own Liberal Party, were to be fundamentally transformed. For the next four decades the career of David Lloyd George was to provide the major catalyst in British political life, the major agency for governmental change in peace and in war. Long before his death, the precise significance of his career aroused bitter controversy among political commentators. There were those, especially before 1914, who romanticized the progress of the 'cottage-bred boy' from 'village green to Downing Street', and who saw him as a messiah for the new democracy. But there were to be many more, across the entire political spectrum from 1916 onwards, who regarded Lloyd George more as a universal scapegoat, 'the big beast', a rogue elephant of politics who brought his own party crashing down in ruins and many of the accepted canons of political morality down with it. He has aroused more extreme and passionate reactions than any other recent politician. One conclusion, however, remains beyond dispute. It was voiced by his one-time colleague and life-long associate, Winston Churchill, in the Commons in March 1945 on the event of Lloyd George's death: that historians, surveying the first quarter of the twentieth century, would come to see how far the history of Britain, in peace and in war, had been moulded by the life of this one man. Now that new sources have become available for a study of Lloyd George's career, in particular the magnificent collection of his private papers housed in the Beaverbrook Library, Churchill's verdict can be conclusively upheld. The forty years that followed the Caernarvon Boroughs by-election in 1890 may, therefore, fairly be termed 'the age of Lloyd George'.

In 1890, the young Lloyd George surveyed the British political scene through the eyes of a foreigner. Although he was born in England, in Manchester in 1863, his upbringing and political education had taken place in Wales. He had been brought up by his uncle, Richard Lloyd, in the tiny village of Llanystumdwy in south Caernarvonshire in the 1860s and 1870s, at a period of immense social,

---

[2] David Lloyd George to his wife, 7 August 1890 (N.L.W., 20,407C, No. 121).

religious and political upheaval in rural Wales. His earliest political recollection was the dramatic triumph of the Liberal candidate, Jones-Parry, in the 'great election' of 1868 in Caernarvonshire, a humiliating defeat for the squires and their Anglican supporters who had ruled the countryside for centuries. Lloyd George also recalled how the landlords took their revenge after the 1868 election by evicting scores of tenant farmers and quarrymen who had dared to challenge the deference vote and to back the Liberal.[3] Soon the young Lloyd George was embarking on a career of radical protest against the social ascendancy of the parson and the squire over Welsh-speaking, nonconformist rural Wales. As a twelve-year-old, he led a kind of strike by his school-fellows against the masters and governors of the local Church School, which, as a Baptist resident in a so-called 'single-school area', he was compelled to attend. He was a relatively poor boy, brought up in the humble home of the village shoemaker, deeply resentful at the crust of custom and 'feudalism' that encased his world. At the same time, he always had the prospect of a middle-class career open to him. He was, in his way, a representative of that newly-emergent middle class that rose up in Welsh society in the later decades of the nineteenth century, initially in local government, and which found its urge for civic status fulfilled through Gladstone's Liberal Party. He was able to work towards a career as a solicitor, and in 1884 set up practice in the small town of Criccieth. With the immense range of contacts open to an ambitious young country attorney, this provided him with the perfect base for a political career. He first began to build a political reputation in February 1886, when he appeared before the quarrymen of Ffestiniog, on the same platform as the Irish Nationalist, Michael Davitt. It was Davitt's rural socialism that captured the young Lloyd George's imagination more than his advocacy of the Irish national cause, but even so Ireland seemed to provide a model for the radical movement in Wales. The tithe campaign in southern Caernarvonshire in 1886–7, during which nonconformist farmers rose up in protest against the payment of tithes which they could not afford to a Church which they did not attend, afforded Lloyd George further invaluable experience of the techniques of political agitation. It was at this time also that he began to explore the potentialities of the newspaper press —always a major theme throughout his career—as he established contacts with the *Genedl Gymreig* and an associated syndicate of radical journals in Caernarvon. In 1889 he was among the legatees of a social revolution in Wales, when the Local Government Act resulted in the

---

[3] Lloyd George's speech at Queen's Hall, 23 March 1910, quoted in *Better Times*, London, 1910, p. 296; cf. Kenneth O. Morgan, *Wales in British Politics, 1868–1922* (Cardiff, revised edition 1970), pp. 22–7.

election of nonconformist-dominated country councils to supplant the squires who had ruled the countryside for centuries as Justices of the Peace. At the youthful age of twenty-five, he was elected an alderman: the Conservative M.P., H. C. Raikes, fulminated that 'his election as a boy alderman was only paralleled by the medieval scandal of child cardinals'.[4] By now, Lloyd George had become a controversial and pugnacious figure in Welsh radical circles, producing belligerent declarations on behalf of Welsh disestablishment, land and temperance reform, even Welsh home rule, at sessions of the North Wales Liberal Federation. But hitherto he was unknown outside his native land. His return to Westminster added a totally new dimension to his career.

The political context in which Lloyd George was to operate over the next forty years cannot be properly understood unless it be made clear that his political assumptions were fundamentally shaped by his Welsh background. From Wales, he derived his characteristic concern with the land question and with the politics of Dissent. From Wales, also, he gained his appreciation of the popular weapons he might use, especially the power of the chapels and of the local press. At the same time, he added to these elements certain qualities all his own, a supreme volatility which not even the influence of his native Wales could restrain. Some aspects of the Welsh national movement, the campaign for higher education for instance, left Lloyd George unmoved. Even in the local politics of Wales itself, he was something of a lone figure. For he was a grass-roots politician who preferred to negotiate at the summit. He operated less through local figures residing among the foothills of power—that was the insulated world of his forgotten younger brother, William, placidly minding the family solicitors' business back home in Criccieth, and of his own wife, from whom the inexorable progress of his own career at Westminster was gradually to drive him apart. Lloyd George's instinct was rather to work through the higher echelons of authority—party potentates rather than election agents, newspaper proprietors rather than local journalists, bishops rather than parish priests. For him it was decision rather than doctrine that provided the ultimate yardstick. This gave him a flexibility of which there were striking indications even in this early phase of his career. Thus in 1895 he was apparently the spearhead of a vigorous rebellion of backbench Welsh Liberal M.P.s, protesting at the failure of his own party to make Welsh disestablishment the foremost plank in its programme. And yet, at this very time, he was secretly making an astonishing overture to the Welsh bishops, offering them a compromise over disendowment so as to secure a self-governing church

4 Speech quoted in *The Times*, 9 April 1890.

in a self-governing Wales.[5] Here was the tribune of the nonconformist chapels trying to by-pass the narrow denominationalism of the Calvinist 'clerisy', whose bigotry and snobbery often disgusted him. Mundane party objectives would be subsumed in a supreme national cause, that of independence for Wales. 'Non-contentious' issues like disestablishment and disendowment would be set aside as matters of detail. But his overtures were rejected by the Welsh bishops, and the moment of possible coalition passed, as it was to pass in British politics in the future, in 1910 and again in 1920. The would-be coalitionist again turned to severe partisanship. By temperament, however, as well as by background, Lloyd George approached British politics as an outsider and an outsider he remained.

The Liberal Party which he served in the 1890s was still undergoing a profound process of internal upheaval. Despite the recent improvement in its electoral fortunes, the traumatic effects of the crisis surrounding the schism over Irish home rule in 1885–6 were still all too visible in the structure, the organization and the morale of the party. Gladstone still remained the leader of the party in 1890, but the survival of his personal ascendancy seemed almost the one focus of unity for a party otherwise deeply torn and disillusioned. The great majority of its Whig patrons, already shaken in their allegiance during the campaign for the 1884 Reform Bill, finally left the party when it followed Gladstone in championing Irish home rule. Henceforth the leadership and largess of the old Whig gentry, a crucial element in the coalition that made up Gladstonian Liberalism, was to be lost. In the centre, Liberalism now lost much of its intellectual support amongst professional and academic opinion—men like Matthew Arnold, Dicey, Seeley, 'authoritarians' like Froude and Maine seceded from the Liberal tabernacle. Most serious of all, the Irish crisis also cost the Liberals their most dynamic radical element, Joseph Chamberlain, along with many of his nonconformist followers in the West Midlands. From 1886, the severance between Gladstone and Chamberlain was complete, as the tragi-comedy of the 'Round Table' conferences of 1886–7 inevitably confirmed.[6] Certainly, the bulk of radical Liberals remained faithful to Gladstone. The National Liberal Federation swung to his support in 1886, for all its Birmingham antecedents, while even in the Midlands Chamberlain's authority as a 'Liberal Unionist' was for some years under severe challenge. But the loss of Chamberlain,

[5] See Eluned E. Owen, *The Early Life of Bishop Owen* (Llandyssul, 1958), pp. 179–81.
[6] See Michael Hurst, *Joseph Chamberlain and Liberal Reunion* (London, 1967).

together with the departure of most of the remaining Whigs, severely shook the 'broad Church' that had been Gladstone's Liberal Party, and narrowed the political base of Gladstone himself. The years that followed saw the younger leaders of the party—Harcourt, Morley and Rosebery prominent among them—engaged in a desperate attempt to remould their party anew, to create a new Liberal coalition that would be truly national rather than sectional in its composition. Their efforts, their successes and failures provided much of the framework for the history of British party politics in its crucial *fin de siècle* phase.

The assembly of the National Liberal Federation at Newcastle in October 1891 (Doc. 1) illustrated very clearly the different approaches adopted towards Liberal revival at this time. On the one hand, the party was now irreversibly pledged to the supreme cause of Irish home rule. John Morley, indeed, welcomed the predominance of the Irish issue as it would provide one great theme, one transcendent moral cause that would unify the various disparate elements within the party. On the other hand, the split of 1886 had released in the party a vast array of sectional or, in the terminology of the time, 'faddist' groups, all of which fought for their place in the sun. Most of them had been active, and were endorsed by successive National Liberal Federation conferences, since 1887, but the 'Newcastle programme' of 1891 gave them all a new status. Conspicuous among these 'faddists' were the land reformers, a motley array ranging from apostles of peasant proprietorship like Francis Channing in the East Midlands to outright land nationalizers like Dr G. B. Clark in the Scottish highlands. Their demands ranged from modest reforms like the repeal of the laws of entail and primogeniture, through 'free trade' in land, to radical programmes like the taxing of ground rents and of the site-value of rural and urban land. The cry for land reform owed much to the agrarian radicalism sparked off by the crusades of the American Henry George in the early 1880s. The prolonged agricultural depression of that decade lent it added momentum. At the same time, more traditional demands for fair rents and fair compensation for evicted tenants, inspired by the land warfare in Ireland and given a national impetus by radicals in Wales and Scotland, added to the pressure for 'free land' at Newcastle. Another 'faddist' group powerful at the conference was that of political Dissent. The chapels were increasingly dominant in local Liberal Associations, especially since the schism of 1886, the loss of Chamberlain notwithstanding. Pressure at Newcastle for the disestablishment of the state churches in Wales and in Scotland were impressive testimony to the political power of the chapels, as also was the cry for temperance reform, preferably through a local veto upon licences and the steady contraction of the liquor traffic.

A totally different strain was contributed by the London 'progressives', notably the Metropolitan Radical Federation which had won such striking triumphs in the London County Council elections in 1889. Its advocates, with their working-class backing, now tried to supply the 'urban cow' that the Liberals had lacked in 1885. They demanded, in effect, a sweeping programme of municipal socialism and municipal home rule, including the ownership of public utilities such as tramways and water and gas supplies. The taxing of ground values and housing legislation were also inserted into the Newcastle programme by the London radicals. Indeed, the achievements of Liberal local authorities in London, Birmingham, Glasgow and elsewhere were to lead to American civic reformers seeing in the British cities (along with the German) the one true 'hope for Democracy'.[7] Other issues also figured on the new Liberal platform, including the 'mending or ending' of the House of Lords (Liberals disputed over which alternative they preferred), and the democratic reform of the franchise, generally summarized as 'one man, one vote'. Finally, a new spectre arose to haunt the delegates at Newcastle—the spectre of organized labour, recently galvanized by the 'new unionism' among the dockers and other skilled and unskilled workers. The adoption at Newcastle of an eight-hour day for miners, a proposal bitterly contested by Liberal coal-owners like D. A. Thomas in South Wales, was testimony to the way in which the split of 1886 had helped to give the voice of Labour a new importance within the Liberal Party. At the same time, the failure of the Newcastle conference to adopt the eight hours principle more generally was an omen of the tension now looming between middle-class and working-class Liberals.

This Newcastle Programme committed the Liberals to a vast range of reforms. Chamberlain derided it as a 'political conglomerate' while Balfour, preferring a theatrical metaphor, dubbed it 'a programme of varieties'. Certainly, it was hard to see how the traditional individualism of the free churchmen and the free traders could be properly reconciled with the collectivism of the London radicals and their Fabian allies. In time, Liberal leaders like Lord Rosebery were to complain that their party was hopelessly hamstrung by a huge list of measures, most of which challenged head-on some powerful vested interest, instead of being unified by some great national theme like imperialism or Ireland.[8] If anything held together this varied programme (of which the young Lloyd George was a belligerent advocate), it was the principle of

[7] Cf. Frederick Howe, *The City: the Hope of Democracy* (New York, 1905); *The British City* (New York, 1907).
[8] Earl of Rosebery, *The Pressing Question for the Liberal Party* (London, 1895).

democracy, the age-old Liberal assault on monopoly and privilege in a new and more sophisticated guise. But this Liberal creed was capable of interminable variations among different sections of the electorate. Welsh disestablishment or temperance reform were of scant interest in London's East End, or municipal tramways in East Anglia, or registration reform in the Scottish highlands. The term 'Liberal' had now become a vast umbrella which sheltered most of the active and assertive protest movements in late Victorian Britain, a coalition of pressure groups held together only loosely within the framework of the National Liberal Federation, and by Gladstone's waning leadership.

In any event, the fate of the Newcastle Programme depended upon the inclinations of Gladstone himself. And his speech to the Newcastle delegates (Doc. 2) shows that, whatever the radical enthusiasms surging throughout Liberal Associations, Gladstone's own Liberal faith remained relatively unmoved by them. In order to keep his party 'firm for Irish Home Rule', he made indefinite pronouncements on behalf of temperance reform, church disestablishment, registration reform and free education. But he gave few indications as to their priority, if any, in the legislative programme of any future Liberal government. He totally ignored any proposal tainted by collectivism, except for a vague pledge to introduce free allotments for rural labourers. He was willing to provide a few modest offerings for Labour—registration reform, parish councils and the full panoply of 'peasant democracy' in local government. But on the role of the state in intervening between capital and labour, notably on the eight-hour issue, he offered only a few depressing generalities. His followers acquiesced, and much of the next fifteen years were to be spent by Liberals in the search for a 'social programme' which could somehow be reconciled with the grand old causes of retrenchment and reform.

For Gladstone at Newcastle, the Liberal Party essentially stood for one overpowering moral cause—the national liberation of Ireland. He claimed that Ireland 'blocked the way' to reform in other fields; but critics like Chamberlain correctly asserted that Gladstone actually welcomed this obstruction that kept his party from unwelcome ventures along the collectivist path. In fact, Gladstone's attempt to identify Liberalism with the Irish question alone soon foundered. The general election in July 1892 gave the Liberals a disappointing majority of only forty, and that wholly dependent upon the Irish vote. The presence of 'Labour' candidates in several seats—to the particular embarrassment of John Morley at Newcastle—and the return of Keir Hardie and John Burns in London constituencies, foretold that Gladstone no longer had complete control over his own party. The session of 1893 was largely taken up by the ritual passage of the second Irish Home Rule Bill and its inevitable rejection by the Lords. Gladstone failed to persuade the Cabinet to go to the country on the issue and, as a result, retired from the leadership in March 1894. After a fierce internecine conflict, Rosebery triumphed over Harcourt and became Prime Minister. Far more crucial was that, apart from Morley, now an isolated and embittered figure, none of the leading Liberals henceforth had a prime commitment to Irish home rule. With Gladstone's departure, Liberalism ceased to revolve around the dominant theme of Ireland. 'Faddism' was now in the ascendant.

For some years to come, after the disastrous general election of 1895 which saw the Unionists returned by a majority of 152, the Liberals lurched along, desperately striving to impose some kind of discipline upon the warring pressure groups that made up their ranks. The party seemed at times so hopelessly torn that it scarcely presented a serious challenge to the Unionists at all. The fierce personal warfare between Rosebery and Harcourt continued until Rosebery's unexpected resignation as party leader in October 1896. The succession of Harcourt, however, hardly served to restore harmony, and in 1899 he gave way to an obscure *tertium quid*, Sir Henry Campbell-Bannerman, an elderly Scotsman whose alleged mishandling of the 'cordite affair' had helped to bring his own government down in June 1895. Successive conferences of the National Liberal Federation provided a commentary upon the Newcastle programme in emphasizing the multiplicity of interests that now composed the Liberal Party. In Chamberlain's uncomfortably accurate phrase, they were 'politicians in search of a cry'.

Many historians have taken a pessimistic view of the state of the Liberal Party in the 1890s, seeing it rent by irreconcilable divisions within the leadership and at the grass roots. Paul Thompson's excellent study of London politics suggests that in urban areas Liberals, still largely wedded to the employing middle class and the chapel vote, were quite unable to develop a new approach that could win over working-class voters.[9] Since the Liberals were in any case on the defensive in rural areas, at least in England, some writers have seen the Liberals in this period as a fundamentally doomed party, and the 'strange death' of Liberal England (if not Wales or Scotland) as dating from this time. However, a close study of Liberal strength in the constituencies suggests a modified picture. The different elements that made up 'faddism' could be a source of strength as well as of weakness, by releasing new elements, hitherto politically dormant.

[9] Paul Thompson, *Socialists, Liberals and Labour: the Struggle for London, 1885-1914* (London, 1967).

The campaign for land reform, for instance, brought the Liberals new strength in the East Midlands, the West of England and East Anglia. Mrs Janet Howarth has shown how the organizational base of the Liberals was re-formed in Northamptonshire between 1880 and 1895.[10] A determined radical like Francis Channing could weld into unity both tenant farmers, anxious for secure tenancies and free allotments, and urban workers concerned with employment and housing, without losing any of the Liberals' traditional nonconformist, professional and commercial support. In the East Midlands, the Liberals were a growing, not a declining, party in the early 1890s. In Wales and Scotland, the Liberals again found strength hitherto untapped, and were able to link the Celtic national cause to the Liberal call for civic and religious liberty.[11] National freedom and religious freedom became identified. In Wales, the only moment of real danger for the Liberals arose in 1895 over the *Cymru Fydd* crisis (Doc. 3) when the young Lloyd George argued that only in a Welsh parliament could the national aspirations of Wales be satisfied. But, at a fateful meeting of the South Wales Liberals at Newport in January 1896, Lloyd George lost control of his own movement; the relentless hostility of the mercantile Liberals of Cardiff, Newport and Swansea ended for ever his dream of merging Liberalism in a national crusade for Welsh home rule. But there were causes far more profound than simply the divisions of north and south Wales for the failure of *Cymru Fydd*. Most Welsh Liberals agreed with Jenkyn Thomas that progress towards Welsh demands such as disestablishment were possible only through the national Liberal party. The achievements of Gladstone's government of 1892–4 —a Welsh disestablishment bill, a Welsh land commission and a federal university of Wales—were proof enough of that. Why, then, should Welsh Liberals opt for the impotence of isolation? Lloyd George, for once, had to give way, and the attachment to Liberalism of Wales, and to a lesser extent of Scotland, stood secure.

However, other aspects of the 'Old Liberalism' were less obviously suited to winning over the mass democracy. Conspicuous among these was the cause of temperance, advocated with indefatigable zeal by the veteran Sir Wilfrid Lawson. A body like the United Kingdom

---

[10] Janet Howarth, 'The Liberal Revival in the East Midlands, 1880–1895', *Historical Journal*, XII, I (1969), 78–118. For other local studies of the Liberal Party at this period see Kenneth O. Morgan, 'Cardiganshire Politics: the Liberal Ascendancy, 1885–1923', *Ceredigion* (1967), pp. 1 ff.; and Peter Clarke, *Lancashire and the New Liberalism* (London, 1971).

[11] Kenneth O. Morgan, *Wales in British Politics*, Chaps. III–V; and James G. Kellas, 'The Liberal Party in Scotland, 1876–95', *Scottish Historical Review* (April 1965), pp. 1–16; and 'The Liberal Party and the Scottish Church Disestablishment Crisis', *English Historical Review*, LXXIX (January 1964), 31–46.

Alliance, which championed the direct veto upon liquor licences, represented a reversion to the sectional pressures of the days of the Anti-Corn Law League in the 1840s rather than a movement suited for the age of mass parties, while its immoderate call for prohibition alienated many working-class voters. Similarly, many of the demands voiced by nonconformists, especially their attack on Church schools, aroused the anger of Liberal churchmen without striking any noticeable chord among the working class. As a result, to critics like Sidney and Beatrice Webb, the Liberal Party in the later 1890s seemed enervated and empty (Doc. 4). In 1891 it had stood at the 'parting of the ways' between its old economic and civic individualism, and a new systematic creed of social progress. But, six years later, there had been no advance. The party's paralysis of will seemed to them exemplified by the pessimistic negatives of John Morley, once the close ally of the London Fabians, but now sunk in nerveless contemplation of an alien world, mindlessly repeating the old shibboleths of disestablishment and free market economics at home, non-intervention and non-expansion overseas, without attempting to shape the political society into which he had been unwillingly propelled. Of course, Morley's pessimism was to some extent peculiar to his own strange temperament, more suitable in many ways to the literary world of London clubland than to party politics. He was soon to retire from the fray to write his biography of Gladstone. Again, the Webbs' analysis ignored many factors—the way in which by-elections in 1896-7 had again turned the Liberals' way, the mass support that the party still enjoyed in mining and textile areas, and the party's ability still to seize the political initiative, as shown by its effective campaigns against the government's Education and Agricultural Rating Bills in 1896. But the Webbs correctly sensed that the Liberals were in danger of becoming a party of negation, united in rallying against great vested interests like the Church, the brewers or the squirearchy, but inert when the moment came for positive advance.

These divisions crippling the party were intensified by the impact of imperialism. Throughout the 1890s, the imperial theme plagued the Liberal Party; at the turn of the century it threatened finally to destroy it. After all, imperialism had originally been an experience that took place within the Liberal Party. The main theorists and practitioners of imperialism, Dilke and Seeley, Chamberlain and Rosebery, Cromer and Rhodes, had grown up within the Liberal tabernacle, and the early advocates of imperial federation in the 1880s had nearly all been Liberals. The Liberal ministries of 1892-5 had been tortured by divisions over imperial policy, especially over Uganda where the expansionists, Rosebery, Asquith and Grey, were in repeated conflict with the Gladstonian wing, headed by Harcourt and Morley, and, of course, the venerable Prime Minister himself. Over South Africa, however, the Liberal divisions were at their most acute. Rosebery's aggressive policy as Foreign Secretary there in 1892–3 of 'pegging out claims for posterity', by lending support to Rhodes's expansionism in southern Africa, led to frequent governmental crises; this internal conflict was heightened by the years of opposition that followed after 1895. No coherent Liberal attitude at all emerged during the inquiry into the Jameson raid in 1896–7, although the effect was to polarize the divisions within the party between 'Lib. Imp.' and 'Little Englander' factions. All this reduced social critics like the Webbs to near despair. In their view a 'forward' foreign policy was the obverse of a constructive social policy at home. Conversely, little Englandism and *laissez-faire* were two sides of the same coin, as Morley's negative outlook showed. Imperialists like Rosebery or Haldane, however, were prepared to associate imperial expansion abroad with new and imaginative roles for the state at home, just like the American Progressives, most of whom were imperialists also. The Webbs, however, vastly underestimated the extent to which 'Little England' Liberals could also become apostles of state intervention.

The South African War in 1899 brought these internal party divisions to a disastrous climax. While the Unionists were almost at one in their approach to the war, apart from a rare eccentric like Leonard Courtney, and easily retained their majority at the 'khaki' election in 1900, the Liberals were rent into three factions. The feeblest of the three at Westminster, the 'Little Englander' or 'pro-Boer' opponents of the war, were the most powerful in the National Liberal Federation. Lloyd George himself belonged to this section; an ardent supporter of the British position at Fashoda in 1898, an advocate of the annexation of the Boer republics in 1899, he was neither at this nor any other time an anti-imperialist on principle. However, as a mordant critic of 'Chamberlainism', who denounced the way in which the war was being fought and the classes who were making money out of it during its course, he was now carving out a national reputation for himself for the first time. At the other extreme were the Liberal Imperialists, headed by Rosebery, Asquith and Grey, who in 1902 were to form the Liberal League to promote the cause of imperial unity. In between, the moderate majority of the party observed an embarrassed neutrality under Campbell-Bannerman, their nominal leader. These divisions in the party were highlighted by a vote in the Commons on 25 July 1900 in which the party voted three ways simultaneously. At the 'khaki' election in October, the popular mood seemed overwhelmingly 'jingo' and the advocates of a negotiated peace found the going hard. Lloyd

George barely clung on to his seat at Caernarvon. However, the last eighteen months of the war saw a distinct change, and the revival of the Liberal Party in the country can be dated from this period. This was the period of prolonged 'guerrilla' warfare during which the British administration incurred international odium by maintaining concentration camps on the Rand, with appalling loss of life amongst Boer women and children. During this last period, the Liberal centre moved steadily towards the 'pro-Boer' position, concentrating less on the objectives of the war than on the methods by which it was being fought. A decisive episode was a speech by Campbell-Bannerman, hitherto a fairly anonymous figure, to the National Reform Union in June 1901 (Doc. 5). During this speech he coined the memorable phrase, 'methods of barbarism', to describe the British concentration camps on the Rand. It was the first clear indication of 'C.–B.''s growing security in his leadership, and of the political and moral recovery of his party.

From this time onwards, the committed imperialists in the Liberal Party were distinctly losing ground. Within two years, all the party's regional federations were to be won over by non-imperialists. For the first time since Gladstone's retirement, the party seemed to present a united front on foreign and imperial policy. More and more of the younger Liberals felt that imperial expansion, especially at such financial and human cost, was holding back reform at home, instead of helping to promote it as the 'Lib. Imps.' claimed. This argument was powerfully advocated in J. A. Hobson's *Imperialism: a Study* (Doc. 7), published in 1902 after a visit by the author to the Rand during the South African War. Hobson was an open admirer of the isolationism of Cobden, whose biography he later wrote. His main thesis was to provide a fundamental critique of imperialism as the inevitable result of underconsumption at home, and the consequent need for the export of capital overseas.[12] But he also underlined the political consequences. He argued that Liberals in Britain, as elsewhere in western Europe, were being prevented from turning from the assault on political privilege to the more fundamental battle with social and economic privilege, as a result of their association with the imperial cause. By sacrificing social reform for the phantasm of imperial grandeur, Liberals were reinforcing the very vested interests, old and new, that they existed to demolish. Hobson's assaults were compromised by his somewhat crude version of a conspiracy theory, reminiscent of the American Populists, in which international financiers,

[12] For a good discussion of Hobson's views, see Bernard Porter, *Critics of Empire* (London, 1968), pp. 207 ff.

often of Jewish origin, were seen as pursuing a vast manipulation of society for corrupt ends. Even so, Hobson's influence was immense, especially among younger radicals. He helped to annex anti-imperialism for the collectivist cause, and to seize the moral initiative from the imperialists. The union of the Old Liberalism and the New was becoming possible.

In the face of this growing anti-imperialism in his own party, an imperial prophet like Rosebery, whom most Liberals had continued to regard as their real leader, was becoming a more and more isolated figure. Campbell-Bannerman's strictures on the 'methods of barbarism' in South Africa angered him deeply. But he had little enough now to offer instead. In a notable speech at Chesterfield in December 1901 (Doc. 6), Rosebery called for a 'clean slate', from which the more contentious items of the Newcastle programme would be erased, and on which new and contemporary principles would be inscribed. Lloyd George welcomed the speech for pointing the way to peace terms that all Liberals could accept.[13] But the positive proposals on Rosebery's 'slate' seemed to include little enough apart from the message of empire, now made tawdry and obscene by the horrors of Kitchener's concentration camps. His cry for 'efficiency', a '*réchauffé* of Sidney Webb', as Campbell-Bannerman wryly observed, was an appeal for administrative improvement, not for social reform. By the latter stages of the war, in fact, the Webbs were disillusioned with their imperialist protégés (Doc. 9). Elitists like Haldane, Asquith or Grey had little sympathy with the new social reformers of the Hobson stamp, and it was the 'anti' coalition now being rebuilt by Campbell-Bannerman that had both mass appeal and radical passion.

The conclusion of the South African War in May 1902 ended the most painful phase of Liberal disunity. In the 'war to the knife and fork' also, between imperialist and anti-imperialist at Liberal dinners, 'methods of barbarism' were being put aside and the flag of truce was waved. Even so, the party remained in a shattered condition, ill-prepared either to challenge the Unionists at Westminster or to ward off the threat from labour in working-class constituencies. It was, indeed, by rallying their traditional sources of strength, that the Liberals again made themselves credible challengers for power. Now indeed the men of Newcastle came into their own. The first instance of this came with the revolt that surged up against Balfour's Education Act of 1902. This remarkable measure, which placed all elementary and secondary education, Church and 'provided' schools alike, under

[13] D. Lloyd George, 'Lord Rosebery and Peace', *New Liberal Review* (January 1902), pp. 767-74.

the control of the county councils, did indeed appeal to a detached Hegelian like Haldane. Even Lloyd George's immediate reaction on 24 March was surprisingly favourable. But the great mass of rank-and-file Liberals were roused by the threat to non-sectarian instruction and by the destruction of their own Board schools. Above all, the chapels, the spearhead of Liberal organization in the constituencies, were given new life and unity after years of flagging energies and uncertainty. Lloyd George, hitherto best-known as a violent critic of 'Chamberlainism', now gave the nonconformist conscience its most forceful expression (Doc. 8). Himself a product of a Church school in Llanystumdwy, he appealed against the injustice of the 'single-school areas'. He drew the stark contrast between Dissenters who maintained their own churches through their own financial efforts, and the Anglican schools, with their ducal acolytes, which asked the state to subsidize their own system of privileged proselytizing. The actual response of the Liberals showed some uncertainty of direction. In England the nonconformist protest, a lively force in some subsequent by-elections, finally petered out amid a mass of individual gestures of 'passive resistance'. In Wales, by contrast, Lloyd George was able to mobilize the county councils, nearly all of which were under Liberal control, to declare their own terms for administration of the act. In the 1904 county council elections in Wales, the Liberals swept the board. It was a more constructive policy than the nihilism of passive resistance and brought Lloyd George unexpected support from Liberal Imperialists like Rosebery and Grey. As time went on, the illusory nature of the revival of nonconformity throughout the land was to be harshly revealed. Their crisis of membership and of morale lingered on. But, in the short term, it was beyond dispute that the protest against Balfour's Act revitalized the Liberals and the chapels that gave them life.

Their opponents went on to challenge a Liberal tenet even more sacred than the defence of the Board schools. This came in Joseph Chamberlain's declaration in favour of the need for tariff reform at Birmingham in May 1903 (Doc. 9). Chamberlain returned from the veld impatient with the inertia into which his Unionist colleagues had lapsed.[14] He now called for a re-direction of British commerce, to respond to foreign tariffs and competition by granting imperial preference to the white dominions (the role of India being much less clearly defined). Equally, his speech made it clear that his objectives were far wider than merely economic. He was concerned with imperial defence, with securing Britain against the dangers of world isolation, and with

[14] Julian Amery, *The Life of Joseph Chamberlain*, Vol. V (London, 1969), pp. 133 ff.

giving Britain a wider vision of world involvement instead of the parochial politics of the domestic arena. Historians in the past few years have adopted an indulgent view towards many of Chamberlain's arguments. Fundamentally, however, his Birmingham speech was an economic illusion and a political disaster. His interpretation of world trade ignored the way in which the dominions were far more anxious to build up their own industries and agriculture than to grant commercial or other preferences to the mother country. Canada, Australia and New Zealand had their own nationalisms now. Politically, the effect was appalling. By the end of September, Chamberlain had left the Cabinet as had the free traders, Ritchie, Hamilton and Balfour of Burleigh. The Duke of Devonshire followed on 6 October. In Lancashire, Unionist 'Free Fooders' were vehemently upholding the grand old Cobdenite cause, while the Prime Minister, Balfour, argued himself into a more and more equivocal position. Even in 1923, after all the economic transformations of the war, a commitment to protection and to 'food taxes' was damaging to the Conservative cause; in 1903, after fifty years of complete free trade, it was fatal.

The defence of free trade, allied to the defence of the free churches, completed the reunion of the Liberal ranks. It brought the Liberal imperialists firmly back into the fold, an effect which the Education 'revolt' had been unable to achieve. In particular, Asquith emerged as the most formidable champion of Gladstonian economics. All over the country, the Liberal party was restored and re-formed. Herbert Gladstone, as Chief Whip, notably tightened up the central party organization. Even in London, where the Liberals had clung on to a mere eight seats in the 1900 'khaki' election, the tide seemed to be flowing strongly in favour of Liberalism once again.

It was, therefore, the Old Liberalism which helped to repair the fortunes of the party—nonconformity and industrial free trade, the very essence of the Liberal faith for half a century. Where, however, was the 'New Liberalism' which could embrace a more positive attitude towards the central government, for which many Liberal ideologues since the time of T. H. Green in 1880 had called? Throughout the 1890s, small groups of intellectual radicals attempted to formulate a revised Liberal creed. Notable among them was the Rainbow Circle, formed in 1893 by men like Hobson, Charles Trevelyan and Herbert Samuel, with the backing of Fabians like Ramsay MacDonald and Sidney Olivier. A new journal, the *Progressive Review*, first published in 1896, publicized their views, while Hobson and Hobhouse, through a combination of under-consumptionist economics and Darwinian sociology, outlined a new attitude to the concepts of community and social organization. In 1897 the radicals of the National Liberal Club captured the executive of that august body, with Labouchere as their chairman, while a meeting of 'forward' Liberal M.P.s under Sir Robert Reid attempted to sway the policy of the party at Westminster in the direction of a new 'social radicalism'. But their influence was limited and their counsels divided. In great labour disputes like the engineers' strike of 1897 and the South Wales coal stoppage in 1898, it was notable that the leading Liberals were silent. The National Liberal Federation was still dominated by the 'faddists' of Newcastle, and not until 1903 did it pass formally a motion in support of social reform. In any case, a party led by a social conservative like Campbell-Bannerman was hardly likely to advance towards any new progressive horizons.

During the years of division during the Boer War, there were many efforts to wrench the party in a new direction. Sidney Webb thought he detected one in Rosebery's renewed appeal for 'a clean slate' in 1901 (Doc. 10). Webb imagined that this heralded a distinct breach with the 'atomism' of the older Liberalism, devoted to individual enterprise rather than to corporate action by the entire community. But it was really only Rosebery's imperialism that indicated a new outlook: at home, his programme contained little that was new. The Liberal Imperialists lacked the imagination to formulate a new 'constructive' faith. Even so, it was the South African War that helped in some measure to make the 'New Liberalism' a real force in contemporary thought instead of a series of disparate initiatives by small groups like the intellectuals of the Rainbow Circle. The war had generated new concern for social problems; in particular, the poor physical condition of working-class recruits to the armed forces had provoked widespread comment. The *Speaker*, a magazine now edited by J. L. Hammond, contained a spate of wide-ranging articles by men like C. F. G. Masterman, which called for Liberals to take up causes like the insurance schemes and the labour bureaux instituted in Germany. During the years 1902–5, which saw renewed controversy over old issues like Church schools and free trade, the whole shape of the Liberal creed was undergoing a radical transformation.

Herbert Samuel's *Liberalism*, much influenced by the writings of Hobson and Hobhouse (Doc. 11), was symptomatic of the new attitude to the state generated by the South African War among many Liberals. As Samuel claimed, a positive attitude to the central government was hardly a novelty for Liberals. The ministries of 1892–5 had gone some way in the direction of state interventionism, for instance in protecting workmen in railways and in government-run factories. Samuel still imposed stern limits on how far the state might intrude: he rejected the socialist view that 'the state is to be the sole capitalist'.

But his retreat from the doctrines of Adam Smith and of Bentham was emphatic enough. Other Liberals turned to a more sweeping attack on the maldistribution of economic power that underlay the evils of society. Leo Chiozza Money's *Riches and Poverty* in 1905 (Doc. 12) concentrated on the consequences of the growing gulf between rich and poor, in which one-ninth of the population enjoyed the product of one-half of the national income. The only alternative that he could see was massive state intervention, the public ownership of major industries, and positive action to redress the social imbalance by the provision of public housing, education and social services. Elsewhere, too, Liberal voices were calling for an end to 'atomistic' Liberalism. The nonconformist churches, aware of their falling attendances in 'darkest England' in the slums of the cities, were turning to preach the gospel of 'social Christianity'. Certainly many of the young 'social Christians' had been in the van of the 'passive resistance' against the 1902 Education Act; but unlike their elder brethren, they viewed their civic disabilities as only marginal to the real crisis afflicting the church. Among the most extreme versions of their gospel was the 'new theology' of R. J. Campbell (Doc. 13), which made an immense appeal to younger Liberals and socialists. It stressed the immanence of God within human society, rather than the transcendence of God from afar, and called for the merging of Christian witness with secular campaigns for social reform. More generally, the 'social Christianity', taken up by other younger free church leaders like Silvester Horne and Rhondda Williams, lent a spiritual force to the 'New Liberalism'. It helped to emphasize the continuity between it and the older creed of which it was the heir.

In practical terms, the New Liberalism meant in particular a new relationship between Liberals and the Labour Party. The 1891 Newcastle programme had marked new concessions to the labour movement; the 1892–5 Liberal ministries had introduced measures like an Employers' Liability Bill and an Inspection of Railways Act. But the party as a whole was conspicuously slow to respond to the cause of labour. Constituency associations, usually dominated by middle-class employers and the local 'shopocracy', were notoriously hostile towards adopting labour candidates, while 'social radicalism' hardly penetrated at all into the parliamentary party of Campbell-Bannerman. Morley's defeat at Newcastle in 1895, after he had refused to endorse the principle of the eight hours' bill, showed the dangers inherent in this inflexibility. After the foundation of a new working-class party, through the formation of the Labour Representation Committee in February 1900, the need for a new harmony between Liberals and Labour became vital. Keir Hardie, who now sat in the

House as member for Merthyr Tydfil, had defeated a Liberal employer in the 1900 election. By-elections at Woolwich and Barnard Castle in 1903 again showed the perils of a conflict between Liberals and Labour at the polls. The consequence was the secret pact (Doc. 14) concluded early in 1903 between the Liberal Chief Whip, Herbert Gladstone, and Ramsay MacDonald, secretary of the LRC.[15] In effect, it offered the LRC a free run in about thirty-five seats at the next general election, and gave a new clarity henceforth to relations between Liberals and the Labour Party. This confirmed what was already happening at a variety of levels. Labour and radical Liberals were working together in close harmony at Westminster, under the chairmanship of Sir Charles Dilke. In the constituencies, radical Liberals like Francis Channing, member for Northamptonshire East (Doc. 15), laid stress on the wide range of agreement that had existed between Labour and Liberals for the past twenty years over such issues as hours of work, graduated taxation, land reform, a trades disputes bill and old age pensions. This was no doubt true enough of Channing himself, but his advanced outlook was hardly typical of the Liberal leadership. Many constituency parties resented pressure from the Chief Whip to enforce the electoral pact of 1903. However, sympathy on the backbenches and in the radical press for collaboration between radicals and socialists for social improvement was an essential key to Liberal revival in the years up to 1905.

On 4 December 1905, Balfour suddenly resigned, and the Liberals unexpectedly found themselves compelled to take office. After three years of triumphant by-elections, it was an embarrassing time for Campbell-Bannerman and his colleagues. Although the Liberal Imperialist wing of the party had long been in retreat, its leaders were still closely associated with one another. Three months earlier, Haldane, Grey and Asquith had concluded the so-called 'Relugas Compact' (Doc. 16), in which it was agreed that Campbell-Bannerman should retire to the Lords in the event of a Liberal victory, with Asquith leading the Commons. A different version of residual Imperialist influence in the party came in Rosebery's speech at Bodmin on 25 November (Doc. 17). In this, he denounced Campbell-Bannerman's statement at Stirling two days earlier, in the course of which the Liberal leader had voiced support for Irish Home Rule, on a 'step-by-step' basis. Rosebery's bombshell at Bodmin, Balfour thought, might split the Liberals into fragments yet again; hence Balfour's resignation as a tactical move. In fact, he completely miscalculated.

[15] There is an authoritative discussion of this pact in F. Bealey and Henry Pelling, *Labour and Politics, 1900–1906* (London, 1958), Chap. VI.

Rosebery was now a largely isolated figure, speaking for hardly any-one but himself, while Campbell-Bannerman was no easier to dis-lodge than any other party leader ambitious for office. Asquith, ever the dedicated Liberal partisan, now calmly informed his colleagues that, since the election had not yet taken place, he considered the Relugas Compact to be null and void, and felt bound to enter a Campbell-Bannerman administration (Doc. 18). Haldane and Grey, very reluctantly, had to follow him, though the offer of the powerful offices of the Secretaryships for War and Foreign Affairs no doubt soothed their ruffled feelings. After years of division and disarray, since the days of Newcastle in 1891, the Liberals were again strong and united. At the general election that followed in January 1906 Campbell-Bannerman led his party to the most massive party majority of modern times.

How far can the immense Liberal landslide at the 1906 election be considered merely a negative reaction to Unionist mistakes during the past ten years ? In many ways, clearly it was. Free Trade, the Education Act, 'Chinese slavery' in South Africa, all identified with the late Balfour administration, were the main issues of the campaign, and the Liberals exploited every one to the full. Yet this is a superficial inter-pretation: certainly, for instance, the correlation between the non-conformist 'passive resistance' campaign and the fate of Liberal candidates at the polls in 1906 is not a clear one. It was generally accepted that the election saw a new emphasis on the role of labour, on unemployment and social conditions in urban areas, and that many Liberal candidates gave these themes quite a new prominence. The Taff Vale verdict (1901), which undermined the right to strike was fiercely condemned. It became clear during the campaign that, contrary to Sidney Webb's scepticism, it was possible for the Old Liberalism and the New to be reconciled. After all, the programme at Newcastle had included several wide-ranging proposals for state intervention to re-shape the rights of property and to intervene between master and man. Nonconformists were anxious to use the state to hack away the age-old endowments of the Welsh Church, and to expropriate liquor licences. Land reformers sought statutory power to enfranchise lease-holds, to provide security of tenure and to set up free allotments. There had long been pressure for taxation of the unearned increment. Pro-posals for municipal housing and ownership of public utilities had been a staple of radicalism in London and other cities for two decades past. On grounds of pure theory, men like Samuel or even Hobson might try to draw a line between radicalism and collectivism—but then so would Keir Hardie himself. In practical terms, their attitudes on specific issues would be largely identical with those of the 'socialists'.

No one illustrated better the possible harmony between the Old Liberalism and the New than did the new President of the Board of Trade, David Lloyd George. He had been in the van of the fight for the old causes: indeed, it was they that had brought him to national prominence. He had crusaded against the war in South Africa; he had campaigned in Wales against the clerical supremacy inherent in Church schools; he had waved the patriotic flag in support of free trade; he had denounced the 1904 Licensing Act. Lloyd George was supremely a rural, Celtic radical directing his attacks against privilege of the old kind. The cause of labour and the trade unions, even when it involved the Penrhyn quarrymen or the railwaymen of Taff Vale in his own community, left him comparatively unmoved, as Keir Hardie complained.[16] Yet the demands of Welsh radicals had long envisaged state intervention in a variety of spheres. Lloyd George of all people could not argue that the state could legitimately fix fair rents on the land, but not fair wages or reasonable hours of work in urban areas. More than most backbench radicals, he was a pragmatist, and his years of office after 1905 were to show how the old creed and the new could be reconciled, how individual libertarianism and state intervention could make common cause. Only a most obtuse observer could really argue that the party which swept all kinds of constituencies in 1906 and captured 401 seats was fundamentally doomed. It was surging with new life, in its organizational structure and in intellectual debate. Far more than Chamberlain's shattered remnant or the staid spokesmen of the Labour Party, it captured the idealism of the young, as the array of new M.P.s bore witness. If later years saw the 'strange death' of Liberal England (and Wales), in the aftermath of 1906 the Liberal Party was undeniably in full and vigorous health.

[16] Keir Hardie, 'The New Government', *Labour Leader*, 22 December, 1905, p. 459. 'Mr Lloyd-George [*sic*] may safely be described as a politician with no settled convictions on social questions.' In 'Lloyd George: a Political Estimate', *Labour Leader*, 16 June 1905, 'Cymro' concluded gloomily that 'Lloyd George will never contribute anything of permanent value to the industrial and social progress of his country'.

2

The Liberals in Power, 1905-15

THE exact significance of the immense Liberal majority at the polls in January 1906 has long been a lively source of controversy among historians. Even at the time there were commentators, especially within the new Labour Party, who regarded the electoral landslide as a political illusion, and the Liberals as essentially doomed. Among the later writers who popularized this theme was George Dangerfield in a brilliantly written but basically misleading work published in 1936, *The Strange Death of Liberal England*. In this volume, which has had a totally disproportionate influence upon later writers, Dangerfield argued that the new challenges, economic, social and ideological, of the years 1910–14 really marked the death of the moral imperatives upon which the Liberal Party was founded. The future replacement of the Liberals by the Labour Party as the major spokesmen for the British Left was thus an inevitable process, for which the conflict between Asquith and Lloyd George in 1916 merely supplied the occasion rather than the cause. From a different standpoint, some recent historians, most notably Paul Thompson and Henry Pelling, have concluded that the middle-class character of Edwardian Liberalism made it basically incapable of accommodating its working-class support, either at the levels of local constituency organization or of national policy, and that the eventual triumph of an increasingly militant Labour Party was inexorable. Mr Thompson, basing his analysis on the situation in London, sees the electoral triumph of 1906 as essentially fortuitous, based on the accidental coincidence of a revival of political nonconformity and the temporary re-alignment of the working-class Liberal vote. Radicalism in the 1900s, he has written, was 'increasingly an outdated political concept'.[1] Dr Pelling, the leading authority on the rise of the Labour Party, has added that it, and

[1] Paul Thompson, *Socialists, Liberals and Labour*, p. 179.

not the Liberals, was equipped 'to take advantage of twentieth-century political conditions'.[2]

Other historians, however, of whom Trevor Wilson stands out, totally reject this view. To Dr Wilson, the Liberal Party was still in an essentially sound condition on the outbreak of war in 1914, when it was suddenly struck down without warning by a series of totally unfamiliar challenges through the advent of total war.[3] Certainly, the thesis that the Liberal Party was fundamentally doomed in the 1906–1914 period is one that would have made little sense to most contemporaries as they surveyed the records of the successive Liberal administrations of Campbell-Bannerman and Asquith. Without doubt, it was a time of immense internal upheaval for the party, especially in London and other major cities. Certainly, the challenge of a self-conscious working class was one that the Liberals found more and more difficulty in meeting, especially in South Wales and other mining areas. Conversely, the nonconformist chapels, on which they traditionally relied, were now a waning force. Even so, the period inaugurated by the 1906 election was one of extraordinary political achievement by the Liberals, newly reorganized and with new inspiration at the top. If the turmoil of the period 1910–14, years of labour unrest, of the Ulster crisis and the suffragettes' demonstrations, posed a crisis for the Liberal ethic founded on reform within a framework of constitutional order and the rule of law, it was not necessarily the Liberal Party as an organization that was faced with extinction. Dr Henry Pelling has shown persuasively that the Liberals were facing severe pressures from Labour candidates in industrial areas like South Wales:[4] it cannot, however, be argued that the Liberals were about to succumb to them. In the December 1910 election in South Wales, for instance, Liberal candidates defeated Labour in three cases where there was a direct clash at the polls; even Keir Hardie never came top of the poll at Merthyr Tydfil in four successive contests. By-elections after 1910 told the same story. Above all, the career of David Lloyd George during this period, first as President of the Board of Trade, then from 1908 at the Exchequer, suggests that the capacity for renewal and regeneration of the party which he served was far from being exhausted. In short, to view these years as a kind of Indian summer for a party on the verge of imminent collapse is a basic distortion of political history.

[2] Henry Pelling, *Popular Politics and Society in Late Victorian Britain* (London, 1968), p. 118.

[3] Trevor Wilson, *The Downfall of the Liberal Party, 1914–1935* (London, 1966), pp. 15–19.

[4] Henry Pelling, *op. cit.*, pp. 110–17.

Without doubt, the essential problem for the Liberal government in 1906 was to try to accommodate the rising power of organized labour. On the surface, the election had throughout been fought over traditional issues—Free Trade, Church Schools, the Licensing Act, the menace of imperialism. Yet members of the new administration were quick to show that they did recognize the new movements that had helped to sweep them into office. No-one showed a more rapid appreciation of them than did the new President of the Board of Trade (Doc. 19). Addressing his constituents at Caernarvon in January 1906, shortly after the election, he spoke with remarkable frankness on the need to satisfy the demands of labour. He pledged himself to support a trade union bill to provide protection for collective bargaining after the Taff Vale verdict in 1901 had menaced the basic right to strike. He outlined also the need for new social provision for unprotected categories of the community: in particular, he pledged the government to the implementation of Old Age Pensions for which Joseph Chamberlain had so often called in vain. Coming from a member of the government thought to be in the van of the new social radicalism, Lloyd George's words appeared to be prophetic. They seemed to find immediate confirmation when the government accepted the Labour Party's own Trades Disputes Bill in 1906, after pressure from many of the Liberal backbenchers. As a consequence, trade unions were granted virtual immunity from financial damages incurred during trade disputes. A wide range of social measures was confidently forecast, which would show that the Liberal government, even one which contained such veteran opponents of collectivism as John Morley, had finally transcended the economic and social creed of Gladstone.

In fact, the social achievements of the Campbell-Bannerman administration proved to be intensely disappointing. Most of the period up to 1908 was spent in 'ploughing the sands' or 'filling up the cup', as the rival metaphors went. In other words, traditional Liberal supporters were presented with their traditional offerings, which in turn met with inevitable nemesis at the hands of the House of Lords. Thus Birrell's Education Bill of 1906, which was designed to meet nonconformist objections to the Balfour Act of 1902, perished in this way, as later did a Plural Voting Bill, two Scottish Land Bills and (in 1908 under Asquith) a major Licensing Bill. Of social legislation there was remarkably little. There were rare and important exceptions like the measure to grant free school meals to children in 1906, but in general there was little new thinking. As a result, by 1908 those back-bench Liberals usually classified as the 'social radicals', and to whom new journals like the *Nation* appealed, were bitterly disillusioned with the government's lack of urgency. 'Social reform has not gone beyond the rhetorical stage,' wrote C. F. G. Masterman in the *Nineteenth Century and After* (December 1906). Demands for reform from Liberals in the constituencies met with scant sympathy from the government; indeed, Campbell-Bannerman himself was outstandingly conservative on the social front. He feared that radical reforms might create new divisions within a party so recently reunited. No leading member of the government was identified with the 'New Liberalism'. Even a radical like Lloyd George, for all his recognition of the needs of labour after the 1906 election, was still essentially committed to the old causes. Certainly, as President of the Board of Trade he showed a remarkably cavalier attitude towards the old Liberal shibboleths: his Merchant Shipping and Patents Acts marked a striking breach with the pure doctrine of Free Trade. Again, his intervention in the 1907 railway strike, when he insisted on compulsory boards of conciliation being set up, reflected a marked sympathy with the trade union position—and an equally marked refusal to be dictated to by cautious civil service officials. It served to give Lloyd George a new standing with organized labour that was to serve him well over the next fifteen years. Still, even he was still basically preoccupied with the sectarian issues of his Welsh youth. After the Lords had thrown out the 1906 Education Bill, he urged his colleagues in vain to dissolve parliament; in 1908 he was to react equally violently over the rejection of the Licensing Bill. In October 1906, addressing the Welsh National Liberal Federation at Cardiff, he could offer only the old panaceas of rural radicalism—temperance, land reform, Church disestablishment and local home rule. It was hardly an index that the government was in tune with the new democracy.

With the advent of Asquith as Prime Minister in April 1908, the mood began to change. In particular, the promotion of Lloyd George to the Exchequer, a shrewd move by Asquith to preserve the balance within the new government, marked a dramatic new phase in the Liberal government's policies. This new course had already received a powerful stimulus the previous month from a dynamic junior minister, Winston Churchill, in an article in the *Nation* on 'The Untrodden Field in Politics' (Doc. 20). In this, he called for his party to move forward from the championing of political liberty to the cause of economic and social liberty. He advocated a 'new constructive policy' which would apply scientific remedies for such evils as pauperism and casual employment; he was even prepared to endorse such selective measures as the public acquisition of railways and canals. All this would strengthen and preserve competitive capitalism as he understood it. Churchill's promotion to the Board of Trade meant that a leading minister could advocate 'the New Liberalism' from within the administration: at last the government was catching up with the intellectual currents that had swept it to power. Churchill gave his creed further expression in the summer of 1908 when he urged 'a big slice of Bismarckianism' upon the government, including labour exchanges and unemployment insurance, national health insurance, and a complete modernization of the old poor law. He sought to apply scientific, measurable solutions to evils such as illness and poverty, hitherto left to the arbitrary ravages of nature.

Throughout 1909 and 1910 Churchill applied his immense energies and powers of advocacy to persuade his colleagues of the urgency of redirecting the efforts of the Liberal government. During this period he was able to secure such notable social landmarks as the passage of the Trade Boards Bill in 1909 for 'sweated industries', and later the introduction of labour exchanges. It was a period in which the Liberal Party seemed to be advancing rapidly towards a new accommodation with state socialism. While the 1908 session saw the last of the age-long sectarian conflicts over denominational schools and licensing reform, with the Liberals finally admitting defeat in each case, the cry on the backbenches and in the press for new social measures was becoming ever more distinct. About forty Liberal backbenchers now voted regularly with the Labour Party on domestic issues. The main intellectual spokesmen of the party were now overwhelmingly committed to social reform. J. A. Hobson in 1909 spoke of a 'crisis of Liberalism' in which the old barriers between liberalism and socialism must of necessity become blurred.[5] 'The old *laissez-faire* Liberalism is dead.' C. F. G. Masterman's *Condition of England* published in 1909 was an eloquent and moving statement by a junior minister (and a close confidant of Lloyd George) of the gulf that lay between the ostentatious wealth of the 'conquerors' in suburban villadom and the spiritual and social destitution of the 'prisoners' in urban slums. Masterman's analysis was given added force by his devout Anglicanism and his concern that society be given a new corporate cohesion and strength. This was 'Christian Socialism' as he understood it.

How far the government was prepared to move in this radical direction, however, remained very uncertain. So many of the Cabinet, men like McKenna, Runciman and Grey, seemed utterly out of sympathy with the collectivist creed. Haldane was immersed in his army reforms and had forgotten most of that concern for social issues he had revealed back in the early 1890s. Asquith himself supplied no new initiatives; he was a man who responded passively to political

[5] J. A. Hobson, *The Crisis of Liberalism: New Issues of Democracy* (London, 1909), pp. 3 ff.

pressures from without, rather than supply any fresh stimulus of his own. However, Asquith had one supreme quality that made him an outstanding leader—a fierce partisanship, and a determination to rule at all costs. It was this that had led him to reject the Relugas Compact at the time of the formation of the ministry back in December 1905. Now in 1908 and 1909 he could see as clearly as any observer the warning signs for his government—the massive loss of by-elections to the Unionists and the probable erosion of the immense majority of 1906 when the next election came. This consideration weighed even more heavily with the Chancellor of the Exchequer. Lloyd George now became a Liberal transformed. Between 1908 and 1910 he turned from being the traditional voice of Cobdenism and the chapel vote to being the tribune for a new social concern, a change of course which gave the flagging administration new life. It was far more than mere political necessity that weighed with Lloyd George now. He shared with Churchill an impatience for the priorities of the older Liberalism. As a Welsh outsider (an outsider like Churchill, the renegade from Toryism), he viewed traditional Liberal causes with an irreverent eye. Lloyd George had already absorbed some of the newer Liberal thinking through reformers like Seebohm Rowntree.[6] He imbibed a good deal more during his highly unorthodox visit to Germany in the summer of 1908 with Harold Spender and Sir Charles Henry, in which the striking achievement of Bismarckian social legislation deeply impressed him. (So also did the emerging military might of Germany, and the way in which its national strength was directly related to an enlightened welfare programme.) As a result, he and Churchill led a new campaign within the government on behalf of social reform. Together in the winter of 1908–9 they devised a new series of priorities for their colleagues, headed by labour exchanges and national health insurance. It was highly significant that Lloyd George's address to the Welsh Liberals at Swansea in October 1908 was markedly different in content from his Cardiff speech two years earlier.[7] Now he stressed the extreme urgency of a social reform programme, lest the British Liberals lapse into the same sterility and decline as their counterparts on the continent of Europe.

Lloyd George's main departmental preoccupation was to base this programme upon budgetary reform. An expanded welfare programme, which would seize the political initiative for the Liberals for years to come, must be related to a reshaped fiscal policy, though one compatible with Liberal free trade traditions. As a result, his famous 'people's budget' of 1909, which inflamed the Lords and led to a

[6] See Asa Briggs, *Seebohm Rowntree* (London, 1961), pp. 62 ff.
[7] *The Times*, 2 October 1908.

massive political crisis which lasted two-and-a-half years, broke completely with traditional budgetary policy. There was already growing
financial pressure upon the exchequer with the implementation of
Old Age Pensions in 1908 (made the more expensive by amendments
accepted by Lloyd George in committee) and the new charges upon
expenditure resulting from the laying-down of the new 'Dreadnought'
battleships. Clearly, new revenue had to be found immediately—
and from the central government, since there was a growing crisis of
finance amongst the local authorities. Lloyd George's budget in 1909,
then, was conceived in terms of a long-term programme, one which
would decisively wrest the initiative from the Unionists. It was directed
largely against the old Liberal enemies—landlords would face new
duties upon the unearned increment and on undeveloped land;
brewers would be savaged by new licensing duties. But if the victims
were traditional, the social objectives of the new budget were essentially novel. Indeed, the whole measure was very much Lloyd George's
own. Even Churchill was very alarmed at the new land duties: as
Lloyd George wryly observed of him, 'he had a soft spot for dukes'.[8]
The budget as a whole was intended to provide an ever-expanding
base of wealth for internal development. The new taxes upon the site
value of urban land, on mining royalties and ground rents would
associate the Treasury with the growing urban wealth of the country,
and also provide an attractive Liberal alternative to the Unionist
policy of tariff reform. In this way, the budget could claim to appeal
both to labour and to middle-class free traders, and provide a new
unity as well as a new impetus for the Liberal ranks.

After a prolonged period of intense crisis that lasted from the
introduction of his budget in April 1909 down to the passage of the
Parliament Act in August 1911, Lloyd George emerged triumphantly
successful. In this period, he clearly took over the leadership of the
radical wing of his party from Churchill. The latter was now increasingly obsessed by the labour unrest in mining areas and in several
major ports: the riots at Tonypandy, which were to do such subsequent harm to Churchill's reputation in working-class areas, severely
weakened his reforming *élan*. Lloyd George henceforth stood almost
alone in the Cabinet as a reformer, but it was a burden he was well
able to sustain. In 1910 his 'people's budget' was passed, and much
social legislation flowed from it. Furthermore, at the two general
elections in January and December 1910, admittedly with Labour
and Irish support and with reduced majorities almost everywhere, the
Liberals were returned with majorities of over 120. The permeation

[8] Randolph S. Churchill, *Winston S. Churchill*, Vol. II (London, 1967),
p. 323.

of the government by the New Liberalism, as interpreted by Lloyd George, now seemed almost complete, as even a hostile critic like Mrs Webb had to admit (Doc. 21). She noted how Lloyd George and Churchill had transformed the political situation, and how the small Labour Party seemed totally eclipsed in popular esteem. The climax came with Lloyd George's National Insurance Bill in 1911 (Doc. 21). This was in many ways one of the most impressive pinnacles of his career. It was at one level an astonishing achievement of political expertise. Only Lloyd George could have got through such an immensely complex measure, one that entailed playing off the industrial assurance companies against the friendly societies, and both against the British Medical Association. It also entailed trying to detach the doctors' rank and file from their own leaders; 'a deputation of doctors is a deputation of swell doctors,' observed Lloyd George.[9] It involved both conciliating the trade unions and satisfying the claims of private industry. In terms of party manœuvrings, it meant a deal between the Liberal Chief Whip, the Master of Elibank, and the Labour Party, as a result of which the latter largely supported Lloyd George's bill in return for the passage of the payment of Members of Parliament (a salary of £400 a year was conceded in 1911). Lloyd George's measure was a typically many-sided one, a characteristically flexible compromise between state socialism and *laissez-faire*. To balance the creation of what was in effect a notable measure of redistributing income, there was the non-actuarial decision of allowing the contributions to the unemployment insurance fund to be divided out amongst contributors.[10] It was a Liberal salute to the Gladstonian principle that wealth ought to 'fructify in the pockets of the people'. But the essential impetus of the bill was clearly towards the founding of a welfare state on collectivist lines. It included a high degree of compulsion, with a consequent vast expansion of the machinery of government. It was through the insurance commissions that men like J. A. Salter and Thomas Jones first made their entry into the public service. With what seemed to be at first an astonishing degree of popular acclaim from the 'stalls' as well as from the 'upper gallery' (as *Punch* observed), Lloyd George had set the seal on the transformation of the Liberal ethic.

Once the main lines of the Churchill-Lloyd George policies were outlined, their contents assumed to some extent a supra-political character. The Unionists, who in any event included enterprising

[9] Bentley Gilbert, *The Evolution of National Insurance in Great Britain* (London, 1967), p. 363.

[10] Though 'dividing-out' was rejected for health insurance: Lloyd George decided to be 'virtuous' and build up an accumulated reserve fund.

young social reformers like Arthur Steel-Maitland, and the 'Round Table' apostles of Milner's 'Kindergarten' like Leopold Amery, were anxious not to appear hostile to measures to relieve the conditions of the working class. Most of the backbenchers on the Liberal side were generally enthusiastic. Doctrinaire opponents of the encroachments of the 'servile state' like Hilaire Belloc and his Catholic friends, extremist advocates of private enterprise like Harold Cox of the Cobden Club, were eccentric exceptions. While the majority of the Cabinet was apathetic on social matters, they offered Lloyd George relatively little resistance in Cabinet discussions, while Asquith gave his Chancellor steadfast support.

However, the fierce flames of party passion soon nullified the advance towards new social objectives. The most long-lasting, though not the most dangerous, clash came over the climax of the warfare between the Liberal government and the House of Lords.[11] In a supreme act of folly, on the advice of Balfour, the Lords threw out Lloyd George's 1909 budget, the first time such an extreme action had been taken for over 200 years. There is no evidence at all to suggest that Lloyd George anticipated such a reaction—on the contrary, his budget was framed in large measure to meet a financial crisis, and he was much embarrassed by the delay in securing new taxes to pay for his social programme. On the other hand, when Lansdowne and his fellow peers responded so foolishly, Lloyd George eagerly seized the opportunity to rally the nation on the cry of 'the peers versus the people'. Asquith appeared to declare at a mass meeting at the Albert Hall in December 1909 (Doc. 22) that the government would curb the Lords' veto and would obtain 'safeguards' by means (it was widely assumed) of a royal pledge to create a sufficiency of Liberal peers to outnumber the Unionist majority. The Liberals won the January 1910 general election by a majority of 124, with Labour and Irish support, but, with no royal pledge forthcoming from Edward VII, the fight went on. Lloyd George was now in the thick of the battle. In speeches remarkable for their abusiveness from a Cabinet minister, he whipped the Lords on to new heights of fury. In speeches at Limehouse and Newcastle in July and October 1909, he had outlined the stark contrast between the entrenched privilege symbolized by his ducal opponents, and the new social needs embodied in the government's programme. 'Five hundred men chosen at random from among the unemployed', was his most telling jibe.[12] In response to this provocation, the Lords abandoned all restraint. Even after allowing

[11] This is very clearly described in Roy Jenkins, *Mr Balfour's Poodle* (London, 1954), and it is not necessary to recapitulate the details here.
[12] Speech at Newcastle, 9 October 1909.

the passage of the budget in April 1910, they fought root and branch the limitations of their veto now propounded by Asquith. After an immensely embittered conflict, but one which seems to have left much of the electorate generally apathetic, the 'ditchers' in the Lords were finally overborne. A royal pledge was given by George V, very unwillingly, which threatened a flood of new Liberal peers, and in August 1911 the Parliament Bill was passed. Asquith and Lloyd George now occupied new positions in the demonology of their Unionist opponents, not least because the ending of the permanent Lords' veto made possible Irish Home Rule, Welsh Disestablishment and other Liberal policies too appalling to contemplate.

This appears superficially to be a time of intense partisanship. Certainly, feelings ran high; yet in fact at the very climax of the conflict with the Lords, Lloyd George made an extraordinary proposal for an all-party coalition. He broached this in August 1910 (Doc. 23), during the conference of Liberal and Unionist leaders, to try to settle the constitutional conflict on the advent of the new monarch, George V. In reality, Lloyd George's penchant for a coalition was not wholly surprising. Even in his early days as a Welsh radical, as in his move for Welsh home rule back in 1895, he had been impatient with the petty orthodoxies of party controversy. The House of Lords crisis seemed to him a supreme instance of how sectional conflict could consume the national energies, while the Germany he had seen at first hand in 1908 went on building up its economic and military might. His plans in 1910 illustrate Lloyd George's illusory passion for a transcendent national synthesis that would soar above partisan strife— the kind of grandiose vision of leadership that attracted him to Joseph Chamberlain in his youth, later on to the 'New Nationalism' of Theodore Roosevelt in the United States, later still to Milner's Prussian 'efficiency', and in the 1930s to a false prophet like Hitler. Often Lloyd George's instinct for supreme executive power could lead his judgement far astray. He could select the wrong messiah. But now in 1910 he could spell out how party deadlock made impossible a coherent or constructive policy on critical social issues like housing, temperance reform (a characteristic demand of his), national insurance, unemployment, and education. Significantly, the obverse of his programme would be the remodelling of the national defences (possibly including some form of modified conscription), though at an economic cost. As Lloyd George himself recalled, his scheme met with a positive response from others with a cross-bench frame of mind, such as Churchill among the Liberals and F. E. Smith among the Unionists. Balfour himself, now wearied with years of party bickering, and personally fascinated by Lloyd George, was also strangely enthusiastic. So, too, were some tariff reformers on the Unionist Social Reform Committee. On the Liberal side, Grey, with whom Lloyd George enjoyed a bitter-sweet relationship throughout these years, also saw real value in the scheme. Lloyd George, years later in his *Memoirs*, was to blame the Conservative die-hards' attachment to Ulster for the eventual failure of his scheme, and Akers-Douglas (the former chief whip) in particular. In fact, the reasons for it were far more profound. Those issues that Lloyd George dismissed as essentially non-partisan—Irish Home Rule, the House of Lords, the Welsh Church, free trade—were in fact intensely controversial. They simply could not be spirited away by verbal formulae or by 'non-partisan' commissions, since they had both decades of traditional conflict and a real cleavage of interests at the present time bound up with them. Not only the die-hards but more moderate leaders like Austen Chamberlain saw with dismay the loss of familiar landmarks that differentiated them from the Liberals. On the other side, Asquith saw in every one of Lloyd George's 'non-controversial' issues a skein of fundamental philosophical issues. The world of Asquith and Austen Chamberlain was one of interest groups and traditional ideologies in conflict, a world in which party battles in the legislature underpinned the formulation of policies at the executive level. The clash between the Lords and the Commons was the prelude in their eyes to the unfolding of more conflicts still to come, not the overture to a coalition. The English political culture, and its deep-rooted alignments, would not be extinguished by the blandishments of the Welsh apostle of coalitions, and Lloyd George's plan abruptly failed. Only an unthinkable crisis like a world war could lend it credibility, and to all contemporaries this appeared utterly remote.

As a result, party strife reached new heights of bitterness in the years that followed the end of the conflict with the Lords over the Parliament Bill. In a few months, the right-wing *National Review* could denounce Asquith's government for having promoted 'national anarchy' (Doc. 24). Further, it was a time when each side adopted a posture of the most bitter partisanship. For the government, Lloyd George now inspired a new hatred of the Unionists, parading himself as the innocent 'St Sebastian of Limehouse', in Leopold Amery's ironic phrase. In the Unionist camp, Balfour's quiescent leadership was widely thought to be too conciliatory, and a fierce journalistic campaign against him, spearheaded by Leo Maxse in the *National Review*, saw him driven out. Balfour's successor was a melancholy Glasgow ironmaster, Bonar Law, who brought a new tone of acerbity to the Unionist leadership. The crises of the next three years are a familiar theme—Dangerfield made them the premises for his argument of an inevitable Liberal decline. Some of these crises led to more violence in rhetoric than in actuality—the dreary controversy over the Welsh Church, which saw Lloyd George and Lord Hugh Cecil locked in combat during the Commons' debates, was in this category. The renewal of the Irish Home Rule controversy, however, posed a new and terrible threat to national unity. The passage of the Parliament Act made Irish Home Rule now a legislative possibility, and Asquith duly introduced a bill on these lines in 1912, a modified version of Gladstone's abortive measure of 1893. In response, Bonar Law went to amazing lengths in endorsing the Ulster covenanters now in revolt against the Home Rule Bill. At Blenheim Palace in 1912, he seemed to encourage open rebellion if Home Rule were forced through parliament, an extraordinary position for a responsible party leader to adopt, and one which reinforced the intransigence and venom of Ulster Orange Lodges even fifty years later. Bonar Law has much to answer for. The conflict over Ireland raged at Westminster for the next two years. A desperate attempt to find a *via media*, inspired by Lloyd George in March 1914, proposed the temporary exclusion of Ulster for a period of years, but it was rejected by Bonar Law.[13] In any case, events at Westminster were secondary to developments in Ireland itself. By the start of August 1914, Ulster Volunteers, armed with open Unionist connivance from such party leaders as Carson and F. E. Smith, and faced with an apparently inert, if not actively disloyal, army high command, seemed likely to force that unhappy island to the brink of civil war.

The lesson of direct action was taken up elsewhere. The suffragettes' movement, active in Britain for the past dozen years, now reached an infinitely more violent phase. As Mrs Pankhurst and her more militant wing of the Women's Social and Political Union made clear, defiance of parliament by Ulster leaders and by organized labour was an open-ended process. The more militant women now took the same course, inflamed by episodes such as the self-inflicted death of Emily Davidson on Derby Day at Epsom in 1913, with dire results to the reputation of the Liberal government. More crucial still was the alarming new militancy of organized labour. From 1909 onwards, the restraint of trade union leaders, in the face of rising unemployment, growing mass membership and new pressures for direct action from rank and file, finally collapsed. In 1911 there were lengthy and violent strikes on the railways, in the mining areas and at several major ports. Hussars patrolled the Welsh valleys, after the calamitous riots at Tonypandy which did such havoc to Churchill's reputation as the workers' friend.

---

[13] Leon Ó. Broin, *The Chief Secretary: Augustine Birrell in Ireland* (London, 1969), pp. 85 ff.

In April 1912, the miners conducted a massive national stoppage
on behalf of a minimum wage, a proposal which Asquith was rapidly
forced to concede. The government seemed almost overwhelmed by
these new developments, especially when they appeared to be spurred
on by syndicalist and other militant doctrines from France and the
United States. Certainly Lloyd George himself continued to avow
his sympathy for the labour cause (Doc. 25), and retained his 'special
relationship' with the trade unions. The Cabinet set up a small committee (Lloyd George, Haldane, Buxton, Beauchamp and McKinnon
Wood) to investigate industrial relations, and made several notable
concessions to militant trade union demands. Even so, by the summer
of 1914 when the Triple Alliance of miners, railwaymen and dockers
came into being, the government seemed on the verge of losing control
over these immense class pressures that threatened to undermine the
very cohesion of British society. Asquith seemed to be presiding over
a land on the verge of revolution.

Can it, therefore, be concluded that these startling new developments made the Liberal Party's demise inevitable? Without doubt,
the government's reputation was severely shaken, while its record in
by-elections was dismal in the extreme. In its working-class strongholds, the Liberals seemed to be losing much of their support, partly
because of the stubborn refusal of local Associations to adopt labour
candidates, while the decline of the nonconformist chapels in industrial
and urban areas was now widely acknowledged. The 1910 Commission
on the Welsh churches suggested that this was the case even in a dis-
senting stronghold like Wales. As a result, the organizational weak-
nesses of the party were underlined, after the striking reforms of the
party machine conducted by Herbert Gladstone while chief whip in
1900–5. In industrial areas like the West Riding and South Wales,
the Liberals were a struggling party; in many rural districts, the local
Liberal Associations were melting away. It must be added also that
the party's preoccupation with issues like Irish Home Rule and the
Welsh Church associated it to an undue extent with the causes of
Celtic nationalism, now something of a waning force in Scotland and
even in Wales. Certainly, its preoccupation with Irish and Welsh
measures severely deflected it from the social policies previously outlined by Lloyd George, and in 1913–14 the tempo of social reform
markedly slackened. In any event, the National Insurance Bill, as a
new kind of poll tax, was far from popular with working-class voters.[14]
Lloyd George himself was somewhat in the shadows at about this
time. The long-drawn-out agony of the Marconi affair, in which he

[14] See Henry Pelling, *Popular Politics*, p. 13.

was widely rumoured to have been involved in improper speculation in shares of the Marconi company, which was under contract to the government, knocked Lloyd George's career off course.[15] It is a curious tribute, among other things, to the partisanship of Asquith, the Prime Minister, that he did not ask Lloyd George and Sir Rufus Isaacs, the Attorney-General, to resign. Lloyd George tried to regain his position by turning anew in the autumn of 1913 to rallying the rural radicalism of his youth. He launched a new land campaign, instituting a Land Enquiry Committee on which Rowntree, Masterman and C. P. Scott of the *Manchester Guardian* served.[16] But this new 'land crusade' fell somewhat flat in urban areas, while it became clear that the pace of social change had eroded the bases of the tenurial radicalism which Joseph Chamberlain had rallied thirty years before. Whatever the means of restoring the fortunes of Liberalism, Lloyd George's new land campaign offered no clear way forward. In any case, the famous 'land duties' of the 1909 'People's Budget' had so far yielded nothing at all.

It cannot be disputed that the Liberals were a struggling party in 1914. But they were very far from being a dead one. After all, many of the disparate challenges now faced by the administration seemed directed more against the constitutional system itself than at the Liberal Party specifically. In many ways, it was the Labour Party, consistently unsuccessful at by-elections and believed (by Keir Hardie, among others) to be contemplating an open electoral pact with the Liberals at the next general election, which was the major victim of industrial militancy. The Unionists anticipated victory at the next election, but they could not be certain. After all, the summer of 1914, with all its turbulence in Ulster and elsewhere, saw Asquith still firmly at the helm, his party still intact, his ministry overtly united and far from showing signs of exhaustion, and with a new generation of younger men like Masterman, Samuel, Hobhouse and Simon rising to high office. Major industrial interests—coal, shipping, textiles— still provided support and finance for the Liberal cause: a magnate like Sir Alfred Mond chose to enter the Commons to make this the more explicit. Banking interests in the City were still held firm to Free Trade, the gold standard and the old Gladstonian imperatives.

Above all, there was David Lloyd George himself. Despite Marconi, despite the troubles of 1913–14, he was still fertile with new ideas and new initiatives. His budget of 1914 was intended to be the prelude to a sweeping programme of national development, as its predecessor

---

[15] See Frances Donaldson, *The Marconi Scandal* (London, 1963).
[16] Asa Briggs, *Seebohm Rowntree*, pp. 64 ff.; Trevor Wilson (ed.), *The Political Diaries of C. P. Scott, 1911–28* (London, 1970), pp. 68–70.

of 1909 had been. It included higher death-duties, a new super-tax, a clearly graduated income tax upon earned incomes, and a new local rate on land values. These would be the springboard for a dramatic policy of house building and other development schemes. The 1914 budget, in fact, ran into severe procedural difficulties at the hands of the Speaker, Lowther, and caused Lloyd George much parliamentary embarrassment. Even so, there is ample evidence to suggest that the government still had the resilience, the determination and, indeed, the potential votes, to discover new reserves of power. Certainly the opposition, discouraged by nearly ten years out of office, hitching its wagon to the improbable stars of die-hard peers, food taxers, Ulster covenanters, the Welsh Bishops and the 'jingo' press, was far from obviously a refurbished, streamlined machine geared for victory.

In times of peace, then, Liberal England (and even more Liberal Scotland and Wales) was a living reality. But its foundations rested upon the alignments of domestic politics. Peace went along with retrenchment and reform in the famous Gladstonian trilogy. Crises in foreign policy were likely to introduce new and unknown hazards. War, however, seemed very far away: even after the assassination at Sarajevo, Lloyd George could assure his audience on 9 July 1914 that 'the sky has never been more perfectly blue'.[17] The vast majority of British Liberals, especially in the reaction against imperial expansion in the post-Boer War period, retained a persistent hostility towards foreign entanglements and towards increased spending on weapons of war. A 'cave' of Liberal backbenchers, amongst whom the Quaker, J. Allen Baker, was conspicuous (Doc. 26), voted steadily against any increase in the arms estimates, often combining this with a sympathetic view of Germany as the fatherland of social and municipal reform. The eighty-strong Liberal Foreign Affairs Committee sharply attacked Grey's policies. Lloyd George himself appeared to champion these views when resisting increased naval estimates proposed by McKenna in 1909 and then by Churchill in January 1914, the latter occasion all but leading to Lloyd George's resignation.[18] But Lloyd George himself was notable in the government for his flexibility in foreign as in domestic affairs. The one-time Little Englander had always had a pronounced vein of nationalism in his make-up. Again, during his visit to Germany in 1908, he had been impressed by the military as well as by the economic resilience of imperial Germany. His national coalition in 1910 had included defence reorganization as a prominent feature of its projected programme. And it was Lloyd George who

[17] Speech at the Guildhall, 9 July 1914.
[18] Lloyd George to Mrs Lloyd George, 15 January 1914 (N.L.W., MS, 20,433, No. 1497).

provided a startling contrast with the government's supposed pacifism in foreign affairs during the second Moroccan crisis in July 1911, when at the Mansion House he appeared to put forward a somewhat indefinite threat to Germany (Doc. 27). Its belligerent tone created a sensation; when Asquith uttered similar views in more restrained language a few days later it caused little comment. In domestic terms the Mansion House speech gave Lloyd George a new celebrity amongst the right-wing press; Maxse in the *National Review* concluded amiably that in the Cabinet 'Baptists' and 'Imperialists' were finally at one in the defence of national honour (Doc. 28). One legacy of the Agadir affair was that Lloyd George became much more involved in the discussion of German war plans through the Committee of Imperial Defence.

But there was so little apparent attention paid by Liberal ministers to overseas affairs that it encouraged a general view that Britain would remain aloof from any European conflict, the Entente with France notwithstanding. Certainly Britain remained detached during the Balkan wars of 1912–13, and the assassination at Sarajevo in June 1914 and the subsequent escalation of tension between Austria-Hungary and Serbia appeared most unlikely to implicate Britain directly. Lloyd George later complained (Doc. 29) that the Cabinet had devoted virtually no attention whatsoever to foreign policy during the eight years up to 1914. His account of his own ignorance of the new commitments entered into by Grey in the light of military conversations with the French after 1906 was certainly exaggerated, but the Cabinet as a whole seems to have been totally unaware of these discussions until after the Agadir crisis in 1911.

When the threat of world war, therefore, loomed up in August 1914, the Cabinet's response was hard to predict. It was widely assumed that a 'peace party', comprising a substantial proportion of the ministers, would resign rather than endorse a British declaration of war; Lloyd George himself was generally assumed to be of their number, perhaps their leader. These illusions, however, were soon exploded. Certainly he fought hard in the Cabinet after 30 July to delay any final British commitment, and the next few days were agonizing ones for him. On the other hand, he had foreseen the prospect of a German invasion of Belgium, together with the strategic threat it posed to Britain. Those Liberal backbenchers who took an openly pacifist position and called for a declaration of non-intervention—men like Ponsonby, Buxton and Morrell—were not influential and had little contact with members of the government. The Cabinet's 'peace group' ultimately proved to be something of a myth. It became clear that hardly any minister could contemplate resigning after the German ultimatum to Belgium—

certainly not Lloyd George who still recalled the impotent isolation he had endured during the South African War fourteen years earlier. In consequence, Churchill's urgings upon Lloyd George on 2 and 3 August 1914 to follow the 'patriotic' line accorded with the Chancellor's own instincts—reinforced by the unexpected 'jingoism' of 'Uncle Lloyd' back home in Wales. In the event, only Morley, a veteran without influence on the rank-and-file, and John Burns, an isolated refugee from the labour movement, resigned from the government; Asquith's government remained essentially intact. After a day or so of catharsis, Lloyd George and other Cabinet ministers found a new buoyancy and confidence after the desperate domestic crises that had so recently been paralysing their party and their government.

Lloyd George rapidly acquired a new national stature when war broke out in August 1914. First, his skilful handling of the 'flapping penguins' of the City in dealing with the complicated financial crisis that war created now won him a new reputation in economic circles. The national credit, fortified by a new issue of treasury notes, was secure, and Lloyd George had confirmed his talent as an outstanding departmental chief. Even sceptical economists like Blackett and J. M. Keynes were impressed.[19] The 'war budget' the following November, though less justifiably so since it eschewed increases in direct taxation, was also thought a great triumph. It was, however, as the government's main voice with the general public that Lloyd George so dramatically enhanced his national standing. His address to a mass audience of London Welshmen at the Queen's Hall, London (19 September 1914) in which he stridently denounced Germany as 'the road hog of Europe' won him a new popular acclaim. He followed it up with a series of equally powerful recruiting speeches and also with several successful approaches to organized labour. In March 1915 he negotiated with the unions the 'treasury agreement' under which labour conceded many traditional demands including, in effect, the right to strike. Thus, by the late spring of 1915, Lloyd George had emerged as the one Liberal minister whose popular standing had unmistakably risen. He was not tarnished with military failure as even Churchill was, after the ambiguous outcome of the Antwerp expedition. Somehow, Lloyd George seemed to stand apart from the government of which he had so long been a member, and to stand on a distinct pinnacle of his own. At Westminster, now that he was well known to be a severe critic of the government's war policies, especially in relation to the supply of munitions, he seemed to have gained a new all-party acceptance, if hardly all-party trust. To the public, Lloyd George, a controversial

[19] Roy Harrod, *The Life of John Maynard Keynes* (London, 1951), p. 197.

Cabinet minister for ten years, seemed somehow a new man, uniquely equipped for the new dangers of total war.

While Lloyd George gained in authority, however, a view sedulously fostered by his allies in the press, the Liberal government rapidly fell into disarray. With the war supposed to be marked by a party truce, local Liberal Associations went into rapid decline, while such a basic component of grass-roots Liberalism as the nonconformist chapels now found themselves confronted by a desperate crisis of conscience. The chapels were deeply rent by moral confusion, pulled one way by the pacifism of many ministers, and the other by the full-throated 'patriotism' of Robertson Nicoll, Lloyd George's admirer who edited the *British Weekly*. Lloyd George's apparent attempt to reunify the nonconformist conscience in April 1915 by a vehement temperance campaign, with proposals ranging from complete prohibition to state purchase, was overtaken by events. The Liberal Party at Westminster was equally confused. Backbenchers found themselves a prey to an immense range of attitudes towards the war, but with virtually no public opportunity for discussing them. Meanwhile, the bases of their party's policy—Irish Home Rule and Welsh Disestablishment—remained in a state of suspended animation, while even such a traditional principle as the protection of individual liberty was now being menaced. The passing of such an extreme measure as the Defence of the Realm Act was an appalling shock to many Liberals; in the government, ministers like Samuel and Simon gave voice to this alarm.

Even so, the government was unlikely to be torn apart by internal factionalisms. Attempts by the London press, such as the *Daily Chronicle*, to portray rival bids for the leadership by dissident ministers, usually attributed to Lloyd George and Churchill, found little evidence to sustain them. Asquith's leadership was still beyond question. It was far more likely that the ministry would simply subside into a kind of paralysis: the early months of 1915 made it all too evident that the war was destined to drag on for a long time to come, with no sign of an Allied breakthrough, either on the western front or in such peripheral and badly-planned enterprises as the Dardanelles expedition. Quite suddenly, a political crisis flared up in May 1915. The apparent cause for this lay in the resignation of Lord Fisher, the First Sea Lord, after a final irrevocable clash with Churchill. But behind it lay a long background of discontent, both in the Commons and within the government itself, with the conduct of the war in general and of the production of munitions in particular. The decisive action was taken by the two party leaders, Asquith and Bonar Law, both anxious to shore up their positions and to side-step attacks on them by backbenchers chafing at the party truce. On 17 May Bonar Law wrote a dramatic letter to

Asquith (Doc. 30) virtually demanding that Asquith should remodel his administration. Asquith did so, but on his own terms. He ensured that the Liberal predominance within the government was preserved. Reginald McKenna was surprisingly promoted to the Exchequer to keep out a Unionist, after a proposal that Lloyd George should hold both Treasury and Munitions fell through; Runciman and Birrell, two other ineffective Liberal ministers, also retained office. The Unionists were granted relatively humble posts, with Bonar Law himself only accorded the Colonial Secretaryship. Nevertheless, it was a decisive moment, a watershed in political history. The great Liberal administration which had held office since December 1905 had abruptly collapsed. There has never been another.

It has often been asserted that the rivalry between Asquith and Lloyd George, which was to tear the Liberals apart within another eighteen months, lay behind the crisis of May 1915. In fact, there is no evidence that relations between the two at this time presented any basic difficulty. There is no indication at all that Lloyd George was in any sense involved in a prior conspiracy with the Unionists. In fact, the latter regarded him with deep distrust, while his acceptance of the new post of Minister of Munitions was of immense political service to Asquith. Indeed, Lloyd George actually seems to have turned down a Tory offer of the premiership. Mr Stephen Koss's attempt to create the myth of a Lloyd George conspiracy, based mainly on a misleading account by Charles Hobhouse, is therefore not convincing.[20] Relations between Asquith and Lloyd George remained amicable for some time to come, and the Prime Monister continued to use Lloyd George in such delicate matters as negotiations with labour over unrest in the mines. Even so, the net effect of the crisis of 1915 was considerable upon the Liberal Party. The party leadership was isolated still further from its own backbenchers and from the party in the country, by the intrigue which formed the new government. Further, the effect was inevitably to lower Asquith's own prestige and authority, and to make him more heavily dependent upon Lloyd George's support. Conversely, the entry of Conservatives into the government and the drastic demotion of his one major Liberal ally, Churchill, left Lloyd George in an increasingly difficult position. From now on, it was that much harder to find any real affinity between himself and the party to which he had devoted his career. His leading associates within the government were all Conservatives, Balfour

[20] Stephen Koss, *Haldane: Scapegoat for Liberalism* (London, 1969), Chap. VII; D. Lloyd George to Mrs Lloyd George, 26 May 1915 (N.L.W., 20,435C, No. 1585). This point is most cogently argued in Cameron Hazlehurst, *Politicians at War* (London, 1971), pp. 234 ff.

notable amongst them; even more did he turn to political allies in the newspaper world, proprietors like Lord Riddell and working editors like his Manchester conscience, C. P. Scott.[21] Conversely, of his close Liberal allies, Rufus Isaacs (now Lord Reading, Lord Chief Justice) had left party politics, while Charles Masterman had lost his seat in parliament (and also Lloyd George's confidence after his refusal to fight for the nomination in Swansea District). To a unique extent, Lloyd George's position now showed how the pressures of war had changed the character of party politics. It had elevated ministers; it had debased the Commons; it had undermined the party machine. Lloyd George, leaving in his wake not only the old Liberalism of Newcastle days but even the newer Liberalism of his early middle age, was now on his own. To an extent that few could perceive, his Prime Minister and his party were in some measure his prisoners, to sustain or to destroy.

[21] See Trevor Wilson, *The Political Diaries of C. P. Scott, 1911–28*, passim. Lloyd George was first connected with the *Guardian* when he became its Welsh correspondent in 1895.

3

The Crisis of War, 1915-18

FROM the start, Asquith's new Coalition was plagued by intrigue and dissension. Long before the end of 1915, it seemed that its days must be numbered. And, at every stage of the crisis, it seemed that the Liberals were the inevitable victims. For it was their principles which the very fact of total war, with the unbridled collectivism and the 'jingo' passions which it unleashed, appeared to undermine. From May 1915, therefore, the Liberal party at Westminster became increasingly riven by internal divisions, while the constituency parties just withered away. Amidst all these new tensions, most Liberals felt that the introduction of military conscription marked a symbolic divide between a whole-hearted commitment to all-out war, whatever the sacrifice, and a respect for the historic cause of individual liberty. The issues involved had already been raised, in a very different context, by Lloyd George himself in April, just before the downfall of the Asquith government. This concerned the supply of alcoholic liquor, which Lloyd George considered a grave menace to the war effort. He had shaken his colleagues with a series of extreme proposals, even including the public ownership of the drink trade, an extremely radical measure which a traditionalist like Asquith resisted to the end. Lloyd George's temperance schemes eventually collapsed, leaving as their curious legacies the nationalized public houses of Carlisle and the diluted quality of 'Lloyd George's Beer'. But the issue of military conscription raised the question of the validity of the Liberal ethic during wartime in a far more acute form.

A significant warning sign came in July 1915 (Doc. 31) when some eight backbench Liberals issued a 'whip' to their parliamentary colleagues to urge them to endorse national service. They included such prominent Liberal capitalists as Sir Alfred Mond and the newspaper magnate, Sir Henry Dalziel. Mond, indeed, was very shortly to resign his connection with the *Westminster Gazette* in protest against that journal's stubborn resistance to any form of conscription. These were still mainly lone voices on the Liberal backbenches. But they had now the most powerful of advocates in the Cabinet, in Lloyd George, the new Minister of Munitions. Lloyd George had been, until the fall of the late government, an advocate of stepped-up recruitment drives rather than of conscription, which would be likely to lead to trouble with the trade unions. But he was now bitterly critical of his government's dilatory handling of the war. His aim was at all costs 'to win a definite victory somewhere' and to try to devise a more imaginative strategy to break through the stalemate on the western front. Quite suddenly, he came to regard military conscription as a unique symbol of the rigorous prosecution of the war; from June onwards, he advocated it boldly. So, too, did almost all the Unionist ministers, and by November the Cabinet was paralysed by dissension over the conscription issue, with Asquith himself, now an increasingly enervated and dispirited figure, unable to offer any lead. The consequences of this conflict over conscription were profound for the future development of the Liberal Party—perhaps even more profound than the later events of December 1916. In particular, as Lord Riddell observed (Doc. 32) in early November, it led to Lloyd George's becoming entirely alienated from his Liberal colleagues. He was aligned with the most unremitting 'patriots' in the Unionist party on almost every major issue. With close associates, usually journalists and press lords like Riddell or C. P. Scott, he frequently discussed the merits of his resignation in view of Asquith's inertia and inability to create effective institutions or instruments of government with which to fight the war (Doc. 32). On 20 December 1915, Lloyd George gave astonishingly public expression to his feelings in his 'too late' speech in the Commons: 'in this war, the footsteps of the Allied forces have been dogged by the mocking spectre of "too late" '. It was a calculated blow at the policies of the government of which he was a member, almost a blatant challenge to Asquith to dismiss him.

To keep his government afloat, Asquith had to make concessions, and his government's Military Service Bill of January 1916 proposed a modified form of conscription dealing with single men only. This produced an agonizing crisis of conscience for many Liberal ministers (Doc. 33). In the event, only Simon, the Home Secretary, resigned from the government; Runciman and McKenna, both stern opponents of the servile state, were somehow induced to stay on, while C. P. Scott in the *Manchester Guardian* used his journal as an outspoken vehicle of protest for fundamentalist Liberals throughout the land. Simon's speech explaining the reasons for his resignation touched some basic Liberal chords, particularly his reference to the ultimate value of the voluntary principle. But at Westminster the effect of his resignation was very slight. By contrast, one influential body now created was the 'Liberal War Committee', a group of perhaps forty Liberal members, headed by Sir Frederick Cawley, and including such notable associates of Lloyd George as Dalziel, Mond and Freddie Guest. This group, still largely ignored by historians, became in effect the spokesman for all those Liberals who sought a redirection of the government's war policies, with the implication of a change of leadership as well. There is no evidence that Lloyd George gave them any direct encouragement, but for the first time Asquith's critics had in embryo their own alternative organization within the Liberal party.

Throughout March and April 1916 the argument over conscription continued to rage. The 'Derby' recruitment scheme and the compromise bill in January were held to be quite inadequate for producing the necessary recruits in sufficient numbers, while Asquith's leadership was more and more indecisive. By early April (Doc. 34) Lloyd George was on the verge of resigning. However, as he was made to recognize, outside the administration he would be more isolated still, with no firm support from the Unionists and no decisive strength amongst his own Liberals. All this time, pro-Asquith journalists like A. G. Gardiner and J. A. Spender kept up a fierce refrain of criticism directed against Lloyd George, alleging that he was implicated in a series of conspiracies against the leadership of Asquith. None of their charges has ever been in the least degree substantiated, but they did much damage, and certainly Lloyd George did seem now an isolated man within his own party. At the same time, however, he was not without some backing. He had close contact with two hitherto obscure backbench Liberals, Christopher Addison, his deputy at the Ministry of Munitions, and David Davies, a fellow-Welshman and a millionaire coalowner. Together with another Liberal, F. G. Kellaway, the member for Bedford, these two had drawn up an unofficial list of perhaps a hundred Liberals who might be expected to back Lloyd George if a confrontation arose with Asquith (Doc. 35). The precise significance of this list is very much open to debate: its composition was shifting and the degree of the commitment of its members most uncertain. There is no evidence that Lloyd George himself tried to foster its growth as a 'connection' sympathetic to himself, and by June, Addison's group seemed to have evaporated. Even so, its very existence did indicate how the suspension of party politics during the war years had weakened the structure and the leadership of the Liberal Party. From now on, Asquith's authority could no longer be taken for granted. On the conscription issue as a whole, he emerged in a poor light. At every stage he was forced to yield and eventually to introduce a whole-hearted Military Service Bill for all males between the ages of eighteen and forty-five, a reversal of policy that inevitably elevated the stature of Lloyd George and undermined that of Asquith.

Lloyd George had by now established himself in a curiously distinct political category. He was prepared to exploit his own Liberal credentials (for instance in rallying 'my teetotal friends nagging me at Rhyl'),[1] but equally he occupied a fluid position hard to locate on the political spectrum. He had potential allies in many varied camps. Through his remarkable work at the Ministry of Munitions, he had reinforced his special relationship with the leaders (if not the rank-and-file) of organized labour. Through the good offices of Sir Arthur Lee, a Unionist lieutenant at the Munitions ministry, he had also achieved contact with Lord Milner and his group of 'Round Table' imperialist protégés.[2] One of the latter, Philip Kerr, was shortly to become the most intimate of Lloyd George's personal advisers. A striking indication of this supra-political position that Lloyd George was now carving out came when Asquith called him in as supreme conciliator in a final attempt to settle the Irish problem. After the government's disastrous mishandling of the aftermath of the Easter rising in Dublin, the rapid growth of Sinn Fein, the position in Ireland had become critical. Asquith even offered Lloyd George the post of Irish secretary—once wryly dismissed by John Morley as 'the back kitchen'—but Lloyd George wisely declined. Still, he did appear to achieve an astonishing degree of success in winning over first the Ulster Unionists and then Redmond and T. P. O'Connor (another journalist ally of Lloyd George) to a compromise agreement over Irish Home Rule. For a tantalizing period in June, Lloyd George appeared on the verge of an extraordinary political breakthrough, a compromise acceptable both to the Nationalists and the Unionists. However, the crucial issue of the exclusion of Ulster—whether it was to be permanent or merely for a period of years—produced the inevitable breakdown. Lansdowne, Long and their Southern Unionist friends forced him to propose new terms that Redmond in his turn had to reject. Henceforth, there could be no Irish compromise, and Sinn Fein's spectacular growth in 1916–18 heralded the final alienation of most of Irish opinion from the government at Westminster. For Lloyd George himself the collapse of his Irish negotiations served to reinforce his disillusion with old-fashioned Liberalism and the Gladstonian past. He turned instead to favour an imperial rather than a home rule solution of the Irish question. However it was noted that the responsibility for the failure of an Irish

---

[1] William George, *My Brother and I* (London, 1958), p. 249.
[2] P. A. Lockwood, 'Milner's Entry into the War Cabinet, December 1916', *Historical Journal*, VII, No. 1 (1964), pp. 127–9.

settlement seemed somehow to be foisted upon Asquith rather than upon Lloyd George himself.

The transformation in Lloyd George's personal position in the government became increasingly marked. On the death of Kitchener, the Secretary for War, in June 1916, Lloyd George, with much reluctance, accepted the War Office, even though its powers had been curtailed by measures previously advocated by Lloyd George himself to curb the authority of Kitchener. But the new War Minister found himself more and more alienated by the conduct of the war. Disaster followed disaster—the bloody failures on the Somme, the equivocal engagement at Jutland, the collapse of the Russian offensive, the gradual petering out of the Salonika expedition which Lloyd George himself had advocated. The Allied position continued to deteriorate— indeed, the failure to provide aid for Rumania in the autumn of 1916 seemed to Lloyd George significantly to strengthen the position of the central powers in the Balkans. These developments drove him to rare depths of depression: on 9 November he told Hankey, the secretary of the War Council, 'we are going to lose this war',[3] and resignation seemed more and more probable. At the same time, press stories multiplied about the plots in which he was supposed to be implicated, especially in the columns of J. A. Spender, editor of the pro-Asquith *Westminster Gazette* (Doc. 36). In fact, no specific 'conspiracy' has ever been unearthed. Without doubt, Lloyd George had his own wide range of contacts with the press and also with friendly junior members of the military and naval staffs. On the other hand, as Lord Esher admitted, Spender provided a ready link for counter-espionage between Asquith and Grey and a commander at the front like Haig. If Lloyd George was engaged in political sub- version and intrigue at this period, there is nothing to suggest that he was uniquely—or, indeed, successfully—engaged in it. In fact, his mounting frustration in the autumn of 1916 was in large measure a consequence of the fact that he had, politically, seldom been more isolated.

The one decisive and determining factor, though, was the grow- ing realization that the Asquith ministry was simply incompetent. On all sides, political and military, critics were almost unanimous that a new leadership was needed to run the war and to force a victory. Opinion, too, seemed to be crystallizing that Lloyd George, with all his known faults, alone could supply it. This was the view even of General Robertson, with whom Lloyd George was later to clash so violently (Doc. 37). As Robertson noted, the War Council Asquith

---

[3] Sir Maurice Hankey, *The Supreme Command* (London, 1961), Vol. II, p. 557.

had set up was clumsy and inadequate, while Asquith's judicial temperament and passive disposition were obstacles to the achievement of firm decisions. The mood of defeatism and despondency was far more widespread than was echoed in occasional debates at Westminister. Whether, however, it could be satisfied without irreparable damage to the government and to the dominant party within it, whether political reform was possible without a political revolution, had still to be seen.

The remodelling of the Asquith coalition was the dominant preoccupation of all political observers by the end of November 1916. Above all, it was the theme of the meetings between Lloyd George, Bonar Law and the Unionist backbench leader, Carson, meetings to which historians have later attached such disproportionate importance, that took place almost daily, from 20 November onwards. These meetings, which owed much to the mediation of the Canadian go-between, Max Aitken, followed a damaging challenge to Bonar Law's leadership from the Unionist backbenchers in a debate on 8 November, with the implication that he should dissociate his party from the failing leadership of Asquith. But, however much the new association of Lloyd George and Bonar Law may have been dramatized by Beaverbrook's later account (partly designed to magnify the role of his patron, Bonar Law), it was far from being a conspiracy. Asquith himself was kept fully informed by Bonar Law from the start, and does not appear to have found the discussions either unusual or alarming. In the event, Lloyd George, Bonar Law and Carson presented a memorandum to Asquith on 1 December which appeared to safeguard his position in all essential details (Doc. 38). It was proposed that there should be a War Committee set up for the supreme direction of war policy, but subject to the supreme control of the Prime Minister who would have a permanent power of veto. There was at this stage no indication that Asquith himself opposed a scheme that seemed likely to make his government a more effective executive instrument of policy. Certainly, there was no suggestion, implicit or explicit, that Asquith should be supplanted as Prime Minister, least of all by Lloyd George. But later, on 1 December, the first ominous signs of a rift began to appear (Doc. 39). Asquith's reply to the memorandum was markedly less conciliatory than had been his conversation with Lloyd George earlier that day. While Asquith fully accepted the need to reconstitute the War Committee, and while he was prepared to be flexible on the delicate question of the personnel of the new body, he insisted that the Prime Minister himself ought to sit on the War Committee as chairman rather than be 'relegated to the position of an arbiter in the background'. But to Lloyd George and to Bonar Law, this was a decisive objection, since it was vital to separate totally the new committee, concerned solely with supreme decision of war policy, from the Cabinet with its multiple concerns. The fatal defect of a tension between the Prime Minister of the Cabinet and the chairman of the new War Committee seemed to be raised in an acute form.

From now on, the pace of events dramatically quickened, and historians have found it hard to work out a coherent chronology. Lloyd George heralded a new phase of the crisis by his famous short note to Bonar Law on 2 December (Doc. 39); this note was first published by Beaverbrook in his *Politicians and the War*, which has so greatly coloured all subsequent accounts of these events. In fact, Lloyd George's position now was a relatively weak one, and many writers have exaggerated his power. His relations with Bonar Law were not easy, and most of the Unionist leaders distrusted him utterly; their suspicions had been reinforced by Lloyd George's attempts to negotiate an Irish settlement during the summer. Again, the 'Lloyd George Liberals' listed by Addison the previous April were in no sense a coherent faction; effectively, they had dissolved. Even so, the prospect of Lloyd George's resignation, which Asquith's letter had clearly opened up, was a most damaging one, and neutral observers of the crisis now strove to repair the breach. Notable among them was Edwin Montagu, the Minister of Munitions and a Liberal who enjoyed good relations equally with Asquith and Lloyd George. Montagu in desperation wrote to Asquith later on 2 December (Doc. 40) urging him to effect some kind of compromise which could uphold both the substance of the new War Committee and the leadership of the Prime Minister. Montagu was intimately involved with the course of events during the next four days, but even he was unable to provide any specific solution to the 'nightmare' in which he found himself. In any case, he realized that McKenna, Runciman, Harcourt and other Liberal ministers were now encouraging Asquith to stand firm, whatever the cost.

The next day, Sunday, 3 December, it became apparent that Asquith's position was beginning to crumble. The new phase was heralded by a remarkably imprecise resolution passed that morning by the Unionist ministers, headed by Curzon, Lord Robert Cecil and Austen Chamberlain (Doc. 41). It urged Asquith to ask for the resignation of his government so that it could be remodelled. The Unionist ministers apparently intended this resolution to strengthen Asquith's hand, though clearly more than one interpretation could be placed upon it. In the event, the meeting that resulted between Bonar Law and Asquith had a most unfortunate outcome, since Bonar Law's version of the resolution, which he failed to quote in full, was apparently misunderstood by Asquith. The Prime Minister saw it, perhaps understandably, as a move directed against his own leadership, and relations between him and the Unionists, never easy, rapidly deteriorated. Nor did later meetings with Curzon and other Unionist ministers make matters clearer. Even so, Asquith's government was still far from lost. No alternative leader seemed to be emerging, Lloyd George being still largely an isolated figure. That evening, 3 December, a new draft of the original memorandum on 1 December was drawn up, mainly by Montagu, Maurice Hankey and Maurice Bonham-Carter, Asquith's secretary, in which it appeared that a modified version of the proposed War Committee would now be acceptable to the Prime Minister.

The next day, Monday, 4 December, began in a mood of amity, or so it seemed. Lloyd George himself now regarded the crisis as over, and the essence of the new War Committee as now agreed upon by all the major parties concerned. And yet, by the late afternoon of that day, the ministry was on the verge of dissolution, and historians have continued to disagree about the responsibility for the breach that resulted. Asquith later cited as the occasion for his break with Lloyd George a strange leading article that appeared in *The Times* that Monday morning which gave a remarkably complete though not wholly accurate account of the recent top ministerial discussions. The article welcomed Asquith's acceptance of Lloyd George's demand for a supreme War Council, and also emphasized Bonar Law's and Carson's association with it. The article as a whole was a strong endorsement of Lloyd George's views, and it is not surprising that Asquith responded by assuming that Lloyd George had inspired it, especially as it was known that relations between Lloyd George and Northcliffe, the owner of *The Times*, had now been resumed. Asquith, therefore, wrote to Lloyd George in stern tones (Doc. 42), urging that the Prime Minister's authority over the new War Committee be made transparently clear and citing the *Times* article as an example of the way in which outside pressure from journalists could distort constructions placed upon the new agreement. Since, however, Asquith did accept by implication that the Prime Minister should not actually serve in the new War Committee, but should supervise it from outside, there still seemed to be no essential difficulty. Lloyd George wrote back in conciliatory terms, and yet again the crisis seemed to have crossed over another dangerous chasm.

But from now on, the position rapidly deteriorated. Asquith's reply to Lloyd George's letter later that day, 4 December, was markedly more belligerent in tone. He returned again to his earlier position in insisting that the Prime Minister must sit on and be chairman of the new Committee, and also demanded that Carson be excluded from any War Committee that might be set up. He also insisted on a larger membership for this new body. These demands, especially the first, were obviously a declaration of war, and Lloyd George at once offered his resignation. Somehow, between the morning and the late afternoon of 4 December, Asquith's views had totally changed. After appearing to accept the new scheme, the vital part of which was that the Prime Minister should not be a member of the new War Committee, he suddenly reversed his position. In effect, he declared that any further negotiations with Lloyd George would be fruitless. Edwin Montagu, in a desperate effort to salvage the situation the following day, 5 December, wrote to discover why Asquith had gone back on his previous proposals (Doc. 43). Montagu gave three main reasons, namely Northcliffe's irresponsible *The Times* article, the pressure from Asquith's Liberal colleagues, especially from McKenna and Runciman, and the difficulty about including such controversial politicians as Carson in any new Committee. Montagu's puzzlement over Asquith's complete change of front has been shared by historians ever since, and no satisfactory explanation has yet been advanced. One authority on the crisis, Dr Hazlehurst, takes the view that Asquith, having won many of the points at issue, simply lost his nerve, and certainly there is difficulty in finding a rational explanation for his conduct. Certainly the *Times* article (in fact written on his own initiative after a talk with Carson by Geoffrey Dawson, the paper's editor)[4] was a trivial enough cause for such a momentous breach with Lloyd George. The pressure of the Liberal ministers may carry somewhat more force as a factor in Asquith's decision. In addition, however, it might well be questioned how long the effective supremacy of any Prime Minister could be sustained with power likely to be sucked away into a committee of which he was not a member. More, there was mounting evidence of a growing personal rift between himself and Lloyd George, made more bitter by the influence of McKenna and Runciman, both bitterly hostile to Lloyd George (Doc. 44). The evidence of the political meetings of the following day, 5 December, indicates that it was Asquith and not Lloyd George who adopted the inflexible view throughout. Whereas Lloyd George insisted that a compromise was still very possible and emphasized to Montagu, Hankey and other go-betweens that he still thought it essential to retain Asquith as Prime Minister,[5] the other Liberal ministers almost unanimously urged Asquith to resign and to leave his opponents to struggle on by themselves. This was the burden of their meeting on the evening of 5

[4] *History of The Times*, Vol. IV (London, 1952), p. 297.
[5] S. W. Roskill, *Hankey, Man of Secrets*, Vol. I (London, 1970), p. 328.

December, in which their hostility to Lloyd George was very pronounced.

Clearly Asquith at this stage had gravely overestimated his political strength. His abrupt reversal of his previous position had made the *de facto* liaison between Lloyd George and Bonar Law an unshakable alliance: in the face of Asquith's open challenge they were inevitably thrown together. Now the Unionist ministers, who had dithered in a pitiful manner during the past two days, submitted their resignations. The ship had foundered at last: by the end of 5 December Asquith's coalition premiership was at an end. Nor was it clear now how far any kind of Liberal administration could be reconstituted. A significant feature of the past few days was a resumption of the movement to assemble a backbench group of Liberal members sympathetic to Lloyd George. Addison, the organizer of the group the previous April, now resumed his inquiries and, with his associates, Kellaway and Glyn-Jones, came up with a large though somewhat unreliable array of over a hundred Liberal backbenchers who were thought likely to support Lloyd George if he were able to form a government (Doc. 45). The exact influence of this upon the subsequent course of events is not wholly clear, but Addison himself henceforth was much involved in the formation of the new government. On 6 December Asquith submitted his resignation to the King. A last effort by the King to effect a reconciliation between Asquith, Bonar Law and Lloyd George came to nothing, and, with Bonar Law predictably declining the offer of the premiership, Lloyd George accepted the King's commission to try to form a government.

In the next three days, 7–9 December, by herculean efforts, he was able to amass enough all-party support to form a government. His ties with Bonar Law ensured that the great bulk of Unionists would now back him—indeed his position here was sufficiently secure that eventually he was able to keep Carson out of his new War Cabinet, as Asquith had also wanted. Addison and other Liberal sympathizers, the Welsh parliamentary party prominent among them, gave him adequate initial support from his own party, although no Liberal front benchers of any note joined the government. Churchill, one of Lloyd George's firmest backers, was at this time a very isolated figure and was not found a place in the new ministry owing to Unionist hostility. For Lloyd George, however, it was the attitude of Labour that would make or break his attempts to form a government. J. H. Thomas, the railwaymen's secretary and another Welshman, was a key figure here: important negotiations took place between him and Dr Thomas Jones, an obscure member of the National Insurance Commission, who played an important role in the political manœuvres of this time. Lloyd George's talks with Thomas on the morning of 7 December bore fruit, and later that day at a crucial meeting, by the narrowest of majorities, he won the support of the trade union leaders for his proposed labour policy.[6] Arthur Henderson was eventually to represent the Labour Party in the new War Cabinet. By the end of 9 December, the main issues were all resolved. A new War Cabinet of five was set up—Lloyd George, Bonar Law, Curzon and Henderson, together with a surprise choice, the apolitical figure of Lord Milner. Without any action from Parliament, with only the incidental involvement of Members of Parliament, a new government had been created, and the future course of British politics totally transformed.

The dramatic events of December 1–9 have long been keenly disputed by historians, and it seems improbable that any completely satisfactory consensus will ever be found. Clearly, these days provide one of the decisive watersheds of recent British politics. The fact of Asquith's being supplanted by Lloyd George, and the manner in which it was done, with the appalling effects upon the Liberal Party that resulted, had had shattering consequences both for the party and for the main combatants in the crisis. Since December 1916, the Liberals have played an increasingly peripheral role; never since then have they shown any sign of a convincing recovery as a party of power. Not surprisingly, accusations of conspiracy have been widespread and certainly the way in which Bonar Law and Lloyd George came together, with the sinister mediation of Aitken, was in some respects clandestine and suspicious. On the other hand, Lloyd George was far from alone in playing politics during this crisis, nor did he precipitate the final breakdown of talks. There seems little reason to doubt that his reluctance to overturn Asquith as Prime Minister was genuine enough, and that the memorandum of 1 December must be regarded as an instrument for rejuvenating the supreme command, and not a personal bid for power. What seems equally clear is that Asquith himself failed to appreciate the manner in which confidence in his own leadership had simply drained away. A sad interview he gave to a sympathetic Liberal journalist, Robert Donald, editor of the *Daily Chronicle*, on 7 December confirms this view (Doc. 46). Asquith insisted again on the crucial role played by the *Times* leading article of the 4th in causing the final rift, though the sum of the evidence available suggests that he was clearly deceiving himself. Asquith's emphasis on the question of the personnel of the new Committee also leaves many questions unanswered in the historian's mind, since all the names put forward were negotiable as far as Lloyd George was concerned. The truth appears to be that Asquith,

[6] There is a full account of this meeting in David Lloyd George, *War Memoirs* (new edition, London, 1933), Vol. I, pp. 625–9.

in this ultimate crisis, showed in extreme form his own characteristic blend of ambitious partisanship and personal detachment. Remote from contact with the press or with his own backbenchers, as Robert Donald noted, Asquith simply exaggerated his own strength. His comments on Balfour, who in fact swung his own influence towards Lloyd George during the crisis, are a good example of this. Conversely, Asquith seriously underrated his opponents, especially Bonar Law, for whom he had a well-developed contempt. In fact, even in his own party, Asquith was losing ground, while his heavy-handed treatment of his Unionist colleagues since May 1915 left him with little hope of gratitude or support from that quarter. Lloyd George's succession to the office of Prime Minister in December 1916 was far from pre-ordained: it was not the cause of the ministerial crisis at all. But Asquith's own intransigence made his own departure from office almost inevitable: he left a vacuum that Lloyd George alone could fill.

For the rest of the war, Lloyd George's personal ascendancy was to be the main agent of change in British politics.[7] With orthodox party alignments still in suspense, the ultimate implications of his premiership as a Prime Minister without a party were far from clear. The machinery and organization of the Liberal Party in the country remained in the hands of Gulland and the official party whips. Indeed, Lloyd George had been projected to supreme office in a manner utterly remote from the normal conventions of the party system. In general, it was assumed in 1916 that his premiership was a temporary wartime phenomenon, and that Asquith was likely to return to lead the Liberal Party as soon as peace was restored.

From the outset, however, it became clear that a basic change in national politics had taken place. Partly this feeling was inspired by the new Prime Minister's style. More than any of his predecessors, he remained aloof from the usual political circles, preferring his own unorthodox self-made associates, and the security of his own intensely Welsh household in Downing Street, to contact with his fellow politicians. Even more, however, did the nature of the new premier's power arouse instant comment—and, soon, accusations of dictatorship. There were divided opinions about the effectiveness of the new War Cabinet he created, but without doubt it enormously enhanced the Prime Minister's authority. It gave him an unprecedented authority over

[7] For general accounts of the wartime premiership, see John Ehrman, *Cabinet Government and War, 1890–1940* (Cambridge, 1958), Chap. III; John P. Mackintosh, *The British Cabinet* (London, 1962), Chap. 13; Alfred M. Gollin, *Proconsul in Politics* (London, 1963), pp. 377 ff.; and Kenneth O. Morgan, 'Lloyd George's Premiership', *Historical Journal*, XIII, No. 1 (1970), 132–44.

supreme decision-making. Again, the new Cabinet secretariat became in effect a kind or Prime Minister's department. Even more symptomatic was his own private 'secretariat' or 'Garden Suburb' whose influence permeated the entire governmental machine and gave him an extraordinary personal ascendancy. Arthur Henderson later commented that 'L.G. was the War Cabinet and no-one else really counted' (Doc. 52).

In political terms, however, Lloyd George's position was always highly precarious. Early in January 1917, he discussed the wider political scene with some of his close Liberal associates, Neil Primrose, his Chief Whip, Sir Alfred Mond and Sir Edwin Cornwall (Doc. 47). Their general feeling was a reluctance to challenge the existing Liberal party organization in such a way as to antagonize party workers in the country. At the same time, it was recognized that Lloyd George's lack of a national party organization was a fatal weakness: already, it seemed, a more permanent division within the Liberal Party was being acknowledged. Lloyd George's first aim was to preserve his position in parliament. He went far towards gaining this objective in July when he secured two outstanding Liberals, Edwin Montagu and Winston Churchill, as members of his government (Doc. 48). As Derby observed, Asquith saw two of his most able lieutenants removed, and the whole operation, conducted in characteristically brisk manner by Lloyd George personally, strengthened his position in the House and in the country. For months to come, he continued to brood, when the military situation allowed, on his anomalous political position. The Prime Minister's future was the theme of many of his private discussions with Riddell and other press advisers (Doc. 50). Lloyd George now developed a favourite thesis that the war had provided that great divide in British politics that he had long foretold, and that the old party conflict between Liberals and Unionists was being superseded. Instead, a new alignment was emerging, based not so much on class as on the basis of authority. A sectional Labour Party, headed by Arthur Henderson (who had left the War Cabinet in August 1917) and fired with revolutionary fervour after the Bolshevik triumph in Russia, would confront a broadly-based national bloc headed by Lloyd George himself, representing property, constitutionality, and law and order. Typically, Lloyd George brushed aside the importance of a formally organized party, with agents, local associations and candidates; but at least the theme of forming some kind of Lloyd George organization was crystallizing in his mind.

But in the short term, his position rested simply on survival. In practice, this largely focussed upon his persistent conflict with the generals on the running of the war. The Admiralty had been effectively placed under the Cabinet's control in May 1917, and by December Jellicoe had been swept aside in favour of Beatty. The army, however, was a far tougher adversary, and over the decision to launch the Flanders offensive in June 1917 Lloyd George had to admit defeat. Haig, the Commander-in-Chief on the western front, and Robertson, chief of the General Staff, were well provided with political allies. Hankey, the secretary to the Cabinet, felt certain that Robertson was 'intriguing like the deuce' with opponents like Asquith (Doc. 49). The crucial turning-point came the following February. Then Lloyd George managed to manœuvre Robertson into an impossible situation in which he had either to retain his present post with much reduced powers, or else move to the unknown hazards of the new military council set up at Versailles. It was a desperate crisis and Lloyd George came nearer than at any other time to resignation. By the barest of margins, Robertson was defeated, even Haig deserting him in the final crisis. The war was henceforth to be largely directed by the so-called 'X Committee' of the War Cabinet, consisting of Lloyd George himself, Milner, now War Minister, and the new chief of the general staff, General Wilson. The ascendancy of the administration over the army was thus largely ensured, and the survival of Lloyd George was now a political certainty. In addition, he was shoring up his position by widespread contacts with the newspaper press, which played a vital part in shaping the popular mood during the Robertson crisis. The Coalition Liberal chief whip, Guest, warned Lloyd George that his contacts with the press were becoming counter-productive (Doc. 51), especially through the sinister activities of Lloyd George's press secretary, 'Bronco Bill' Sutherland. But the special relationship between the government and certain selected press lords was helping to fill the political vacuum which Lloyd George's position as Prime Minister had created. He was beginning to develop independent support.

The possible shape of post-war politics increasingly dominated discussion during the spring and summer of 1918. Although the outcome of the war remained still very much in doubt, until the final allied breakthrough on the western front in August, at least the entry of the United States into the war, with the immense accretion of industrial and military strength that this brought with it, made an allied defeat unthinkable. More and more, therefore, Lloyd George found opportunity to reflect upon his own political role. It was alleged that Beaverbrook was brought into the government as Minister for Information in order to finance a new party. In April (Doc. 53) Lloyd George conducted for Riddell's benefit an illuminating examination of his own political credo, as re-defined by total war. His own anxiety to transcend mundane partisan and sectarian politics, so well illustrated in the coalition scheme in 1910, now found a new credibility as the pre-war issues melted away. His own creed of 'Nationalism-Socialism' consorted well with the Milners, bureaucrats like Hankey and Thomas Jones, and with all the apolitical tycoons he had introduced into his war administration. At the centre he was supreme. He had an army overflowing with generals. The problem, as Riddell acknowledged, was to find a rank-and-file.

For the present, Lloyd George's dream of a new 'National Party' was very remote. He had, therefore, to make what he could of his own shifting groups of supporters in the Liberal Party. The occasion, though not the cause, arose following some startling revelations in the press by General Maurice, until very recently in charge of Military Intelligence (Doc. 54). Maurice alleged on 7 May that recent statements in the House by Lloyd George and by Bonar Law were inaccurate, and that Haig's forces on the western front had been deliberately reduced by government decision during the past nine months. There followed the most serious partisan crisis of the war, the so-called 'Maurice Debate' of 9 May 1918.[8] Lloyd George, using figures that many historians have subsequently questioned (and which he himself, if Hankey's diary is to be trusted, appears to have known were incorrect), was able to rout Asquith's hesitant challenge. Further, he won over almost all the Unionists in the House by an inspired speech, as well as the majority of Liberals present. However, ninety-eight Liberals did vote against the government, and, while the divisions over the Maurice affair did not perhaps have the precise consequences that historians once imagined, still a new bitterness grew up between Liberal supporters and critics of the government.

Soon the gulf between 'Asquithian' and 'Lloyd George' Liberals in the House was extended to the constituencies. By the end of May, an organization was in being to co-ordinate known Coalition supporters within the Liberal Party. Captain Guest and the faithful Addison were behind this move, and by July a 'Coalition Liberal' party could be deemed to exist in Westminster, if not in the country. A much more drastic step then followed, one pregnant with immense consequences for the future course of British politics. This was the electoral pact concluded between Guest and Bonar Law, for the Unionists, in July 1918 (Doc. 55), which originated the notorious 'coupon'. While no rupture with the official Liberal party was overtly mentioned, the pact meant in effect an electoral agreement between the Lloyd George Liberals and the Unionists which would guarantee the former up to

150 seats at the subsequent general election.[9] The position of the Coalition Liberals was indeed curious since their programme consisted simply of the perpetuation of the ascendancy of the Prime Minister. They were numerically much the weaker partner in the alliance. On the other hand, it might be noted how crucial to the Unionists was the presence of Lloyd George. In eighteen months he had become the one indispensable factor in any victorious political alignment. Contrary to the impression given in Dr Trevor Wilson's account of the events of the next few months,[10] it was Lloyd George and not the Unionists who exercised the political initiative and dominated the stage.

Victory in the field greatly enhanced his position. By the end of October, it was clear that the war was almost over, and he and Bonar Law formally concluded an alliance with which to fight the general election. The adhesion of the Unionists, whatever their reluctance to mortgage their future to the unpredictable premier, was guaranteed. What was equally vital to Lloyd George's designs was to win over a substantial portion of his own party also, to give a real bargaining position within the alliance. Decisive here was the attitude of the Liberal members of the government, and Lloyd George had intimate discussions on this point early in November with H. A. L. Fisher, the historian who now served as President of the Board of Education (Doc. 56). Fisher and other Liberals were anxious about compromising some deeply-held principles: for instance, free trade could be sacrificed by too many concessions over anti-dumping and 'key industries' legislation. But the Liberal ministers were duly won over. These Coalition ministers readily saw what they were doing: they were transforming the wartime division of their party into a permanent breach. Churchill, ever ambitious for office, saw that 'here is a great split'. The next day, 7 November 1918, Liberal participation in a post-war government was ensured. Lloyd George placated his colleagues on free trade, Ireland and Indian policy, but they were all too willing to be placated. The immediate pattern of post-war politics had been determined.

Beaverbrook and others on the Unionist side felt that their party had swallowed Lloyd George whole, especially on the question of imperial preference. But Lloyd George argued with considerable force to his fellow Liberals that it was he who had dominated the Unionists. The coalition manifesto issued by him and Bonar Law on 22 November 1918, shortly after the armistice (Doc. 57), went far towards confirming this view. On the main issues of contention—free trade, the House of Lords, India, Irish Home Rule, the Welsh Church—while there were

[9] Trevor Wilson, 'The Coupon Election and the British General Election of 1918', *Journal of Modern History*, XXXVI (1964), pp. 28–42.
[10] Trevor Wilson, *Downfall of the Liberal Party*, pp. 140–56.

concessions to Unionist sentiment, the main lines of policy advocated would follow an unmistakably Liberal direction. Further, the manifesto contained a clear endorsement of a progressive social policy on housing, education and other issues, in the best 'New Liberal' tradition. It was surely through the Coalition rather than through the hesitant clichés pronounced by the Asquithians that the New Liberalism that had swept the party in the pre-1914 period would be best sustained.

The election campaign that followed was a very strange one. On the surface, it was quiet, almost dull, with a good deal of unanimity between rival candidates on the main lines of post-war reconstruction at home and abroad. But the circumstances in which the election had been launched, and particularly the arbitrary way in which 'coupons' of government endorsement were accorded to, or withheld from, various Liberal candidates aroused much bitterness from Liberals up and down the land. The manner in which Liberal opponents like McKenna and Runciman, let alone Labour candidates, were made scapegoats for the 'jingo' mood added to this bitterness. Certainly, the election left an unpleasant memory behind it, one which Keynes was later to perpetuate in memorable terms (Doc. 58). According to him, the punitive Carthaginian terms which he felt to be enshrined in the Versailles peace settlement was the inevitable result of the mood of the 'coupon election'. Keynes saw this election as coloured by a mood of 'hang the Kaiser' hysteria to which Lloyd George himself, especially in a notorious speech at Bristol on 9 December, made a leading contribution. But it is clear that Keynes's celebrated account wildly exaggerated Lloyd George's share in the revanchist atmosphere of the campaign. His own campaign speeches were usually moderate and responsible, though the unscripted peroration of his otherwise balanced speech at Bristol was a most unfortunate impromptu. In any event, Asquithian Liberals such as Donald Maclean and many Labour spokesmen were equally vehement on the need for the trial of the Kaiser, and for exacting heavy reparations from Germany. On the other hand, the circumstances of the election undoubtedly put opponents of the government at an emotional disadvantage. It was not the usual party contest. Far more than any election since at least Palmerston's triumph in 1857, it was a personal mandate for one man, the architect of victory, and for all his supporters from whatever party they came. Edwin Montagu's sycophantic description of the 'one man nature' of the campaign (Doc. 59) was intended as a compliment. But the campaign had an unhealthy background. The man who adopted the 'national' posture had arrogated for himself alone the mantle of patriotism. In that sense, the election resembled the prelude to a personal dictatorship. Much would rest on what residual checks Lloyd George's own Liberal instincts could impose on his conduct of post-war politics.

The 'coupon election' marked a political revolution. Over 520 supporters of the government were returned, over 470 of them with the 'coupon', while the 'un-couponed' Liberals numbered less than thirty. Indeed, most of these few at first claimed to be supporters of the government also, as did many Labour members. The Liberal Party emerged from the election shattered in morale. They had indeed 136 'couponed' representatives at Westminster, but many of these had been forced upon hostile local associations, and the extent to which they still remained Liberals in anything but name was far from clear. At the party level, the electoral triumph belonged to the Unionists—and also to the Labour Party whose small tally of fifty-seven seats masked a notable electoral breakthrough in terms of votes, despite the adverse circumstances in which the election was fought. The serried rival ranks of capital and labour, the dominant features of British society well before 1914, were now reflected at Westminster also. In this situation, an inevitable polarization of politics took place. Many radicals, especially those like Arthur Ponsonby or E. D. Morel associated with the anti-war Union of Democratic Control, turned towards the Labour Party. Conversely, many traditional Liberal supporters in the business and industrial world, especially many shipping and textile magnates, alarmed at the threat to private capitalism from a powerful and militant trade union movement, gravitated to the right. Lloyd George himself seemed to be descending along this same unhappy path. It was hard indeed to reconcile the strident apostle of national unity in 1918 with the fierce champion of the right of dissent (and the rights of Dissent) ten years earlier. As Riddell was to observe of him, 'he has entirely changed'.

More fundamentally, the Liberal Party was now shattered in structure and morale, a supreme casualty of total war. Its organizational machine, the central offices at Abingdon Street and the regional councils, were all securely in Asquithian hands, save only in Wales; but its grass-roots support was rapidly being eroded. In local government, the Liberals, often disguised as 'Ratepayers' now, were in full retreat. In such traditional Liberal strongholds as the West Riding and South Wales, the working-class vote was being thrown massively behind the Labour Party. In Scotland, 'red Clydeside' seemed to be unleashing an even more menacing threat, stemming from the ILP and the new Communist Party.[11] With the growing cohesion and class

---

[11] See Keith Middlemas, *The Clydesiders* (London, 1965).

consciousness of Labour, political and industrial, the forces of capital coalesced in self-protection and inevitably found its political voice in the Unionist Party. Most damaging of all was that two fundamental elements of popular Liberalism for three generations past, two vital bases for Lloyd George's own ascent to power—the nonconformist vote and Celtic nationalism—were now visibly in decline. The nonconformist denominations were demoralized by the war. The wartime years, with their pressures towards social and sexual equality, had imposed immense strains upon the puritan ethic.[12] The 'big guns' of the pulpit seemed to have little to say to the new post-war generation back from the trenches. Nor could nonconformists claim any longer to be in any real sense a victimized minority; indeed, men like Sir William Robertson Nicoll seemed all too obviously members of the new power élite, sometimes zealous in persecuting those dissenters who opposed the war. The old nonconformist struggle for social equality had long since been achieved: even in Wales the old issue, still unresolved, of the disestablishment of the Church, aroused scant public attention now. The traditional cries—Church schools, temperance reform, religious equality—were pitifully out-of-date. The old objectives were now attained and nonconformists, already crippled by financial problems, seemed to have little left for which to fight. Again, the national movements in Wales and in Scotland had lost much of their momentum. The aspirations of Scottish nationalists had always been somewhat ill-defined. Those of Welsh nationalists, centring on the privileged position of the bishop and the squire, had been satisfied long before 1914, as Lloyd George's own career so fully demonstrated. In Clydeside and South Wales, capitalism, not clericalism, was the enemy now. Here again, the Liberal Party's very successes in a half-century of democratic achievement contained the seeds of their own decay. With the decline of the chapels and the passing away of the first, most vital, wave of Celtic nationalism, the Liberal Party was losing something fundamental, social forces that had provided it with a built-in local organization and a transcendent moral appeal. The old Liberalism was in retreat; the new Liberalism was already being pre-empted by the Labour Party as it assumed leadership of the British left. Only one unpredictable force kept Liberalism alive as a major element in post-war politics: the mysterious, uncertain influence of Lloyd George himself. This alone would determine whether his rise to national leadership would relegate his own party to sectional impotence.

[12] For a good discussion of the social and psychological effects of the war, see Arthur Marwick, *The Deluge* (London, 1965), especially pp. 297–9.

4

The Lloyd George Coalition, 1918-22

THE party system that unfolded in the months following the 'coupon election' was barely recognizable in terms of pre-war politics. The absence of the Prime Minister himself at the Paris peace conference until July 1919 added to the air of unreality. There seemed little purpose in day-to-day controversy in the absence of the one figure who lent cohesion both to the supporters and to the opponents of the administration. Everyone seemed to be conducting a holding operation until Lloyd George's return, with occasional interludes such as his brief and majestic flying visit to Westminster in April to flay 'die-hard' critics of the peace negotiations.[1] In parliament many detected a new mood of cynicism that boded ill for the evolution of post-war politics. Among these anxious observers was Edwin Montagu (Doc. 60), who viewed the capitalist supporters and the trade union opponents of the administration with equal contempt. Like many other Liberals at the time, he was torn by a kind of schizophrenia, lamenting the departure of Asquith and other old comrades, yet anxious to cling to the 'national' government, seeking to be both Liberal and Coalitionist at the same time. The result was to drive him to a kind of paralysis of despair. Meanwhile at Westminster, the relation between the Coalition Liberals like Montagu and their Unionist allies remained unclear. Bonar Law had argued at the outset of the new parliament that all the Coalitionist members should sit together as a homogeneous whole, irrespective of party, and that they should have joint whips. But as long as separate Liberal and Unionist organizations continued, this could not be achieved, and in practice the two parties continued to work in parallel rather than in unison, eyeing one another with wariness, both treasuring their independence.

---

[1] *Parl. Deb.*, 5th ser., Vol. 114, pp. 2936–56 (16 April 1919).

In July 1919 Lloyd George finally returned permanently to the domestic political scene. Far from being reviled as the architect of a savage, Carthaginian peace, as Keynes would have us believe, he returned to a Roman triumph, hailed on all sides as the hero of a liberal settlement that combined peace with honour. His prestige was immense, his reputation at its zenith. Now was the moment to translate the apolitical, semi-presidential ascendancy of the wartime years into something permanent.

He himself had little doubt about what the outcome should be. The war had finally increased his impatience with the old politics—and, indeed, with the remains of the old Liberalism. The contemptuous way in which he brushed aside the Welsh disendowment settlement in August 1919, casually tossing £1 million in compensation to the Church in the face of Welsh nonconformist protests, was proof enough of that. For years he had consorted with businessmen and bankers, press lords and bureaucrats, all in their way devotees of a new 'national' politics, based on executive power and national unity. In short, they sought the perpetuation of the coalition on a permanent basis, not as a mere transitional legacy of the war years. Ideally, this would have meant a continuance of the political style of the War Cabinet, but Lloyd George was compelled to recognize that this was no longer feasible. In October he was forced, with much reluctance, to restore the pre-war Cabinet, with nineteen members, though many wartime features such as the retention of the Garden Suburb with the omnipresent Philip Kerr, and the growing influence of the Cabinet Office under Hankey, reminded contemporaries that much had not changed. Just as the War Cabinet had disappeared, however, so too had the party truce, as the fierce campaign being put up by Labour in by-elections now confirmed. After their successful challenge to the Coalition Liberals at the Spen Valley by-election in January 1920, when Labour captured the seat and Sir John Simon forced the government candidate to the bottom of the poll, the Independent Liberals moved to a position of all-out opposition to the government. Party politics had returned, and Lloyd George had now to determine his own relationship to it.

To the Prime Minister, a national government would have to be underpinned by a national party. Since the war had produced the beneficial disappearance of the old conflicts between Unionists and Liberals, the opportunity should be seized to fuse the two into a new national organization. Only thus could the Coalition be perpetuated. Lloyd George first addressed himself to what seemed to be the easier task, winning over the Coalition Liberals. In January and February 1920, he tried to convert the Liberal ministers to the idea of 'fusion'

(Doc. 61). 'Liberal labels' were worthless, he insisted; instead, a new national policy must be pushed through by a united coalition, followed by a period of 'administration' on the non-partisan basis. The Liberal ministers were doubtful, but Lloyd George discounted their reluctance. In any case, two Liberal ministers at least were ardent advocates of the idea of fusion, though on totally different grounds. Addison, the Minister of Housing, wanted it because only in this way could an agreed programme of social reform be carried through; conversely, Churchill, the War Minister, saw in a 'national' party the only effective means of combating the red peril of labour militancy with which he was now obsessed. On the Unionist side, there were favourable omens also. The Lord Chancellor, Birkenhead, wrote some powerful articles in the press on behalf of a coalition (Doc. 62). In these he urged that only a new national party, behind a national administration, could secure united action over such overriding issues as foreign policy and defence, Irish home rule and domestic reform. With some reluctance, Bonar Law agreed to this idea of fusion as the only method of ensuring the leadership of Lloyd George over a Conservative-dominated government.

In March 1920, the fusion of the Conservatives and the Coalition wing of the Liberal Party was generally anticipated. Then, quite suddenly, at meetings of the Liberal members between 16 and 18 March the whole scheme fell through (Doc. 63). To the general astonishment, the Coalition Liberals proved to be a decisive stumbling-block. Most of them were more anxious to keep the way open for reunion with the Asquithians than to unite permanently with the Tory enemy. They could not view as casually as Lloyd George appeared to do the prospect of sacrificing age-old Liberal policies on such questions as free trade. Even more, they had a rooted hostility to abandoning their historic party label: they were still Liberals. Lloyd George's meeting with the Liberal backbenchers was, therefore, anti-climactic, and he called only for a vague 'closer co-operation' with the Unionists at the constituency level. Bonar Law regarded this development laconically, as he had always regarded fusion as more necessary from Lloyd George's standpoint than from that of the dominant Unionist Party. Fusion, in fact, was off. Lloyd George's only real opportunity of remoulding the British party system on his own terms, to create a new national party to replace the old, had gone for ever.

Lloyd George himself remained in a political limbo after this failure, though still apparently impregnable as leader of the nation. His political outlook still heavily emphasized the 'national' aspect of his programmes, with its right-wing implications, in contrast to the sectional demands of Asquithian 'pacifists' and Labour 'bolsheviks'.

As Riddell noted (Doc. 64), he seemed closest in spirit now to self-made captains of industry, whose contempt for democracy was often very marked. By contrast, his hostility to socialism was at this time very pronounced, and he was bitterly reviled by Labour spokesmen for making comparisons of Arthur Henderson with Lenin and Trotsky. His own Coalition Liberals were now out on their own. At the Leamington conference of the National Liberal Federation in May 1920 (Doc. 65), their spokesmen, Addison and Macnamara, were howled down; the schism between Coalition and Independent Liberals, already made plain in several by-elections, was now beyond repair. As the veteran Unionist minister, Walter Long, complained, the Coalition Liberals had attempted to persuade their Asquithian colleagues that the government of which he was a member was essentially Liberal in complexion and that they had sacrificed nothing of their traditional creed. But the Independent Liberals, newly encouraged by Asquith's own return in a famous by-election at Paisley, viewed this claim with as much scepticism as did Walter Long. Henceforth, Lloyd George's Coalition Liberals were in an uncomfortable category of their own, expelled from their own party but without another to cling to, and with little encouragement from their leader.

The pattern of party politics for two more years continued to be dominated by Lloyd George's own manœuvres. Even after the failure of fusion in March 1920, he continued to be fascinated by the prospect of winning over the Unionists to a grand national coalition on the lines of the Peelite-Liberal coalition in the 1850s or alternatively (another favourite analogy) in a great unified command like that led by Foch in 1918. Certainly most of the Unionist ministers seemed congenial and even willing partners. Austen Chamberlain, who succeeded Bonar Law when he retired from the Unionist party leadership in March 1921, apparently permanently, was even closer in contact with Lloyd George, admittedly on a clear master-servant basis. So, too, were other Unionist ministers such as Balfour, Birkenhead, Horne and Worthington-Evans. A new combination of party leaders seemed an ever-present possibility and was, indeed, in many ways the logical outcome of the alignments in parliament between 1920 and 1922.

Whatever the sympathies of ministers for fusion, however, it rapidly became clear that the Unionist rank-and-file became more and more insistent for independence. By 1921, they saw that the Coalition was clearly unpopular in the country, with a sorry record of economic dislocation and severe strikes at home, and the lack of success of its policies abroad. Ireland was another cancer in the body politic. By January 1922, fortified by the conclusion of the Irish Free State Treaty, rank-and-file rebellion among Unionists throughout the land was widespread.[2] In particular, the Coalition Liberals were now held to be a complete incubus, and an unhealthy one, mainly a projection of Lloyd George's own personal entourage. A continuance of the alliance with these adventurers was widely resented. In any case, many Unionists believed, Lloyd George's personal future was now seriously in doubt. Austen Chamberlain and the party leadership treated this with grand indifference, but there was mounting, month after month, growing pressure on the Unionist leadership for the resumption of normal political relations.

On the Coalition Liberal side, now surprisingly aggressive in view of the party's dismal results in by-elections, the response was less clear. A close adviser like Sir William Sutherland, a major participant in the 'honours scandal', urged the Prime Minister to go to the country on a totally new programme (Doc. 66). He argued, with much cogency, that the old Liberal themes—education, temperance, free trade and the rest—were out of date, and that social and economic issues like the cost of living weighed far more with the modern voter. But Sutherland was much more effective in diagnosis than in explaining of what this new Liberal policy should consist. Other Liberals in the government felt that the political manœuvres of the past year or two had put them in a humiliating position. Fisher and Hilton Young, two powerful Liberal intellects (Docs. 67–68), argued that the growing Tory dominance in the government, and the loss of Liberal ministers like Addison and Montagu, had left them with no tenable position. Once the Genoa conference was out of the way, Lloyd George and his Coalition Liberals should resign at once and leave the helpless Tories to flounder about on their own. The outcome, in Hilton Young's view, would be a new and much stronger coalition in which Lloyd George's leadership would no longer be under challenge. Central to the thinking of both Fisher and Hilton Young was the belief that Lloyd George still dominated the political stage. Whatever the gales of backbench criticism and the vitriolic personal abuse to which he was subjected in the right-wing press, he still seemed the dominant factor in current politics. Three years and more after the 'coupon election', he was still, to friend and foe alike, outstandingly the man who would determine the way in which post-war party politics would develop. But the extent to which British politics were still in any valid sense post-war had still to be tested.

The shape of politics after 1918 was much influenced by the immense series of crises with which the administration had to deal. A common theme in all these issues was the personal involvement of the Prime

[2] See Robert Rhodes James, *Memoirs of a Conservative* (London, 1969), pp. 100 ff.

Minister. After his return from Paris in July 1919, he increasingly resembled a kind of minister of all departments, assuming each portfolio in turn and throwing traditional forms of Cabinet responsibility and collective participation to the winds. It is this period that has led some historians to see Lloyd George as inaugurating a new era of 'Prime Ministerial government'.[3] Nowhere were these new tendencies more apparent than in the realm of labour policy, where he grappled manfully, and on the whole successfully, with the threat of a general strike. In an industrial world totally transformed by the war years, with the trade unions infinitely more powerful, and with a slump in the staple industries, there was a persistent atmosphere of crisis. In particular, pressures for 'direct action' became widespread in the trade union movement, especially among the miners. The government appeared to meet this with a stern front, none more so than Churchill, now moving rapidly to the extreme right on domestic issues. Once a leading advocate of 'social radicalism', the architect of labour exchanges and of social insurance before 1914, a champion of radical measures like nationalization of the railways as recently as 1919, Churchill was now a belligerent and uncompromising opponent of labour. The open sympathy of many Labour leaders with the revolutionary régime in Russia added force to his appeals to popular prejudice against the 'red peril'. Yet, in general, neither side wanted a class war. Churchill's belligerence was toned down by a government which passed a notable series of social reforms, including Addison's Housing Act of 1919 and the introduction of unemployment insurance on a general scale in 1920. On the Labour side, most trade union leaders, men like Smillie and Thomas, basically sought conciliation. There was, however, one famous occasion when trade union threats of 'direct action' turned into something approaching reality. This involved the creation of 'Councils of Action' in August 1920 when the Trades Union Congress decided to set up committees throughout the land to ensure the prevention of arms shipments to Poland to aid the White Russian armies.[4] Shortly afterwards, Lloyd George announced that British arms in fact would not be sent to Poland, and that the Poles were being urged to conclude peace. This gave rise to the later legend amongst Labour supporters that the Councils of Action were themselves the cause of the British government's decision. In fact, Lloyd

[3] For instance, Humphry Berkeley, *The Power of the Prime Minister* (London, 1968), pp. 48, 77; R. H. S. Crossman, introduction to Walter Bagehot, *The British Constitution* (Fontana edition, 1963), pp. 48 ff.; and, with modifications, John P. Mackintosh, *The British Cabinet* (London, 1962), pp. 348 ff.

[4] L. J. Macfarlane, 'Hands off Russia in 1920', *Past and Present* (December 1967), p. 138.

George had himself long reached the conclusion that it would be impractical and unpopular to mortgage British arms in an open-ended war in eastern Europe, and certainly at variance with his attitude of appeasement in foreign affairs.

The Councils of Action again brought Lloyd George to the forefront in the handling of labour policy. He had long employed all the varied weapons in his formidable armoury in the attempt to placate labour. In 1919 he had been as ready to use armed force to quell workers on strike as had Churchill himself. In October he was prepared to starve the striking railwaymen into submission, while the Cabinet discussed the possibility of enlisting university-trained stockbrokers and other loyalist groups in a Citizen Guard.[5] On the other hand, conciliation and diplomatic guile were more in accord with Lloyd George's typical approach. His most remarkable triumph came in March and April 1921, when a renewed miners' dispute over the contentious issue of a national wages' pool brought a threat of a national stoppage by the Triple Alliance. On 'Black Friday', 15 April 1921 Lloyd George seized on an unlucky impromptu by Frank Hodges, the secretary of the Miners' Federation and another Welshman; he isolated Hodges and obtained a virtual suspension of support for the miners by the other trade unions. In effect, the Triple Alliance dissolved and never rose again. Thereafter, after several more serious disputes in the summer of 1921, the worst-ever year for industrial stoppages, the industrial situation improved; by 1922 the loss of workdays in strikes was infinitely less serious. On the purely tactical front, Lloyd George had won a series of brilliant victories, a tribute to the endless fertility, resource and imagination that he could apply in cutting through the complexities of labour disputes. He could claim that the threat of a general strike had been averted and, at a time when Italy, France and other countries were plunged into industrial turmoil, the fabric of British society survived intact. On the other hand, in political terms the consequences for Lloyd George's future were to prove disastrous in the long run. His manœuvres, especially the sidetracking of the recommendations of the Sankey Commission in 1919, which included a proposal for the nationalization of the mines, as well as his biting attacks on 'bolshevist' and 'unpatriotic' labour leaders, robbed him henceforth of the support of the organized labour movement. His attempt to rally 'patriotic' labour, on the lines of the small National Democratic Party and the British Workers' League, proved a hopeless illusion. Throughout this period, the Labour Party grew steadily in membership and polled notably well in by-elections, in

[5] R. K. Middlemas (ed.), *Thomas Jones: Whitehall Diary*, Vol. I, 1916–25 (Oxford, 1969), p. 101.

large measure in reaction to the government's industrial policy; by 1922, Labour was a far more convincing challenger for power than were the ragged and demoralized ranks of the Independent Liberals. Lloyd George himself was never trusted by Labour again: the special relationship, dating from his period at the Board of Trade in 1905–8, had evaporated. When Lloyd George made approaches to the Labour Party in his later career, in 1927 just after the general strike, and in 1931 just prior to the financial crisis, Labour was almost united in rebuffing him. Labour's memories were longer than were Lloyd George's own, and his future as any kind of leader of the British working-class was hopelessly doomed.

If his industrial policies, with which he was so closely associated in a personal way, forfeited Labour support for Lloyd George, his government's treatment of Ireland cost him the bulk of Liberal and radical sympathy. By 1920, with the failure of its Government of Ireland Act in winning any support outside Ulster, the government was committed to complete coercion of the Sinn Fein movement, even to civil war. The use of auxiliary forces like the 'Black and Tans' was a profound shock to the Liberal conscience, and to one-time supporters of Gladstone's home rule policy. Lloyd George himself does not seem to have played much part in the determination of Irish policy until early 1921. He left matters largely in the hands of the Irish secretary, Sir Hamar Greenwood, a Liberal minister but a notable hard-liner. However, Lloyd George's own utterances on the 'time of troubles' in Ireland were remarkably belligerent and insensitive. At Caernarvon in October 1920 he committed the government to a policy of forcible retaliation towards the 'murder gang' in southern Ireland. In words of Old Testament ferocity, reinforced by the strident nationalism he had picked up during the war years, he spelled out the impossibility of ever granting Ireland complete independence, because of the consequent threat to British national security on its western shores. This kind of rhetoric may have gone down well with the nonconformist patriarchs at Caernarvon, but many Coalition Liberals, even in Wales, reacted with disgust. When, to these coercive policies in Ireland, was added the government's open flouting of free trade in the Safeguarding of Industries Act (1921), with its 'key industries' and 'collapsed exchanges' provisions, the Coalition Liberals' allegiance to their leader was strained to the limit.

The exact pressures that led Lloyd George to a reversal of his Irish policies in May and June 1921 are not yet wholly clear, though clearly Liberal and Labour criticism played some part.[6] He perhaps realized

---

[6] The best account of the peace negotiations is still Frank Pakenham, *Peace by Ordeal* (London, 1935).

also that he had grossly underestimated the difficulty of subduing southern Ireland by force, and the extent of the sympathy of the civilian population for the IRA. In the event, serious negotiations eventually began with Arthur Griffith and the other Sinn Fein leaders in October 1921, with the negotiations very much under the personal direction of Lloyd George himself. He spent two anxious months in conclave with Griffith, Michael Collins and the other delegates, searching for a compromise over such complex issues as finance, defence obligations, the oath of supremacy and the status of Ulster. The negotiations were further hampered by President de Valera's insistence on staying in Dublin throughout, while the Ulster government was not represented at the talks. The final achievement of agreement on 5 December 1921, after many final moments of anxiety, was a dramatic vindication of Lloyd George's negotiating methods. He had personally managed to win Michael Collins over beforehand by man-to-man diplomacy. Then Collins, under severe pressure from de Valera, appeared to go back on the agreement. Finally, by a supreme bluff, Lloyd George won over the Irish delegates by threatening an immediate resumption of hostilities: even the recalcitrant minority, Barton and Gavan Duffy, now felt compelled to sign the articles of agreement. The following month, by a vote of sixty-four to fifty-seven, the Irish Dail agreed to endorse the Irish Free State treaty, and the partition of Ireland was now a political fact. Many anxious months elapsed before anything like order was restored in Ireland, months that saw the murder of Sir Henry Wilson at his London home by IRA gunmen. There followed bitter civil war in Ireland between supporters and opponents of the treaty that dragged on until May 1923. Some crucial issues, above all the Boundary Commission that was to report on the geographical demarcation between northern Ireland and Eire, and which Griffith and Collins had imagined would inexorably lead to a unified Ireland, were left ambiguous.

Nevertheless in practical terms the Irish question had been removed from the forefront of British politics. No longer would it overshadow public life as it had done ever since the days of Cromwell. When the Irish question re-emerged in British politics in the late 1960s through the Ulster civil rights movement, it was as intractable as ever, but now basically peripheral. Lloyd George, then, in some sense could claim to have solved the Irish question, where Pitt, Peel and Gladstone had failed, and where Palmerston and Disraeli had not even tried. But, as in the case of his labour policies, his triumph was bought at a terrible cost. The years of reprisals and coercion in Ireland had alienated so much Liberal and intellectual support that he lost credibility among radical voters henceforth, especially among the young. To Oswald

Mosley, writing of these events nearly fifty years later,[7] Ireland divided the generations in Britain almost as sharply as the war in Vietnam was to do in the United States in the 1960s and 1970s. A man like C. P. Scott of the *Manchester Guardian*, prepared to forgive and forget even the Black and Tans, in the light of the achievement of peace in Ireland, was a very rare phenomenon. Here again Lloyd George and the Liberal ethic seemed to be parting company. Conversely, while Liberals wrung their hands at coercion in Ireland, many Unionists felt deeply unhappy at the granting of self-government to the land run by that Sinn Fein 'murder gang' so eloquently denounced by the Prime Minister. The achievement of the Irish Free State thus added to the pressure from the Unionist rank-and-file for a final breach between their party and the volatile and unpredictable Prime Minister.

Foreign policy added further strains to the political bases of the coalition. Soon the euphoria that followed the Treaty of Versailles gave way to increasing disillusion, for which the writings of Keynes set the mood. Conference followed conference, and still German reparations were not forthcoming, and still the Kaiser remained safely aloof in Holland, and still such basic issues as Franco-German relations and a settlement of the Greek-Turkish conflict in Asia Minor remained unresolved. More than any feature of the government's operations, foreign policy bore the personal stamp of Lloyd George himself. He was the only one of the three major peacemakers of Versailles to survive with his political power and personal energies undimmed. Now, in a series of over twenty major international conferences between 1919 and 1922, he tried to create the new international order to which he had pledged himself at the 'coupon election'. Two themes in particular exercised his attention.[8] First, he was anxious to bring Germany back into full association in the comity of nations, instead of turning her into an international pariah, weighed down by savage reparations. At Paris in 1919 he had pressed, in his Fontainebleau memorandum and elsewhere, for a relaxation of the reparations imposed upon Germany and a modification of her national frontiers in relation to the Rhineland, Danzig and Upper Silesia. Now at Spa, San Remo and other conferences he preached the gospel of moderation and conciliation. Lloyd George, in short, was the first appeaser of Germany after 1919. Secondly, he was anxious to restore the fabric of European trade, credit and industry, ravaged beyond

---

[7] Oswald Mosley, *New Outlook* (April/May 1970), pp. 33–4.

[8] For discussions of Lloyd George's views on foreign affairs at this time see Arno J. Mayer, *Politics and Diplomacy of Peacemaking* (London, 1968), especially Chap. 18; and Martin Gilbert, *The Roots of Appeasement* (London, 1966), pp. 60–79.

recognition by the war. Thus at a series of conferences he tried to pioneer proposals to restore traditional markets in central and eastern Europe through long-term credits and a stabilization of currencies. In particular, he attached great importance, in commercial as well as in political terms, to the establishment of normal diplomatic relations with the Soviet Union after the winding up at the White Russian and Allied intervention. Advisers like Philip Kerr and E. F. Wise, his personal assistant on eastern European affairs, pressed advice upon him in this sense. In short, Lloyd George sought to restore the economic and political system of pre-1914, based on the balance of power and the Bank of England, with the two great outcasts of Europe, Germany and Soviet Russia, restored to full association with the community.

But the political implications of these courageous policies were once again damaging for Lloyd George. The anti-German nationalist hysteria of the 'coupon election' was still widespread, while Soviet Russia was deeply distrusted during the red scare and labour unrest of the 1919–21 period. Again, Lloyd George's choice of methods was politically controversial. Churchill argued in 1920 that Lloyd George had virtually taken over the running of the Foreign Office himself. In addition, Philip Kerr, the key member of the 'Garden Suburb', exercised a wide-ranging influence upon foreign affairs, without any of the usual constitutional or parliamentary safeguards. In practice, the Foreign Office accepted its demotion with remarkably little protest. Balfour, the Foreign Secretary until the end of 1919, willingly acquiesced in Lloyd George's handling of foreign policy. His abiding philosophy was 'a free hand for the little man'.[9] Curzon, who succeeded him, was a more abrasive personality. Lloyd George treated him with scant respect and brushed his protests aside time and again. At the same time, Curzon's protests usually involved matters of protocol. On the substance of policy on a wide front—French security, German reparations, naval negotiations with the United States, he was content to follow Lloyd George's lead. Not until the flare-up of hostilities in the Near East at the end of the administration did any more fundamental conflict develop between the Foreign Office and the Prime Minister. In the meantime, the interference of the Premier's personal aides, first Philip Kerr and then Edward Grigg, into foreign policy and international diplomacy, went on largely unchecked.

For much of the time, Lloyd George still had real hopes of fulfilling his vision of a new world order. In particular, the Washington naval conference in the autumn of 1921 achieved considerable agreement with the United States and Japan over capital ship construction. In

[9] Blanche Dugdale, *Arthur James Balfour* (London, 1936), Vol. II, p. 196.

Europe, throughout 1921, relations between Britain and Germany steadily improved, and Lloyd George's hopes for reconciling French fears for her security on her eastern frontier, and German hopes for financial and economic assistance, still appeared to be realistic. However, the Cannes conference in January 1922, which saw the fall of Briand's government in France and the succession of Poincaré, a bigoted and intransigent nationalist, was disastrous for Lloyd George's hopes. Undeterred, he turned anew to one grand effort to secure an international European settlement. This was the ill-starred Genoa conference in April 1922, intended partly as a means of restoring Lloyd George's sagging fortunes at home. But the conference yielded nothing. It was ill-prepared on the British side, and plagued by Poincaré's and Barthou's dogged refusal to scale down their demands on Germany. Even worse, the bombshell of the Rapallo treaty between Germany and Soviet Russia on the eve of the conference made its subsequent negotiations largely meaningless. French suspicions of German revanchism, right-wing detestation of Bolshevik dictatorship were re-kindled anew, and Lloyd George's foreign policies lay in ruins. All this had inivitably severe repercussions upon his political fortunes, so intimately intermeshed were his foreign and domestic manœuvres. Labour and Liberal critics were vocal in denouncing the delay in providing a realistic reparations settlement with Germany; man like Ramsay MacDonald built up a new reputation in denouncing 'the system of Versailles'. Conversely, the great mass of Conservative opinion, finding a platform in Wickham's Steed's articles in *The Times*,[10] was deeply alienated by the fear that Genoa would see the diplomatic recognition of the Soviet Union. In March, on the eve of the conference, Lloyd George was outvoted by his Cabinet colleagues; even a loyal lieutenant like Austen Chamberlain now averred that the *de facto* recognition of Russia was politically unacceptable. Churchill was even more implacably hostile to the idea, and, as the second-in-command in the Coalition Liberal (rechristened the 'National Liberal') organization, his political stature was considerable. After Genoa, the issue continued to rankle as Churchill insisted on his blank opposition to any kind of formal relationship with the Soviet government. The entire issue was deeply damaging to the Prime Minister's prestige; Thomas Jones thought that three-quarters of his Cabinet was now actively disloyal to him.[11] Foreign policy joined with labour and Irish issues in serving to undermine the Lloyd George government, and to polarize political opinion again on party lines.

---

[10] *The History of The Times*, Vol. IV, pp. 656 ff.
[11] *Thomas Jones: Whitehall Diary*, Vol. I, p. 197.

These different crises underlined the growing malaise that seemed to be affecting the government's position throughout 1921 and early 1922. By-elections, press criticism, lobby gossip all tended to a relentless condemnation of the unpopular coalition and, to a lesser extent, of the volatile leader who alone lent it cohesion. Two curious issues lent substance to this malaise, and they largely preoccupied political commentators in this later period.

The first concerned the slogan of 'economy'. A series of right-wing candidates triumphed at by-elections on the platform of retrenchment. Conservative opinion had called for the dismantling of the government's controls over industry, commerce and agriculture after the war, but its consequences in runaway inflation they refused to face. A favourite target was the housing programme of the Liberal minister, Addison, widely distrusted for his social radicalism, and soon to be thrown to the wolves in July 1921; his subsidized housing had become ruinously expensive, since it was not underpinned by controls over the cost of building materials. In the face of this right-wing clamour, and against all his own instincts, Lloyd George gave way in August 1921 (Doc. 69) and appointed a 'business committee' under Sir Eric Geddes which would investigate the nature and scale of government expenditure. The committee was strongly resisted by reforming ministers, mostly Liberals like Fisher and Montagu, and the eventual report of the committee confirmed all their fears (Doc. 70). Geddes and his colleagues went even further towards the target of £100 million of economies than had been anticipated and made slashing cuts in all aspects of central government expenditure. Oblivious to the social consequences, the economy-minded businessmen who made up the committee made huge inroads into spending on education and the social services, and the consequences for domestic reform were calamitous. Lloyd George had henceforth to preside over the dissolution of his government's own enlightened social programmes. Addison's houses, Fisher's day-continuation schools were largely swept aside, and the feebleness of the government in the face of a mounting right-wing reaction was amply displayed.

The 'honours scandal' was an even greater embarrassment for the government. Through the government's bountiful Coalition Liberal Whip, Captain Freddie Guest, a vast distribution of honours was carried out, to provide Lloyd George with a personal fighting fund of several millions. Meanwhile the faithful 'Bronco Bill' Sutherland engaged in 'the trafficking of baronetcies' in London's clubland. In retrospect, much of the moralistic outcry of the critics seems hypocritical. The sale of honours was a practice long indulged in by Prime Ministers since the time of Palmerston, while criticisms that the calibre of the House of Lords, still an entirely hereditary assembly, was being impaired by its recently-ennobled recruits could hardly be taken seriously. Nevertheless, by the summer of 1922 the 'honours scandal', so-called, was a serious political liability for the government. Above all, it drew attention to the uniquely personal character of Lloyd George's ascendancy, and the way in which he had vaulted above the orthodox party system. By July he had to reply to his Tory critics (Doc. 71): he claimed (probably correctly) that he had paid little attention to the award of recent honours, and that lieutenants like Sutherland and Guest had been largely given their heads. He was forced to set up a Select Committee and to stand in a white sheet before the enraged Tory rebels. He remained unrepentant. Years later, he argued with much cogency that the sale of honours was far healthier than the sale of policies, which was what the Tory and Labour parties indulged in. He preferred his own, supposedly open methods; indeed, the activities of J. C. C. Davidson, one of his most scandalized Tory critics, recently hinted at delicately by Robert Rhodes James, would not bear too close examination. The semi-espionage indulged in by Joseph Ball with the connivance of the Conservative Central Office was widely known, and winked at. It might be added that the Unionist party had itself shared fifty-fifty in the proceeds of the 'Lloyd George Fund'. Nevertheless, it cannot be denied that another factor tending to the resumption of normal party politics in the summer of 1922 was the way in which the public was partially persuaded that Lloyd George was somehow flouting the moral canons of respectable politics. 'Normalcy' became an ever more compelling cry.

Throughout 1922 the government staggered on from one crisis to another. Montagu, like other Liberal ministers, felt that the condition of politics was quite deplorable (Doc. 72). Lloyd George virtually ignored his Liberal colleagues, except for Churchill, and consorted almost entirely with Tories like Chamberlain, Horne, Birkenhead and Worthington-Evans. The Cabinet as traditionally known was a thing of the past. Three months after his letter, in March 1922, Montagu was driven to resign after a severe clash with Curzon over the government's aggressive attitude towards Turkey; the government seemed more right-wing than ever. Lloyd George really did seem now the prisoner of the Tory majority, as he had not been in 1919–20. Even the right of dissolution, a traditional weapon of all prime ministers, was taken from him in January 1922, when his Conservative colleagues under severe pressure from their party chairman, Sir George Younger, and from the constituency parties, resisted Lloyd George. Austen Chamberlain argued strongly (Doc. 73) that the time was inopportune because work still remained to be done. More to the point, his own party would not accept it, since it clearly wanted an election fought as an independent entity rather than as the rear legs of the Coalition horse. Unionist hostility to the Prime Minister mounted inexorably. Lord Salisbury, a typical bell-wether for 'die-hard' opinion, bitterly denounced Lloyd George to Bonar Law in March (Doc. 74), and certainly the wave of right-wing opposition to the premier was even more alarming than the hostility of labour. Edward Grigg and Thomas Jones sensed the new atmosphere of decay (Doc. 75). Cabinet ministers were largely disloyal to their leader, especially after the differences over Genoa and the recognition of Russia, while Lloyd George's own isolation from party politics was more marked than ever. 'The P.M. seemed to be losing his punch and grip.'

Even so, until the late summer of 1922, it would be wrong to over-emphasize Lloyd George's political weakness. Despite the honours scandal and the Geddes 'axe', despite Genoa and the Irish and Lord Salisbury, his influence and authority were still the dominant features of the political scene. As high summer approached, the waters appeared a little calmer, the economic scene at home more tranquil, the inter-national situation from Belfast to Delhi more peaceful. Then came the disastrous débâcle of the Near Eastern crisis, associated with Chanak.[12] Foreign policy in this area had from the outset borne the personal stamp of Lloyd George's own views. He had encouraged the Greeks to take up arms against the Turks and had encouraged the dis-memberment of the Turkish empire at Sèvres in 1920. He had a fine Gladstonian contempt for the 'unspeakable Turks' as an inferior race unfitted to rule. Then in late August the Turkish army under Kemal smashed through Greek resistance in Asia Minor, captured and sacked the city of Smyrna, and advanced towards the British position at Chanak on the Dardanelles. Lloyd George's response, backed up by Birkenhead and Churchill, was instinctively belligerent. But his threats of war met with little support from the French or the Italians, and with virtually none from the member states of the Empire. A British quarrel in Asia Minor meant nothing to the Australians or the Canadians. Above all, British opinion was now in a thoroughly isola-tionist mood and in no frame of mind for a bloody engagement with the Turks for the sake of such a theoretical goal as the freedom of the straits.

All over the country, the Unionist party rose up in rebellion. It was known that Cabinet ministers like Stanley Baldwin and Arthur Griffith-Boscawen were threatening resignation, and a complete revolt of the Unionist rank-and-file against the Coalition seemed in prospect.

[12] The most recent account is David Walder, *Chanak* (London, 1968), pp. 168 ff. For Bonar's Law's views, see Robert Blake, *The Unknown Prime Minister* (London, 1955), pp. 450 ff.

The decisive factor was Bonar Law. He had surprisingly re-emerged in political life after his serious illness, and his attitude towards the Coalition, though formally correct, was still sufficiently ambiguous to encourage Tory rebels. There was a potential alternative Prime Minister to hand at last. Bonar Law's letter to *The Times* on 7 October (Doc. 76) gave the rebels the leadership they had hitherto lacked. In general, he endorsed the main lines of British policy in the Chanak crisis, which was shortly to find a peaceful solution at the treaty of Mudania, negotiated by Curzon and General Harington. But Bonar Law's phrase about the impossibility of Britain's alone acting as 'policemen of the world' struck a responsive chord. It chimed in with the isolationist mood. The break-up of the government was now visibly under way.

In defiant mood, Austen Chamberlain called a meeting of the Unionist Members of Parliament to the Carlton Club for 19 October; but events were overtaking him. Like Asquith in 1916, Austen Chamberlain had become isolated from the major currents within his own party; like Asquith in 1916, he seriously exaggerated his strength. Ministers were now resigning, there was a 'revolt of the private secretaries', and even Curzon, who had little cause to be loyal to Lloyd George, decided to throw in his lot with them. Most decisive of all, Bonar Law had reluctantly agreed at Beaverbrook's home the previous night, before the Carlton Club meeting, to speak out in opposition to remaining in the Coalition. Beaverbrook carefully ensured that every leading newspaper carried the news the following day. At the Carlton Club, therefore, the outcome was not in doubt once Bonar Law had spoken; only the extent of the majority was uncertain. Although most of the leading figures in the party—Chamberlain, Balfour, Birkenhead, Horne, Worthington-Evans, Lee of Fareham— stayed loyal to Lloyd George—the mass of their party was in revolt. The convolutions of Lloyd George's Near Eastern policy, although conducted with a strident belligerence that might have been expected to appeal to the Conservative mind, had provided the decisive occasion for a breach. Lloyd George himself, indeed, in this final crisis seemed to lose all sense of direction. His activities seemed quite irrational. After urging Fisher, Mond and other Liberals to stay firmly with the Coalition, in a speech at Manchester on 14 October he openly flouted Conservative sensibilities and made a passionately pro-Greek speech. His reputation for irresponsibility seemed amply confirmed. There was a ready audience among the sober middle-class for the pungent remarks of the hitherto obscure Unionist minister, the president of the Board of Trade, Stanley Baldwin, who described graphically the dangers of following the lead of a 'dynamic force' (Doc. 77). The

Liberal party, he claimed, lay in ruins; the Conservatives, even with their highly-developed sense of survival, might well follow them into disaster. By a majority of ninety-seven the Unionist members voted to detach themselves from the Coalition, and Lloyd George resigned later that day.[13]

The following general election showed dramatically how fragile his position had really become. He fought with his own 'National Liberals' to defend a dead cause—to support a Coalition that no longer existed and a mood of bi-partisan unity that had disappeared. He now faced the bitter hostility of the Independent Liberals and also of Labour; this last aspect assumed particular importance as the majority of National Liberal seats lay in industrial areas where the Labour Party was powerful. Even with the generous support of Bonar Law, who prevented Conservatives from opposing Lloyd George's Liberals in most constituencies, Lloyd George could not avert a débâcle. His own Liberals lost over seventy seats, most of them in working-class areas like South Wales and the West Riding, and their tally fell to a mere fifty-seven, less even than the rejuvenated Asquithians who claimed sixty. More crucial still, Liberal England (and, to a lesser extent, Liberal Wales) lay in total ruin, along with the career of the man who had done so much to create it.

As soon as the Lloyd George government had fallen from power, the post-mortems began; historians have continued them avidly ever since. Even though out of office, Lloyd George still dominated the political stage. His fall created a massive vacuum. British politics were still in most senses 'post-coalition' rather than restored to their pre-war polarity. The Conservatives were in considerable disarray. Chamberlain and other former ministers refused to join Bonar Law's new Conservative government, and rejected with intense bitterness the approaches of renegades like Curzon. But it was on the Liberal side that the inquest was most painful. To many Liberals, not only those close to Asquith, Lloyd George had betrayed his party. The 'coupon election' had split his party beyond repair, while his government's policy subsequently had been the reversal of everything Liberalism stood for (Doc. 78). As C. F. G. Masterman and others contended, the demise of the old land duties of 1909 symbolized the passing away, indeed the assassination, of pre-war Liberalism. Such policies as the retaliation in Ireland, the Geddes 'axe' at home and the

[13] See K. Middlemas and J. Barnes, *Baldwin* (London, 1969), pp. 122–4. The correct result of the vote at the Carlton Club (185 votes for breaking with the Coalition, 88 for remaining) is given in Robert Rhodes James, *Memoirs of a Conservative: J. C. C. Davidson's Memoirs and Papers, 1910–37* (London, 1969), pp. 129–33.

'jingo' policies in Asia Minor merely confirmed this process. While some Coalition Liberals, notably Fisher and Mond, still preserved friendly relations with their Asquithian former comrades, towards Lloyd George himself the reaction of most constituency Liberals was one of unforgiving bitterness.

Lloyd George himself was quite impenitent. He pointed out to the ever-sympathetic C. P. Scott that his government had in fact pursued a wide range of Liberal policies (Doc. 79). There had been self-government for Ireland, a pacific foreign policy, education, land and constitutional reform. This claim, selective though it was, was not without justice. Whatever Lloyd George's government had been, it was not a die-hard one. On the front of social reform, in particular, whatever the later havoc wrought by the Geddes 'axe', his government's record compared favourably with its pre-war predecessors. The redefinition and redirection of Liberalism in the post-war field, for which Sutherland and Kerr had called, had indeed been substantially achieved, without sacrificing the fabric of free trade, free enterprise and individual liberty for which Liberalism traditionally contended.

On grounds of policy, Lloyd George's claim, then, had much substance. But politics concerns hard structures as well as theoretical policies; they are the product of the interaction of interest groups and social classes no less than of the instincts of gifted individuals. Lloyd George's policies may have been 'Liberal' in the Gladstonian or even the Hobsonian sense; they had nothing to do with the Liberal Party. Indeed, they seemed a positive alternative to that party, since their prerequisite had been a new political organization, a national coalition which would reduce the old Liberal party to sectional impotence. To lend any credence to Lloyd George's claim to have preserved Liberalism rather than to have destroyed it, he required organized supporters. In March 1920, at the time of the 'fusion' negotiations, he came tantalizingly near to acquiring them. With the failure of fusion, he was again on his own; ultimately, he had no political future. After Chanak he had again to turn to his own much-abused Coalition Liberal party, to try to salvage something which would enable him to bargain with the dissident Unionists and with the 'wee Frees' on something like equal terms. But his downfall showed how insubstantial his position had really been, how the cohorts of Coalition Liberalism were really only a 'stage army' emanating from Downing Street. The dead weight of party was too strong for Lloyd George. The war had not transformed the essence of British political life. Rather had it reinforced the polarization of parties into the rival camps of capital and labour, with the mass of former Liberal voters in Scotland, Wales and the

North fleeing to left or to right according to their class predilections. The individual adventures of wartime politics died at Versailles. His downfall confirmed that in the final analysis Lloyd George must revive his Liberal loyalties and create a new Liberal party to play any part in determining the political future.

5

The Liberal Decline,
1923-9

AFTER the 1922 election, the fate of Lloyd George, and of both wings of the Liberal Party, was wholly obscure. The logic of the National Liberals' position seemed to be to support the Conservatives, and in fact they continued to co-operate with Bonar Law's government throughout the 1923 session. Some prominent Coalition Liberals, like Churchill, Hamar Greenwood and Guest, seemed well on the way to union with their former Conservative colleagues, to form a united front against the menace of Labour. But the prospects of the Conservatives again accepting Lloyd George to their bosom was highly remote. When Baldwin unexpectedly succeeded Bonar Law as Prime Minister in May 1923, this prospect became unthinkable: Baldwin, otherwise an amiable figure, was 'obsessed' (in Thomas Jones's word) by loathing of Lloyd George and haunted by memories of his amoral Coalition. Instead, the National Liberals and Independent Liberals made several indirect approaches towards possible reunion during the 1923 session, headed by intermediaries like Mond and Hogge on each side. But little headway was made, with the glittering millions of the 'Lloyd George Fund' as a supreme obstacle. The 1923 session ended with agreement between the rival Liberal factions at Westminster no nearer, whatever the moves towards reconciliation at the constituency level.

Then Baldwin's Plymouth bombshell in October 1923 gave the Liberals a new vision of power (Doc. 80). Baldwin's speech was not the complete surprise to his colleagues that was once thought. Certainly, some kind of nod towards protectionist solutions as a means of remedying unemployment was discussed by Cabinet ministers, although no commitment to any specific solution was recorded. At Plymouth, in fact, Baldwin called openly for protection of the home market, and asked for a mandate from the electors in support. Why Baldwin took this hazardous step has led to much conjecture: the recent biography by Messrs Barnes and Middlemas sheds light upon his decision, without providing a complete explanation.[1] One certain conclusion is that Lloyd George was central to Baldwin's calculations. Lloyd George was at this time on a lecture tour in the United States, pondering a new political initiative which would recover his former authority. A likely objective would be to win over the former Unionist ministers like Birkenhead, Horne and Austen Chamberlain, now in the political wilderness; friendly press lords like Rothermere and even, perhaps, Beaverbrook might be called upon also, and a new centre grouping re-formed. That Lloyd George visualized any commitment to imperial preference as part of his programme, as Mr Frank Owen has implied,[2] is very unlikely: it would have doomed any prospect of Liberal reunion. Clearly, though, Baldwin regarded the possible return to power of Lloyd George as an imminent threat. He proceeded to spell out his policy including imperial preference upon imports but no tax upon wheat or meat. Free Trade, for the first time since Joseph Chamberlain's Tariff Reform campaign twenty years earlier, seemed threatened at the base.

At once, Baldwin's speech gave Lloyd George a political niche to occupy: for the first time for twelve months he became politically relevant. The post-mortems of December 1916 and the 'coupon election' were forgotten, and, as in 1906, the most traditional of the Liberal articles of faith was made the focus for unity. Once Lloyd George returned from the United States, negotiations at once began to reunite the two Liberal factions (Doc. 81). Asquith and Lloyd George at once came together, through the mediation of Mond and Simon; they agreed on a common slate of candidates and a joint election campaign, with Asquith clearly installed as leader of the united party. Again the Liberals spoke in unison. In every constituency in the land they agreed on a common candidate, save only in Camborne and in Cardiganshire, where the old rivalry between Lloyd Georgeites and the Wee Frees was fought with tribal Celtic ferocity. The Liberal election programme was almost entirely backward-looking in tone (Doc. 82). It did contain, on Lloyd George's insistence, some hints on the need for a national development programme, for economic reconstruction and for the release of credit for industry, but in the main the Asquithian orthodoxy provided the basic framework. Free trade was presented by Asquith and by Lloyd George alike as the only feasible alternative to the two extremes of Tory protectionism on the one hand and a socialist capital levy on the other. Several leading Liberals, apparently alienated from their party by the internecine

---

[1] K. Middlemas and J. Barnes, *Baldwin*, pp. 212–29.
[2] Frank Owen, *Tempestuous Journey* (London, 1954), p. 672.

bitterness of the past year, now returned to uphold the old Free Trade orthodoxy. In particular, Churchill, who had appeared to be moving to the right with precipitate speed since his defeat at Dundee in the 1922 election, now emerged again as the most doctrinaire of free traders and stood as the Liberal candidate for Leicester. He told Lloyd George, 'We are in for a big fight—and I am glad to think *together*.'[3] The election as a whole was a vital test of how far the divisions of the coalition period could be set aside, and how far the Liberals could rally their old pre-war supporters in Scotland, Wales and the North. Lloyd George himself played a somewhat subordinate role in the Liberal campaign: as the architect of the 1906 Merchant Shipping Act and the 1921 Safeguarding of Industries Act, he could hardly claim to be a doctrinaire advocate of undiluted free trade. Yet to the other party leaders Lloyd George's was still the dominant personality. In particular, Baldwin regarded him with a peculiar hatred. He was still obsessed by the threat from the 'dynamic force' which had stirred him to rare eloquence a year earlier at the Carlton Club.[4] To the electors, the campaign seemed at times almost a dialogue between the reunited Liberals and their varied opponents, with Baldwin and MacDonald in partnership in exorcizing the ghost of Lloyd George.

The results of the election were very tantalizing for the Liberals. Their total rose sharply to 157, with many unexpected gains in rural areas of England, in cathedral cities and in seaside towns. The West country and Lancashire swung markedly to the cause of free trade. Indeed, the Liberals emerged as the leading challengers to the Conservatives in rural constituencies in England and in Scotland, where they made inroads into the Labour as well as the Conservative vote. However, it was noticeable that almost all of the Liberal victories were gained in three-cornered contests, and that many of their majorities in these contests were alarmingly small. In any event, Labour, with 191 seats, emerged as the larger of the two opposition parties. On Lloyd George's insistence, agreed to with reluctance by Asquith, the Liberals voted against Baldwin in the vote of no confidence, and Labour then took office. Whether, however, the Liberals' role of kingmaker was one of supreme power or of impotence still remained to be seen.

After the heady hopes rekindled by the 1923 election, the fortunes of the Liberal Party and of Lloyd George himself steadily slumped. Relations between them and the governing Labour Party were never

---

[3] Churchill to Lloyd George, 8 November 1923 (Lloyd George Papers, G/4/4/6).

[4] *Thomas Jones, Whitehall Diary*, Vol. I, pp. 255–6.

cordial. MacDonald regarded Lloyd George himself with suspicion or hostility, and in July 1924 Lloyd George tried in vain to persuade his colleagues to turn the government out. The Liberals themselves were still riven by internal dissension, a legacy of the desperate divisions of the coalition period in 1918–22. The one issue that focussed attention on these divisions was the unhappy dispute over the disposal of the 'Lloyd George Fund'. The position was basically simple—the official Liberal Party had the organizational machine but was virtually penniless; Lloyd George had no organization at all, but his personal campaign fund ran to several millions. Could these assets be merged for the mutual sustenance of both Liberal factions? The dilemma this posed for the Liberals was a painful one, exacerbated by the lack of trust that old enmities bequeathed. Throughout the 1924 session, Viscount Gladstone and Donald Maclean, for the official party leadership, were engaged in long and difficult negotiations with Lloyd George in the search for a substantial long-term donation from the fund (Doc. 83). From the first, negotiations went badly. Initially, Lloyd George imposed terms about the committee that was due to administer the fund, insisting that close advisers of his like Guest and Captain Edge should be brought onto it. Even more fundamental, there was a basic difference of view as to the form that any grant from the fund should take. Lloyd George in effect proposed a series of short-term gifts, up to £50,000 or so, limited for certain very specific purposes. Gladstone and Maclean, however, wanted a permanent fund, to guarantee a regular endowment income for years to come. It is easy to see that Gladstone and Maclean, attempting to create a new and permanent base for their party, had ample justification in seeking a long-term solution. In addition, the circumstances in which a personal party chest of this kind (for which no accounts were ever published) had been acquired, were undeniably suspicious, if not sinister. Yet Trevor Wilson's dismissal of Lloyd George's manoeuvres as essentially irrational, perhaps the natural response of a rapacious Welsh peasant, seems inadequate.[5] After all, Lloyd George's financial strength was his one major weapon—the organization and the Liberal parliamentary party were overwhelmingly dominated by men from the Independent Liberal faction. There was every reason why Lloyd George should be reluctant to sign away his one real source of bargaining power, at bottom his only effective means of shaping party programmes and tactics, without adequate safeguards. In the event, when the Labour government ignominiously collapsed in October after MacDonald's mishandling of the Campbell prosecution, Lloyd George donated a

[5] Trevor Wilson, *The Downfall of the Liberal Party*, p. 297.

mere £50,000, less than half the minimum requirements of the Liberal party organizers. Perhaps he sensed the débâcle that was to follow: it was notorious that Liberal constituency organization in most parts of the country was in an advanced stage of decay. The results were utterly disastrous for the Liberals: their political representation fell to only forty. In Sidney Webb's words, it was 'the funeral of a great party'.[6] Only rural Wales and Cornwall presented any solid front of Liberal strength: in any case, the Liberals had put up only 346 candidates, 110 fewer than in 1923. The great Liberal party, shorn of its gains in middle-class constituencies by a revitalized Conservative party, was crippled. When the new parliament met, the *Nation* was left to lament the futile impotence of the broken rump of Liberals that remained in the House, and the curious irrelevance of Lloyd George himself (Doc. 84).

The next two years saw the internal rifts within the Liberal camp become more bitter than ever. Lloyd George himself was more and more isolated, with several of the old Coalition Liberals, like Guest and Grigg, well on their way to association with Conservatives, and old Wee Frees like Runciman, Maclean and Simon keeping their distance. Above all, relations between Lloyd George and Asquith, never close, now became exceptionally delicate. There was the continuing rift over finance, and the failure of the party organizers to obtain any real satisfaction in their demands for aid from the Lloyd George Fund. The final breach between them came over the Liberals' attitude to the General Strike in May 1926. Lloyd George had ostentatiously taken a line far more sympathetic towards the TUC than had Asquith and his former followers. He declined to attend a meeting of the Liberal 'shadow Cabinet' on 10 May, on account of Asquith's attitude towards the strike, and issued a public statement sternly critical of the government's intransigence and its consequences for the economy. Lloyd George declined to yield in the face of Asquith's protest and, as the majority of the forty Liberal members of parliament were, in general, heirs of the Coalition Liberals rather than of the Wee Frees, Asquith had to submit and to resign his leadership. The parliamentary party now reluctantly elected Lloyd George as its leader instead, with both the National Liberal Federation and the Candidates' Association backing him up, for all their loyalty to Asquith. With renewed troubles over finance and over policy, the internecine warfare of the Liberals seemed more hopeless than ever.

It would be easy to assume, as many writers have done, that the Liberals in this period were wasting away as a political anachronism,

---

[6] Margaret Cole (ed.), *Beatrice Webb's Diaries, 1924–1932* (London, 1956), p. 48, citing a speech by Sidney Webb.

and that Lloyd George himself now only played a subordinate role, having nuisance value but not much else. In fact, this is very far from the truth. Even after the final schism with Asquith over the General Strike, contemporaries still regarded a come-back by Lloyd George as a major possibility, as Baldwin had done in 1923. After the General Strike, there were active rumours that Lloyd George was moving to the left and attempting a liaison with the Labour Party; but Ramsay MacDonald's intense animosity to Lloyd George prevented any progress on these lines.[7] Alternatively, there were always cross-bench personalities like the press lords Rothermere and perhaps Beaverbrook who could conceivably be enlisted for a final Lloyd George crusade on a revived 'fusion' ticket. In a sense, by action or reaction, Lloyd George shaped the pattern of party politics throughout the 1920s. The political structure was dominated essentially by two men whose real claim was that they had positively no connection with Lloyd George—Baldwin, the Tory rebel who had led the breach of his party with the Coalition in October 1922; MacDonald, the anti-war socialist who stood in some vague sense for a new international order after the failure of Lloyd George's 'diplomacy by conference'. In many ways it seemed during the middle and later 1920s that Baldwin and MacDonald were conducting their main debate not with each other, but jointly with the great war leader and peacetime premier against whose ascendancy they had rebelled. Just as so much of the economics of the twenties was concerned to restore the pre-war system, the primacy of the City, the gold standard and the old international banking system, so the politics of the twenties were essentially a nostalgic echo of the revolt against Lloyd George.

There was another, and more direct, sense in which Lloyd George still largely determined the course of events in these years. Such new ideas and policies as enlivened the political and economic debate of the mid- and late-twenties came almost entirely from the Liberal Party, or at least from Lloyd George's segment of it. Even an old opponent like Masterman was compelled to admit that 'when LG came back to the Liberal Party, ideas came back to it'.[8] After the 1924 election, which appeared to confirm the demise of pre-1914 Liberalism, Lloyd George turned again to executive action. He built up again a general staff of advisers, experts and intellectuals that he had previously created during the first world war. Some of his advisers now were old colleagues like Seebohm Rowntree and William Beveridge; others were newcomers not hitherto associated with political affairs, younger

[7] D. Lloyd George to C. P. Scott, 19 October 1927 (B.M., Add. MSS. 50,909, f. 230).
[8] Lucy Masterman, *C. F. G. Masterman*, pp. 345–6.

economists for instance, like Lionel Robbins and Hubert Henderson. Most striking of all was the adhesion of Keynes, so recently a mordant critic of the 'Carthaginian' peace terms and the strident 'jingoism' that had allegedly marked the coupon election, but now newly associated with Lloyd George, if not with his party, in the search for a new policy of social and economic reconstruction. Keynes was newly attracted to Lloyd George as a result of a series of articles in the *Nation* in 1924 in which Keynes called for a massive injection of expenditure by the state on behalf of capital works programmes to further housing, transport services and national development; here alone, Keynes thought, was the true remedy for unemployment, not in a sterile policy of deflation.[9] It was an expansive attitude that had immediate appeal for Lloyd George. The following year Keynes and Lloyd George were united in criticizing Churchill's decision to revert to the Gold Standard, at the pre-war parity, and they were subsequently to co-operate closely in Lloyd George's new campaigns.

Characteristically, the first of the new programmes with which Lloyd George galvanized the politics of the 1920s concerned the land. He was still fascinated or even obsessed by agriculture as a vital key to industrial recovery. In 1925 his Land Enquiry Committee, an echo from the great days of 1913, published its findings. It was apparent from the first that the proposals were likely to prove controversial. Old-fashioned disciples of free enterprise like Walter Runciman were apprehensive at the implied interference with the landlord's rights of sale. In Lloyd George's own Wales, which had seen a considerable revolution in the land market since 1918 and the break-up of many large estates, freeholders were vigorous in protest. Lloyd George, however, persevered and in 1925 his *Land and the Nation*, popularly known as the 'green book', was published (Doc. 85). Its most controversial section was one that proposed the creation of 'cultivating tenure', a form of quasi-nationalization which would appropriate cultivable land for the state, paying adequate compensation to the landlord. This was totally objectionable to Sir Alfred Mond, for long a close associate of Lloyd George's and once a radical Liberal, but now obsessed by hatred of socialism. Early in 1926, after a most bitter public exchange with Lloyd George, he left for the Conservative Party.[10] Hilton Young was another former ally alienated by the 'green book', although his personal relations with Lloyd George remained amicable, and he delayed his final move to the Conservatives until

[9] Roy Harrod, *Life of John Maynard Keynes* (London, 1951), pp. 375 ff.
[10] Mond to Lloyd George, 25 September 1924 (Lloyd George Papers, G/14/5/8).

after the 1929 election.[11] On the other hand, among younger and radical Liberals—the kind of Liberals attracted to the annual summer schools—Lloyd George's proposals seemed exciting and inspiring. Here he managed to kindle much of the old crusading radical zeal. New and equally striking policy statements followed on coal and power. Later there appeared in January 1928 the 'yellow book', *Britain's Industrial Future*, two sections of which were written by Keynes. In this he proposed a widespread policy of state intervention in the economy, including the creation of new semi-public corporations, a public investment board and a general stimulus to domestic investment programmes. It was clear that Lloyd George was now occupied in systematically recasting the old Liberal philosophy in a way that the 'New Liberals' had promised to do before 1914 until their work was destroyed by the war. He was proposing to call in the powers of the central government to redress the disequilibrium of the capitalist economy, to save capitalism from itself. Keynes himself outlined the character of the new Liberal creed at the summer school in 1927 (Doc. 86). As he spelled out for the benefit of the Runcimans and Simons, the old Liberalism of the Gladstonian past, wedded to old themes like free trade and religious liberty, was essentially economic conservatism; so, too, was the philosophy of the Labour Party. Only by recognizing the total transformation of the economy since the end of the war, which had made the old rigid distinctions between private and public enterprise out-of-date, could Liberals apply the radical remedies which alone could rejuvenate a tired nation.

The most dramatic formulation of the new ideas of Lloyd George and his 'brains trust' of advisers came in the 'orange book', *We Can Conquer Unemployment*, early in 1929 (Doc. 87). This advocated sweeping new remedies for dealing with unemployment and economic stagnation. A massive new programme of public works and of government spending was outlined, including a huge programme of road construction and vast housing schemes. This document did not apply the full Keynesian critique as later evolved in Keynes's *General Theory* in 1936. It claimed that these public works schemes would be financially self-supporting, and that the expenditure involved would be more than balanced by savings in the Unemployment Benefit Fund and elsewhere. The magic solution of deliberately budgeting for a deficit to stimulate demand had not yet been conceived. Even so, these formed a radical, even revolutionary set of proposals which dominated public discussion of the economy for the remainder of that election year. Baldwin and MacDonald were both haunted by the

[11] Hilton Young to Lloyd George, 26 August 1924 (*ibid.*, G/10/14/18).

fear that they might result in another return to power by Lloyd George, and both the major parties trained their fire on the Welshman's new schemes, varying this tactic by claiming the authorship of them for themselves. In the 1929 general election, for the first time he poured his funds out freely on behalf of Liberal candidates—even though some of them, like Donald Maclean in North Cornwall, declined his assistance.[12] Lloyd George seemed to be dominating the campaign, and the bulk of the publicity went his way. In an otherwise sterile election, in which Baldwin appealed for 'safety first' and MacDonald promised that a Labour government would lead to 'no monkeying', Lloyd George alone provided radical and novel economic solutions. But for the bulk of the electors they were too novel to be immediately understood. In any case, a set of policies, however appealing, was quite inadequate without the political mechanism to support them. Somehow the Liberal campaign, for all its brilliance, resembled the one-man band of the unhappy days of 1918. As a result, while the Liberal vote rose appreciably to over five million, they failed to bid effectively with Labour in appealing to working-class opinion. The Liberals lost 19 of their old seats, and captured 35, their total tally in parliament rose from 40 to only 59, while Labour members now numbered 287. Lloyd George's last crusade had failed.

Thereafter, the history of the Liberal Party, as long as Lloyd George was active in party politics, was indeed a long diminuendo. The parliamentary Liberal party in 1929 was a distinguished and able body, and at first it promised well (Doc. 88). The old acrimony seemed to have dissolved, and Lloyd George to have recaptured his old power and authority. But life under another Labour government, with the Liberals again in the unhappy position of holding the balance of power, was a harsh experience. Lloyd George, writing to Churchill, despairingly revived the notion of a 'working understanding' with the Conservatives.[13] By 1930, the parliamentary Liberals were again torn by internal dissension over tactics and policy; early in 1931 a section of them, headed by Simon and Ernest Brown, broke away from Lloyd George's leadership. They included old allies of Lloyd George, like Hore-Belisha and his former private secretary, Geoffrey Shakespeare. When the political crisis broke in August 1931, the Liberals presented a pitiable spectacle, their feebleness being emphasized by the absence of Lloyd George himself, prostrated by a severe operation. When MacDonald formed the National government, the Liberals divided

[12] Donald Maclean to Viscount Gladstone, 19 May 1929 (B.M., Add. MSS. 46,474, f. 209).
[13] Lloyd George to Churchill, 16 October 1929 (Lloyd George Papers, G/4/4/24).

into three sections—the Simonite National Liberals, who now became virtually indistinguishable from the Conservatives; a moderate group led by Herbert Samuel which first joined the National government but later seceded, early in 1932, over the tariff question; and a family group of four Welsh members headed by Lloyd George. At last the great outsider of British politics was truly isolated, if not alone.

The latter phase of Lolyd George's career is not central to the main stream of British politics, apart from occasional episodes. He emerged as a bitter, indeed a jaundiced critic not only of the policies of the National government but of the democratic system itself. In 1935, he launched a movement that echoed his earlier great campaigns, his 'Council of Action for Peace and Reconstruction', which he first announced in his own constituency, at Bangor, in January 1935.[14] The association of so many of the nonconformist ministers with this programme emphasized the traditional nature of his appeal, though several ministers began to break away from the 'council of action' as the radical nature of Lloyd George's schemes unfolded. He advocated a massive programme of government expenditure on counter-cyclical lines to promote public works, a revived War Cabinet on the lines of that in 1916, and the creation of a kind of economic general staff. It had many parallels with the dynamic programmes of Franklin Roosevelt in the United States at the same period, and indeed became popularly known as 'Lloyd George's New Deal'. Lloyd George's deliberate rejection of the pure doctrine of free trade, or at least his willingness to use the tariffs imposed since the Ottawa conference in 1932, confirmed his break with the old Liberalism. But his campaign was now out-of-date. His platform won over many publicists, younger independent-minded Tories like Robert Boothby, and a Labour veteran like Lord Snowden. It aroused the active concern of the Cabinet to whom Lloyd George was invited to propound his ideas; for a time, there was a possibility that he might actually be offered a post in the government, but Baldwin's relentless animosity ended this idea.[15] At the general election campaign that October, Lloyd George's 'Council of Action' made little impact. He now seemed to most people, not a radical innovator at all, but a figure from the past, more concerned with refighting the old battles in his *Memoirs* than with solving the trials of the time. The Liberals finished up with only twenty-one seats, seven of them in Wales.

In the thirties, Lloyd George's main preoccupation, as with most of his contemporaries, was with foreign affairs. The first great apostle of appeasement of Germany, he now called for new foreign policies

[14] *The Times*, 17 January 1935.
[15] K. Middlemas and J. Barnes, *Baldwin*, pp. 808–10.

to satisfy the legitimate national claims of Germany. There should be frontier concessions over the Saar, Danzig and the Polish Corridor, while Hitler's proposal for a twenty-five-year non-aggression pact should be accepted. Lloyd George's old adviser, Philip Kerr, now Lord Lothian, was a leading figure amongst those calling for Anglo-German amity. In 1936 Lloyd George even made a startling visit to Germany, meeting Hitler at Berchtesgaden; he expressed his warm, even un-critical admiration of Hitler's economic schemes, which so closely resembled his own. This view of Lloyd George's consorted oddly with his other main theme in discussions of foreign policy during these years, his strong support for the League and for collective security. In 1936 he delivered a resounding indictment of the British govern-ment for failure to apply sanctions in aid of Abyssinia,[16] while he also called for belligerent action on behalf of the Spanish Republican government. Yet even after Munich, his criticism of Chamberlain's policies concerned the ineptitude of Chamberlain's diplomatic methods rather than the basic error of appeasing Hitler by frontier concessions over the Sudetenland. While he was a severe critic of the open-ended pledge to Poland in March 1939, and called for a defence treaty with the Soviet Union, he continued to believe that peace with Germany was possible. Even after the second world war broke out, in October 1939, he startled the Commons by a call for a determined effort to renew negotiations with Hitler.[17] This was still his view when he met Sumner Welles, Roosevelt's special ambassador to Europe, in March 1940 (Doc. 89). Lloyd George's attitude on this occasion may perhaps serve as an epilogue for this later phase of his career. He delivered a bitter philippic against the entire course of British foreign policy in the thirties, the way in which the Baldwin and Chamberlain govern-ments had been dominated by events, and in which the initiative presented to the allies in 1919 had been cast aside. His opportunity for revenge came shortly afterwards. In the great debate in the Commons in May 1940, he exacted retribution from the men of 1922. His biting criticisms of Chamberlain played a major role in swaying opinion in the House, and in the eventual downfall of the Chamberlain government. The heirs of Baldwin and MacDonald, or some of them, had gone at last. It was his last decisive intervention in politics. There was no real likelihood that he would accept any of the half-hearted offers of office made by Churchill, the ambassador-ship at Washington amongst them. He settled into an uneasy and often petulant old age, a mordant critic of the government, and a

[16] Parl. Deb., 5th ser., Vol. 313, pp. 1221–32 (18 June 1936).
[17] Parl. Deb., 5th ser., Vol. 351, pp. 1870–4 (3 October 1939).

surprisingly avid listener to the radio broadcasts of 'Lord Haw-Haw'.[18] The German *Abwehr* documents proposed Lloyd George, Pétain-like, as a putative 'Gauleiter for Wales'.[19] On 1 January 1945, it was announced that Wales's great commoner had been made an earl. Two-and-a-half months later, he was dead. An ironical epitaph on his career was that in the general election of July 1945, his seat at Caernarvon Boroughs, which he had held continuously since 1890, was captured by a Conservative. His son, Gwilym, also joined that party, and served as a Cabinet minister under Churchill in 1951. Lloyd George's daughter, Megan, conversely, joined the Labour Party. In 1966, Megan Lloyd George, now the Labour member for Carmarthen, died also. After three-quarters of a century, the Lloyd George connection with British politics was finally snapped. Perhaps appropriately in some ways, the Carmarthen seat was captured, in the by-election that followed, by a Welsh Nationalist. Wales had had a final revenge over the Lloyd George tradition.

*   *   *

The age of Lloyd George was one which saw first the rejuvenation and later the death agony of the Liberal Party. For the bulk of this period, Lloyd George himself was the dominant element in its progress. Prior to 1905 he was a supreme embodiment of the fusion of the Old Liberalism with the New, the champion of the chapels, of 'Little Englandism' and of the national claims of Wales, yet also a symbol of a new social concern. After 1905, his and Churchill's programmes appeared to have transformed the social outlook of their party; then the outbreak of war interrupted the process and revealed how much remained of the old Liberal animus towards the state. During the war years Lloyd George, by his flagrant challenge to conventional politics, became, almost in spite of himself, the main agent in a schism which shattered his party into fragments and decisively altered the course of British party development. In the peacetime premiership, he tried to preserve the name and something of the substance of the old radicalism within the framework of a new national government. When the realities of party politics proved that this circle could not be squared, even by Lloyd Georgian geometry, he had perforce to return to his old Liberal 'back kitchen'. The final phase after 1922 was a valiant, enterprising and unavailing effort to turn his party into the agent for a new social critique, and thereby make it again a challenger for power. His failure was his party's last stand, and it has shown no sign of permanent recovery since that time.

[18] Frances Lloyd George, *The Years that Are Past* (London, 1967), p. 269.
[19] D. McCormick, *The Mask of Merlin* (London, 1963), pp. 279–80.

On many counts, Lloyd George's career as a politician was one of failure, like that of his old idol, Joseph Chamberlain, and it is all too easy to imagine that this failure was inevitable. Cradled within the Gladstonian Liberal Party, he was one of the major architects of its ultimate ruin as a party of government. Lloyd George's policies have certainly created much of the Britain of today. His social reforms of the period before 1914 laid the basis for the welfare state. The war years saw new forms of collective control absorbed into the governmental system. The peace-time coalition passed several enlightened measures of social progress. The last phase after 1922, though disastrous in electoral terms, was one in which Lloyd George was the inspiration of a massive recasting of economic thought which has since become the general orthodoxy. Throughout, he was a creative force without parallel, one whose influence will surely be seen to have been far more enduring for our society than that of his colleague and contemporary, Winston Churchill. The tragedy of Lloyd George, however, was that his political style presupposed a totally different political world, one where power would be vested in the executive rather than in the legislature, where there would be shifting interest groups coalescing behind short-term crusades rather than permanent parties. In the United States, Lloyd Georgian radicalism would have been immediately intelligible: it found its parallels in the presidencies of Theodore and Franklin Roosevelt. But in Britain, with the slow evolution of its political groupings and of the social classes behind them, the volatile genius of one man was in conflict with the conservative mould of a conservative country. The Labour Party was able to survive and prosper after 1922, unlike the Social Democratic parties in so many other countries, because it was able to identify itself with the political culture of Britain: it took over the mantle of the older radicalism. Lloyd George's failure lay in his increasing inability, at least after 1916, to remain a part of that culture: British politics simply would not be reconciled with the presidential mode. Hence, Lloyd George's tendency in his later years to seek out alien examples, a Hitler or a Roosevelt, as alternatives to the political system of his own land.

Throughout the period from 1890 to 1929, Lloyd George's Liberalism was a permanent phenomenon: whatever he was during this period, he was never a conservative. His Liberalism had many constant features that persistently recurred—its links with the chapels, with rural radicalism, with the popular press, and with the vital national culture of Wales. But his Liberalism, equally, bore only an intermittent and erratic relationship to the Liberal Party as such. Nor did Lloyd George trouble unduly to identify himself with that party. His instinctive democracy, his hatred of privilege, his roots in the warm chapel-bound populism of his native Wales conflicted with his urge for supreme executive power, the kind of instinctive reaction that made him ultimately more at home with imperialists like Milner and Kerr than with individualistic Welsh 'pro-Boers'. The democrat and the dictator were at odds with one another. During the period up to 1914, indeed, it seemed that these rival aspects of Lloyd George's character could be reconciled. Under Asquith's judicious leadership, the Liberal Party was well able to graft new strains of social and economic reform on to the old stock of provincial radicalism, free trade and the chapel vote. Lloyd George's own career showed how a traditional Liberal's concern with social equality could be harmonized with a new Liberal's search for economic justice, how the basic Gladstonian urge for greater democracy could be extended. The Liberal Party, with its middle-class core and massive working-class attachment, was very far from being a dying party in this period: it showed some evidence of turning itself into the kind of grand popular coalition of the dispossessed represented by the Democratic Party in the United States after 1932. But, in the event, the harmony of the Old Liberalism and the New depended too much on their identification with Lloyd George himself. As a result, confronted by the obscene tragedy of the first world war, which mocked at every moral value that Liberalism embodied, Lloyd George's own manœuvres were not merely damaging to the Liberal Party as an organization, but fatal for the union of the various strands which it contained. As a result, after 1918 the Liberal Party, without Lloyd George, was an outdated, backward-looking movement which had lost contact with the New Liberalism of the pre-war period. Lloyd George, without the Liberal Party, was a volatile, erratic individual, full of radical impulses which the harsh facts of the Coalition (created by his own 'coupon election') forced him to suppress. When the Liberal Party and Lloyd George were again reunited after 1923 it was already too late. The Labour Party, a struggling organization before 1914, had taken over the old radical tradition, winning over old Liberals from Ponsonby to Haldane, and had assumed the role of the party of protest. In spite of all Lloyd George's new initiatives and his profusion of multi-coloured 'books' in the later 1920s, his party had been forced into the nebulous 'middle ground' of politics. It was surrounded by a reformist 'Lib.-Lab.' Labour Party, and an utterly moderate Conservative Party. For the first time in their history, the Liberals had been forced into the position of becoming a 'centre party', crusading against two class extremes which did not exist. The Liberals were henceforth neither very obviously a party of the right nor one of the left, while the middle ground of politics proved to be a no-man's-land. Eventually only Lloyd George was left in unwilling occupation of it, and this was the measure of his ultimate failure.

This cannot, however, be the final verdict. From Lloyd George's political failures—for which many others, including Asquith, bear much responsibility—there emerged a new society, emerging from the late Victorian past, leaving behind many of its class stereotypes, its out-dated economic shibboleths, its obsessive and neurotic imperial clichés. The transition was made from nineteenth-century radicalism to twentieth-century social democracy. In this process, the Liberal Party in the age of Lloyd George was both the main agent of change and the major victim of some of its consequences. The permanent legacy of Lloyd George, and the testimony to his vision and his greatness, lie not in a shattered party, but rather in a more just and more civilized society.

PART II: SELECTED DOCUMENTS

A. The Old Liberalism and the New (1890-1905)

a. The Old Liberalism

1. From *Proceedings* of the National Liberal Federation, Newcastle, 1891, pp. 6, 8. This conference devised the so-called 'Newcastle programme'.

IRELAND

Moved by Sir Edward Grey, Bart., MP; seconded by Mr J. Rowntree, MP:

That this Council holds that the case for Home Rule in Ireland has been still further confirmed by the steadfastness, sound judgement, and moderation with which the great body of the Irish people have, during the last year, successfully faced one of the sharpest ordeals in political history;

And it looks with unshaken confidence to Mr Gladstone, upon his return to power, to frame and—in spite of idle menaces from the House of Lords—to pass a Measure which shall fully satisfy the just demands of Ireland, and leave the Imperial Parliament free to attend to the pressing claims of Great Britain for its own reforms....

'OMNIBUS' RESOLUTION

Moved by Sir Wilfred Lawson, Bart., MP; seconded by the Right Hon. H. H. Fowler, MP:

That this Council again affirms its declaration in favour of—A thorough Reform of the Land Laws, such as will secure—

(a) The Repeal of the Laws of Primogeniture and Entail;
(b) Freedom of Sale and Transfer;
(c) The just taxation of Land values and ground rents;
(d) Compensation, to town and country tenants, for both disturbance and improvement, together with a simplified process for obtaining such compensation;
(e) The Enfranchisement of Leaseholds;
    The direct and popular veto on the Liquor traffic;

The Disestablishment and Disendowment of the Established Church in Scotland;

The Equalization of the Death Duties upon real and personal property;

The just division of rates between owner and occupier;

The taxation of Mining Royalties;

A 'Free Breakfast Table';

The extension of the Factory Acts; and

The 'mending or ending' of the House of Lords.

2. Gladstone's speech during the National Liberal Federation meeting at Newcastle Town Hall, 2 October 1891: from *The Times*, 3 October 1891.

The question—the important question—is, how are we to decide upon the title to precedence? Among the many subjects that are before us one name that would leap to the lips of any man addressing you is Ireland (hear, hear). As to the question of the title of Ireland to the precedence, there is no question at all about it (hear, hear) . . . There is another question which I think the Liberal party, with much reason, are disposed to place in very forward rank and that is registration (cheers). The question of registration is one that diverges, severs itself, into two branches, one of them the amendment of registration, properly so-called, the necessity for which is urgent; and the other the establishment of the principle of one man one vote (cheers). . . . But I go to a more complex subject . . . which can best be presented to you at this time of day by the single word labour (cheers). We have performed on behalf of labour that operation which is the most essential of all by the enfranchisement which in 1885 added three millions to the constituencies of this country (cheers). But there is much remaining to be done (hear, hear). One of the things essential to be done is the rectification and reform of what is termed the lodger franchise, a franchise which, constituted as it now is, works entirely in favour of the wealthy lodger, and is entirely against the labouring man who is a lodger too. . . . That is the first item; and the second item I should put down as necessary to be considered is undue [*sic*] labour representation, which, I think you will heartily agree with. It ought to be a great effort of the Liberal party to extend the labour representation in parliament. . . . There is another branch of this question that we must not forget. Although rural interests are little connected with the town of Newcastle, I have no doubt they are very familiar to many members of the Federation. I will run very rapidly over the different points, though, in my opinion, they are points long ago inscribed in the Liberal creed.

We have done, perhaps, more than justice to the Government in acknowledging that they deserved well of the country by passing a County Councils Bill, but we are not satisfied with the County Councils Bill except for the principle it embodies. . . .

We affirm that it is among the high and indispensable duties of the party, when it has the power and influence in Parliament, to seek to provide for the establishment of district councils and parish councils (cheers), to bring self-government within the power of the labouring man throughout the country—I will add boldly, to enact compulsory powers for the purpose of enabling suitable bodies to acquire land in order to place the rural population in nearer relations to the produce of the soil which they till for the benefit of others, but for themselves almost in vain. . . . Let me add yet one more . . . , that which is known as the reform of the land laws, a great subject, economical and political, both the one and the other. That reform of the land laws, that abolition of the present system of entail, together with just facilities for the transfer of land, is absolutely necessary in order to do anything like common justice to those who inhabit the rural districts of this country. . . .

Upon the question whether it is possible to enact compulsory laws binding upon all labourers for reducing their labour to a certain time of day, to a certain number of hours, I will say this. Before giving my assent to that principle, I should be very glad to be assured, I should be very glad to see demonstration, that those who now receive for long hours low wages were to receive in full at least those low wages for the short hours. It will require more than a mere majority in certain trades that are highly organized, it will require more than a majority even in all trades over the country, so to bend the minority so that they shall be the subjects of coercive proceedings, if they are unwilling, or if they find themselves, through injustice to those dependent upon them, unable to conform to the new standard. I give no absolute judgement upon a question which has not yet, I believe, by an appeal to the country been sufficiently examined. . . .

3. From W. Jenkyn Thomas, 'An Independent Welsh National Party', *Young Wales*, March 1895, pp. 57–9.

The question of a separate Welsh party, independent of the Liberal party, and all other political combinations, is being more and more discussed in the Principality, but as yet it can hardly be said to have grown out of the academic stage. As yet, at any rate, it is possible for a Welshman to declare himself opposed to the idea without forfeiting his character as a good Nationalist. In this article, therefore, I purpose, according to the faith which is in me, to point out what I consider grave objections to the proposal to sever the old historic connection between Wales and the Liberal party. Before I go any further, I wish to make my position perfectly clear. It is not to a Welsh National party, but to an independent Welsh National party that I am opposed. I would have every good Welshman exert himself to the utmost to spread the gospel of Welsh Nationalism, and every representative of Wales in Parliament do all that in him lies to push on the national questions of Wales, and to obtain for them the precedence which they deserve. But, in my humble opinion, the best way to promote Welsh interests in Parliament is to leaven the Liberal party from within, and not to form a Welsh party distinct from, and independent of, that organization.

....

The case for an independent Welsh party rests mainly on the alleged neglect of Wales by the Liberal party. Mr Lloyd George said in a speech at Bangor, on May 16th 1894, 'Our support has fetched nothing in the political market, and it is time in the interests of Wales to initiate a new policy.' Even if the Liberal party had not satisfied any of the distinct claims of Wales, it would still be entitled to the everlasting gratitude of Welshmen. Wales has supported the Liberal party since 1868. Since that date the Elementary Education Act, the Ballot Act, the Corrupt Practices Prevention Act, the Extension of the Franchise Act, and the Parish Councils Act—to mention only a few of the great achievements of the Liberal party—have been passed. It would be impossible to exaggerate the benefits which Wales has derived from these reforms. Further, it is not fair to say that even distinctively Welsh demands have been neglected. The fact of the matter is that whenever Wales articulates her demands with sufficient clearness they are granted by the Liberal party. The question which Welshmen should ask themselves is not 'What have we had from the Liberal party?': but, rather, 'What has the Liberal party refused to give us that we have asked for?' We got three University Colleges, the Burials Act, and the Welsh Sunday Closing Act because we asked for them. We ought to have had more, no doubt, but we did not ask for more.

....

For the first time since the demands of Wales have been adequately voiced by its representatives, the Liberal party is in power and the experiment of working in and with that party is being tried now for the first time. How is that experiment progressing? Disestablishment is the *pièce de résistance* of the present session, and the Government is straining every nerve to pass Mr Asquith's Bill. Light has been thrown upon the dark corners of Welsh social life by the Royal Commission on the tenure of land in Wales and Monmouthshire, and its report, which is now being prepared, will undoubtedly be a charter of Welsh agrarian and social reform. The University of Wales has been established and endowed. The majority of the schemes framed under the provision of the Inter-mediate Education Act of 1889 have become law, and the Government has done its best to prevent their mutilation by bishops and other evil-disposed persons. The home language of Wales has been placed in its rightful position in its elementary school system. The Quarries Act has been passed, making necessary greater precautions for the safety of those employed in the important slate industry of Wales. Much quiet work has been done to secure more firmly and unmistakeably the ad-ministrative unity of Wales—a step towards Welsh Home Rule. Many other proofs can be brought forward to show that, considering the enormous difficulties against which the Government has had to contend, Lord Rosebery was perfectly right when he said, at Cardiff, 'You have not done so badly under a Liberal Government'. When the Liberal party ceases to sympathize with Wales, and refuses to lend its aid to redress Welsh grievances, and to realize Welsh aspirations, then and then only can it be said that the experiment of influencing the Liberal party from within has failed—then and then only will the attempt to coerce it from without be justified.

4. From *Beatrice Webb, Our Partnership*, B. Drake and M. I. Cole (ed.) (Longman's, 1948), p. 143. John Morley (1840–1923) was the leading champion of the Gladstonian tradition in the Liberal Party.

(*18 October 1897*.) . . . Met John Morley at a *tête-à-tête* dinner at the Courtneys. He and Sidney anxious to be pleasant to each other. A charming person for a talk on literature; but a most depressing spectacle as a Liberal leader. In sympathy with no single one of the progressive ideas, he clings to his old shibboleths of non-intervention and non-expansion abroad, and Church disestablishment and a sort of theoretical 'home rule' at home. When I suggested that, if I had supreme power, I would hesitate before I disestablished the Church he seemed aghast. And yet he dare not pronounce in favour of his own convictions: he feels instinctively the country is against him. To do nothing, and to say nothing, to sit and wait for the tide to ebb from this Government is the long and short of his policy. Naturally enough he is pessimistic: thinks that all things are going to the bad and that the country has lost its intellect and its character. On politics he is like a theologian who has begun to doubt his theology: in argument he always shrinks away from you, as if he suspected you of laying traps for him out of which he could not struggle. A closed mind and lack of pluck in asserting the dogmas that dominate him, give a most unpleasant impression of narrow-mindedness and nervelessness. . . . John Morley is a pitiable person as a politician; all the more so because he is conscientious and upright. It makes one groan to think of that moral force absolutely useless.

5. Campbell-Bannerman's speech to National Reform Union, Holborn Restaurant, 14 June 1901: from *The Times*, 15 June 1901. Sir Henry Campbell-Bannerman (1836–1908) became Liberal leader in 1899 and served as Prime Minister, 1905–8.

What was this policy [of unconditional surrender]? . . . It was that now we had got the men we had been fighting against down, we should punish them as severely as possible, devastate their country, burn their homes, break up their very instruments of agriculture and destroy the machinery by which food was produced. It was that we should sweep— as the Spaniards did in Cuba; and how we denounced the Spaniards— the women and children into camps in which they were destitute of all the decencies and comforts and many of the necessaries of life, and in some of which the death-rate rose so high as 430 in the 1,000 (shame). He did not say for a moment, because he did not think for a moment, that this was the deliberate and intentional policy of His Majesty's Government, but it was the policy of the writers in the press who supported them, and at all events it was the thing that was being done at that moment in the name and by the authority of this most humane and Christian nation (shame). On the previous day he asked the leader of the House of Commons when the information would be afforded of which we were so sadly in need. His request was refused. Mr Balfour treated them to a short disquisition on the nature of war. A phrase often used was that 'war is war', but when one came to ask about it one was told that no war was going on, that it was not war. When was a war not a war? When it was carried on by methods of barbarism in South Africa.

6. A speech by Lord Rosebery at Chesterfield: from *The Times*, 15 December 1901. Lord Rosebery (1847–1929), a leading Liberal Imperialist, had been Prime Minister 1894–5, and Liberal leader until 1896.

It is six years since the Liberals were in office. It is sixteen since they were in power. Meanwhile, the world has not stood still; but there is Toryism as great in Liberal circles, as great and deep, though it may be less conscious, as in the Carlton Club. There are men who sit still with the fly-blown phylacteries of obsolete policies bound round their fore-heads, who do not remember that while they have been mumbling their incantations to themselves, the world has been marching and revolving, and that if they have any hope of leading it or guiding it they must march and move with it too. I hope, therefore, that when you have to write on your clean slate, you will write on it a policy adapted to 1901 or 1902, and not a policy adapted to 1892 or 1885. . . .

My advice is not to move much faster than the great mass of the people are prepared to go. If the Liberal Party has not learnt that lesson in its many years of affliction, then it has learned nothing. My last piece of advice to the Party is that it should not disassociate itself, even indirectly, from the new sentiment of Empire which occupies the nation.

Campbell-Bannerman to Herbert Gladstone, 18 December 1901: from J. A. Spender, *The Life of the Right Hon. Sir Henry Campbell-Bannerman*, Vol. II (Hodder and Stoughton, 1923), p. 14.

I have your meditations upon Chesterfield. I agree that the views on peace and war go very far and are not unreasonable, though it is unfortunate that they run counter to the very two things our people in the country care most about—Milner and Camps. . . .

All that he said about the clean slate and efficiency was an affront to Liberalism and was pure claptrap. Efficiency as a watchword! Who is against it? This is all a mere *réchauffé* of Mr Sidney Webb who is evidently the chief instructor of the whole faction.

It is not unfavourable to the chance of unity on the war and peace issue: but ominous of every horror in general politics, if it is meant seriously. However, we can talk this over.

What is a 'fly-blown phylactery'? . . .

7. From J. A. Hobson, *Imperialism: a Study*. (Constable, revised edition, 1905), pp. 124–7. Hobson (1858–1940) was a commentator on political and social matters, and a writer on the *Daily News*.

Every important social reform, even if it does not directly involve large public expenditure, causes financial disturbances and risks which are less tolerable at times when public expenditure is heavy and public credit fluctuating and embarrassed. Every social reform involves some attack on vested interests, and these can best defend themselves when active Imperialism absorbs public attention. When legislation is involved, economy of time and of governmental interest is of paramount importance. Imperialism, with its 'high politics', involving the honour and safety of the Empire, claims the first place, and, as the Empire grows, the number and complexity of its issues, involving close, immediate, continuous attention, grow, absorbing the time of the Government and of Parliament. It becomes more and more impossible to set aside parliamentary time for the full unbroken discussion of matters of most vital domestic importance, or to carry through any large serious measure of reform.

It is needless to labour the theory of this antagonism when the practice is apparent to every student of politics. Indeed, it has become a commonplace of history how Governments use national animosities, foreign wars and the glamour of empire-making, in order to bemuse the popular mind and divert rising resentment against domestic abuses. The vested interests, which, on our analysis, are shown to be chief prompters of an imperialist policy, play for a double stake, seeking their private commercial and financial gains at the expense and peril of the commonwealth. They at the same time protect their economic and political supremacy at home against movements of popular reform. The city ground landlord, the country squire, the banker, the usurer, and the financier, the brewer, the mine-owner, the ironmaster, the ship-builder, and the shipping trade, the great export manufacturers and merchants, the clergy of the State Church, the universities, and great public schools, the legal trade unions and the services have, both in Great Britain and on the Continent, drawn together for common political resistance against attacks upon the power, the property, and the privileges which in various forms and degrees they represent. Having conceded under pressure the form of political power in the shape of elective institutions and a wide franchise to the masses, they are struggling to prevent the masses from gaining the substance of this power and using it for the establishment of equality of economic opportunities. The collapse of the Liberal party upon the Continent, and now in Great Britain, is only made intelligible in this way. Friends of liberty and of popular government so long as the new industrial and commercial forces were hampered by the economic barriers and the political supremacy of the *noblesse* and the landed aristocracy, they have come to temper their 'trust' of the people by an ever-growing quantity of caution, until within the last two decades they have either sought political fusion with the Conservatives or have dragged on a precarious existence on the strength of a few belated leaders with obsolescent principles. Where Liberalism preserves any real strength, it is because the older struggle for the franchise and the primary liberties has been delayed, as in Belgium and in Denmark, and a *modus vivendi* has been possible with the rising working-class party. In Germany, France, and Italy the Liberal party as a factor in practical politics has either dis-appeared or is reduced to impotence; in England it now stands convicted of a gross palpable betrayal of the first conditions of liberty, feebly fumbling after programmes as a substitute for principles. Its leaders, having sold their party to a confederacy of stock gamblers and jingo sentimentalists, find themselves impotent to defend Free Trade, Free Press, Free Schools, Free Speech, or any of the rudiments of ancient Liberalism. They have alienated the confidence of the people. For many years they have been permitted to conduct a sham fight and to call it politics; the people thought it real until the South African war furnished a decisive dramatic test, and the unreality of Liberalism became apparent. It is not that Liberals have openly abandoned the old principles and traditions, but that they have rendered them of no account by dallying with an Imperialism which they have foolishly and futilely striven to distinguish from the firmer brand of their political opponents. This surrender to Imperialism signifies that they have preferred the economic interests of the possessing and speculative classes, to which most of their leaders belong, to the cause of Liberalism. That they are not conscious traitors or hypocrites may be readily conceded, but the fact remains that they have sold the cause of popular reform, which was their rightful heritage, for an Imperialism which appealed to their business interests and their social prepossessions. The mess of pottage has been seasoned by various sweeter herbs, but its 'stock' is class selfishness. The majority of the influential Liberals fled from the fight which was the truest test of Liberalism in their generation because they were 'hirelings', destitute of firm political principle, gladly abandoning themselves to whatever shallow and ignoble defences a blear-eyed, raucous 'patriotism' was ready to devise for their excuse.

It is possible to explain and qualify, but this remains the naked truth, which it is well to recognize. A Liberal party can only survive as a discredited or feeble remnant in England, unless it consents definitely to dissever itself from that Imperialism which its past leaders as well as their opponents, have permitted to block the progress of domestic reforms.

There are individuals and sections among those who have comprised the Liberal party whose deception has been in large measure blind and involuntary, because they have been absorbed by their interest in some single important issue of social reform, whether it be temperance, land tenure, education, or the like. Let these men now recognize, as in honesty they can scarcely fail to do, that Imperialism is the deadly enemy of each of these reforms, that none of them can make serious advance so long as the expansion of the Empire and its satellite (militarism) absorb the time, the energy, the money of the State. Thus alone is it still possible that a strong rally of Liberals might, by fusion or cooperation with the political organizations of the working classes, fight

Imperialism with the only effectual weapon, social reconstruction on the basis of democracy.

8. *Education*—Mr Lloyd George (Caernarvon Boroughs): from Hansard, *Parliamentary Debates*, 4th Ser., Vol. 107, pp. 1102, 1104–5, 8 May 1902. Lloyd George was a fierce opponent of the 1902 Education Bill.

I say that, by common consent, there is a Nonconformist grievance. . . . Special advantages and privileges are given to the Anglican denominational schools which are not given to the Nonconformists and to the board schools. The Church have [*sic*] over 12,000 schools in the country, which are mission rooms to educate the children of the poor in the principles of the Church. In 8,000 parishes there are no other schools, and the whole machinery of the law is there utilized to force the Nonconformist children into them. You tell them: 'You will have no religious instruction at all unless you are prepared to take the instruction of the Church of England'. The total expense for the staff of these schools is £3,400,000 yearly, and the State gives £3,600,000 per annum, so that the staff engaged in teaching Church of England principles is wholly paid by the State. Another advantage possessed by the Anglican Church is the patronage of 60,000 excellent appointments in the Civil Service—exclusive patronage to 60,000 appointments to one of the best, most remunerative, and most honourable careers that a child can possibly enter upon. A Member on the other side said yesterday that the Nonconformists have a grievance there. So they have. Out of 2,000,000 children in Anglican schools, 1,000,000 are Nonconformists. Are Hon. Members aware that there are 700,000 Methodist children in these Church schools? . . . These are the advantages—60,000 positions in the Civil Service, the control of these commercial institutions, the machinery of the law to force children into the schools to be taught the doctrines of their particular faith—and what do they give for them? They give £650,000 a year, as against £4,000,000 from the State. Taking their own claims as to the number of the adherents of the Church in this country, that is exactly a farthing per week per head for every adult adherent. This is the intolerable strain for all these privileges, but the maintenance of the schools is now to be thrown entirely on the rates; they have simply to keep the schools in repair. They are grumbling even at that. The Duke of Northumberland writes to complain of it. At the very outside, the repairs will come to £60,000 a year, representing, say, one-tenth of a farthing per week for every adult adherent of the Church of England—one fifth of the widow's mite, and Dukes grumble at it! There is no coin of the realm sufficiently trifling and insignificant to mark the maximum of sacrifice which these fierce religious zealots are prepared to make for their faith. . . .

9. Joseph Chamberlain at Birmingham Town Hall, 15 May 1903: from *The Times*, 16 May 1903, p. 8. Joseph Chamberlain (1836–1914) was Colonial Secretary until 15 September 1903, when he resigned from Balfour's government.

When you are 6,000 miles away from the House of Commons, it is perfectly extraordinary how events and discussions and conflicts of opinion present themselves in different—I think I may even say in truer—proportion. You are excited at home about an Education Bill (laughter), about temperance reforms (loud laughter), about local finance. Yes, I should be if I had remained at home. But these things matter no more to South Africa, to Canada, to Australia than their local affairs matter to you; and, on the other hand, everything that touches Imperial policy, everything which affects their interests as well as yours, has for them, as it ought to have for us, a supreme importance. Our Imperial policy is vital to them and vital to us. Upon that Imperial policy and what you do in the next few years depends that enormous issue whether this great Empire of ours is to stand together, one free nation, if necessary against all the world (hear, hear), or whether it is to fall apart into separate States, each selfishly seeking its own interest alone, losing sight of the commonweal, and losing also all the advantages which union alone can give. . . .

Look into the future. I say it is the business of British statesmen to do everything they can, even at some present sacrifice, to keep the trade of the colonies with Great Britain (cheers), to increase that trade, to promote it, even if in so doing we lessen somewhat the trade with our foreign competitors (hear, hear and cheers). Are we doing everything at the present time to direct the patriotic movement which I see not only here, but, in fact, by our legislation, by our action—are we making for union or are we drifting to separation? That is a critical issue. In my opinion, the germs of a federal union that will make the British Empire powerful and influential for good beyond the dreams of anyone now living—the germs of that union are in the soil; but it is a tender and delicate plant and requires careful handling (hear, hear). . . .

I have admitted that the colonies have hitherto been rather backward in their contributions towards Imperial defence. They are following their own lines. I hope they will do better. But in the meantime they are doing a great deal, and they are trying to promote this union which I regard as of so much importance in their own way and by their own means.

And first among those means is the offer of preferential tariffs (cheers). . . . Last year at the Conference of Premiers the representatives of Australia and New Zealand accepted (this) principle. . . . So far as the principle was concerned they pledged themselves to recommend to their constituents a substantial preference in favour of goods produced in the mother country. [He explains that Canada is to follow the same policy.]

We cannot make any difference between those who treat us well and those who treat us badly (cries of 'shame'). Yes, but that is the doctrine which I am told is the accepted doctrine of the free-trader; and we are all free-traders (cries of 'No, no' and laughter). Well, I am (loud laughter). I have considerable doubt whether the interpretation of free trade which is current amongst a certain limited section is the true interpretation (hear, hear). But I am perfectly certain that I am not a protectionist. But I want to point out that if the interpretation is that our only duty is to buy in the cheapest market without regard to whether we can sell, if that is the theory of free trade which finds acceptance here and elsewhere, then in pursuance of that policy you will have to forgo the advantage of a reduction, a further reduction, in duty which your great colony of Canada offers to you manufacturers in this country; and you may lose a good deal more, because in the speech which the Chancellor of the Exchequer, the Minister of Finance as he is called in Canada, made to the Canadian Parliament the other day, which he has just sent me, I find he says here that if we are told definitely that Great Britain, the mother country, can do nothing for us in the way of reciprocity we must reconsider our position and reconsider the preference that we have already given.

[Chamberlain goes on to describe German retaliation against Canadian goods, which Britain is unable to counter.]

I said just now is this free trade? No, it is absolutely a new situation (cheers). There has been nothing like it in our history. It was a situation that was never contemplated by any of those whom we regard as the authors of free trade. What would Mr Bright, what would Mr Cobden, have said to this state of things? I do not know. It would be presumptuous to imagine; but this I can say. Mr Cobden did not hesitate to make a treaty of preference and reciprocity with France (hear, hear) and Mr Bright did not hesitate to approve his action; and I cannot believe if they had been present amongst us now and known what this new situation was, I cannot believe that they would have hesitated to make a treaty of preference and reciprocity with our own children (loud and prolonged cheers). Well, you see the point. You want an Empire (hear, hear). Do you think it better to cultivate the trade with your own people or to let that go in order that you may keep the trade of those who, rightly enough, are your competitors and rivals? I say it is a new position. I say the people of this Empire have got to consider it. I do not want to hasten that decision. They have two alternatives before them. They may maintain if they like the interpretation, in my mind an entirely artificial and wrong interpretation, which has been placed upon the doctrines of free trade by a small remnant of Little Englanders of the Manchester School who now profess to be the sole repositories of the doctrines of Mr Cobden and Mr Bright. They may maintain that policy in all its severity, although it is repudiated by every other nation and by all your own colonies. In that case they will be absolutely precluded either from giving any kind of preference or favour to any of their colonies abroad, or even protecting their colonies abroad when they offer to favour us. That is the first alternative. The second alternative is that we should insist that we will not be bound by any purely technical definition of free trade, that, while we seek as one chief object free interchange of trade and commerce between ourselves and all the nations of the world, we will nevertheless recover our freedom, resume that power of negotiation, and, if necessary, retaliation (loud cheers), whenever our own interests or our relations between our colonies and ourselves are threatened by other people (cheers). I leave the matter in your hands. I desire that a discussion on this subject should be opened. The time has not yet come to settle it; but it seems to me that for good or for evil this is an issue much greater in its consequences than any of our local disputes (hear, hear). Make a mistake in your legislation, yet it can be corrected; make a mistake in your Imperial policy, it is irretrievable. You have an opportunity; you will never have it again.

b. *The New Liberalism*

10. From Sidney Webb, 'Lord Rosebery's Escape from Hounds-ditch', *Nineteenth Century*, September 1901, pp. 366–71.

What then is the matter with the Liberals? For fifty years, in the middle of the last century, we may recognize their party as 'a great instrument of progress', wrenching away the shackles—political, fiscal, legal, theological and social—that hindered individual advancement. The shackles are by no means wholly got rid of, but the political force of this old Liberalism is spent. During the last twenty years its aspirations and its watchwords, its ideas of daily life and its conceptions of the universe, have become increasingly distasteful to the ordinary citizen as he renews his youth from generation to generation. Its worship of individual liberty evokes no enthusiasm. Its reliance on 'freedom of contract' and 'supply and demand', with its corresponding 'voluntary-ism' in religion and philanthropy, now seems to work out disastrously for the masses, who are too poor to have what the economists call an 'effective demand' for even the minimum conditions of physical and mental health necessary to national well-being. Its very admiration for that favourite Fenian abstraction, the 'principle of nationality', now appears to us as but Individualism writ large, being, in truth, the asser-tion that each distinct race, merely because it thinks itself a distinct race (which it never is, by the way), has an inherent right to have its own gov-ernment, and work out its own policy, unfettered by any consideration of the effect of this independence on other races, or on the world at large.

Of all this the rising generations of voters are deadly tired. When they hear the leading Liberal debater shouting the Liberal war cry of fifty years ago, 'Peace, Retrenchment and Reform,' and explaining it as a claim for absolute quiescence in Downing Street, with the Treasury cutting down all expenditure, and the Cabinet doing nothing but tinker with the electoral machinery, what can they say but 'You are old, Father William'? And when they turn from Whig aspirations to Whig pro-posals, they see the official Liberal leaders, for lack of any live principle, committing themselves to a medley of projects which the man in the street, no less than the experienced administrator, regards as imprac-ticable.

Unable to conceive their own obsolescence, the Liberals of the old rock account for the collapse of their party by the personal quarrels of their leaders. They have haled those leaders to the Reform Club, and insisted on a public outpouring of affection and esteem to reassure the nation as to their solidarity. The leaders have outpoured accordingly in moving copiousness, and we have now no excuse for doubting the warm friendship for Sir Henry Campbell-Bannerman that underlies the resolution of so many of his colleagues to allow no public utterance of himself or his admirers to pass without prompt and explicit repudiation. But though this Reform Club farce has imposed on nobody—not even on the actors themselves—it has reduced the illusion of Liberal solidarity to absurdity, only to confirm another and more dangerous illusion, namely, that it is the South African War that has wrecked the Liberal Party. On the contrary, the war has raised the old Liberal guard from insignificance to unpopularity, for the party had fallen so low that even unpopularity was a promotion. Lord Rosebery is only emphasizing the obvious when he insists that the impotency of the Liberal Party, as an instrument either of opposition or of government, dates from much further back than the Boer ultimatum. Have we so soon forgotten the contemptuous disgust with which, in 1895, the great mass of Englishmen turned away from the Liberal Party? The collapse does not date even from Mr Gladstone's proposal in 1886 to set up Ireland as a self-governing state. The smashing defeat of 1895 was only the culmination of a steady alienation from Liberalism of the great centres of population, which began to be visible even in 1874. London and Lancashire have ever since persisted in this adverse verdict. The most startling feature of the election of 1885—still prior to the Home Rule Bill—was the extent to which Liberalism was rejected by the boroughs. All that has happened since that date has but confirmed the great centres of population in their positive aversion to Gladstonianism. This, and not the ephemeral dispute about the war, is the bottom fact of the political situation. Thirty years ago the great boroughs were enthusiastic for Liberalism. By an uninterrupted process of conversion they have now become flatly opposed to it. The fact that to-day the Conservative Party finds its chief strongholds not in the lethargic and stationary rural counties, drained of their young men, but in the intellectually active and rapidly growing life of the towns (containing two-thirds of the nation), proves that the Liberalism of Sir William Harcourt and Mr Morley is not the Progressive instinct of the twentieth century. The Progressive instinct always exists, and will always, in time, raise up an opposition to the party which strives to maintain the vested interests of the existing order. The Liberal Party can be strong only in so far as it is the political organ of that Progressive instinct. It held that position for so large a part of the last century that it came to believe that it held it by natural right. How is it that it has now lost it?

The answer is that, during the last twenty or thirty years, we have become a new people. 'Early Victorian' England now lies, in effect, centuries behind us.

....

In short, the opening of the twentieth century finds us all, to the dismay of the old-fashioned Individualist, 'thinking in communities'.

Now the trouble with Gladstonian Liberalism is that, by instinct, by tradition, and by the positive precepts of its past exponents, it 'thinks in individuals'. It visualizes the world as a world of independent Round-heads, with separate ends, and abstract rights to pursue those ends. We see old-fashioned Liberals, for instance, still hankering after the disestablishment and disendownment of all State Churches, on the plea of religious equality; meaning that it is unfair to give any public money or public advantage to any denomination from which any individual taxpayer dissents. But if it be so, all corporate action is unfair. We are all dissenters from some part or another of the action of the communities of which we are members. How far the maintenance of a State Church really makes for national well-being—how otherwise than by national establishment and public endowment we can secure, in every parish, whether it cares and can afford to pay for it or not, the presence of a teacher of morality and an exponent of higher intellectual and social life —is a matter for careful investigation. But the notion that there is any-thing inherently wrong in compelling all citizens to help to maintain religious observances or religious instruction of which some of them individually disapprove, is part of the characteristically Whig con-ception of the citizen's contribution to the expenses of the social organi-zation, as a bill paid by a private man for certain specific commodities which he has ordered and purchased for his own use. On this conception the Quaker is robbed when his taxes are spent on the Army and Navy; the Protestant is outraged by seeing his contribution help to support a Roman Catholic school or university; the teetotaller is wronged at having to provide the naval ration of rum. What nonsense it all sounds in the twentieth century! The Gladstonian section of the Liberal Party remains, in fact, axiomatically hostile to the State. It is not 'Little Englandism' that is the matter with them; it is, as Huxley and Matthew Arnold correctly diagnosed, administrative Nihilism. Hence in politics they are inveterately negative, instinctively iconoclastic. They have hung up temperance reform and educational reform for a quarter of a century, because, instead of seeking to enable the citizen to refresh himself without being poisoned or inebriated, and to get the children thoroughly taught, they have wanted primarily to revenge their out-raged temperance principles on the publican and their outrated Non-conformist principles on the Church. Of such Liberals it may be said that the destructive revolutionary tradition is in their bones; they will reform nothing unless it can be done at the expense of their enemies. Moral superiority, virtuous indignation, are necessaries of political life to them; a Liberal reform is never simply a social means to a social end, but a campaign of Good against Evil. Their conception of freedom means only breaking somebody's bonds asunder. When the 'higher freedom' of corporate life is in question, they become angrily reactionary, and denounce and obstruct every new development of common action. If we seek for the greatest enemy of municipal enterprise, we find him in Sir Henry Fowler. If we ask who is the most successful opponent of any extension of 'the Common Rule' of factory legislation to wider fields of usefulness, the answer is Mr John Morley. And when a leader is needed by those whose unalterable instinct it is to resist to the uttermost every painful effort towards the higher organization of that greatest of co-operative societies, the State itself, who than Sir William Harcourt, at his most eloquent, can be more surely depended upon? Not that I have any right to reproach these eminent ones for standing by their principles. The principles were fresh once—in the last quarter of the eighteenth century. Their exponents' minds were fresh, too—about the middle of the nineteenth. But Adam Smith is dead, and Queen Anne, and even Sir Robert Peel; while as to Gladstone, he is by far the deadest of them all. It is kinder to say so bluntly than to encourage his survivors to attempt to conjure themselves into office by a name which, in its owner's lifetime, ended by being hardly able to command even a Scotch constituency; for we cannot believe that Midlothian would have proved safer than Newcastle or Derby had its greatest Liberal representative contested it in 1895. And I confess that I feel the hopelessness, even the comic absurdity, of seeming to invite his more elderly lieutenants, at their ages, to change their spots—to turn over a new leaf and devote themselves to obtaining the greatest possible development of municipal activity, the most comprehensive extension of the Factory Acts, or the fullest utilization of the Government departments in the service of the public. I know too well that they quite honestly consider such aims to be mischievous. They are aiming at something else, namely, at the abstract right of the individual to lead exactly the kind of life that he likes (and can pay for), unpenalized by any taxation for purposes of which he individually disapproves. They are, in fact, still 'thinking in individuals'.

This same atomic conception of society, transferred from the State at home to the British Empire as a whole, colours the Liberal propaganda of Home Rule for Ireland, and its latest metamorphosis, the demand for the independence of the Transvaal. There is good argument for the devotion, within the United Kingdom, of local business to provincial assemblies, in the interest of the efficiency of the House of Commons itself. There is every reason to prefer, for the rebuilding of the civilization of British South Africa, the model of the Australian Commonwealth rather than that of Malta or Mauritius. But Irish Home

Rule and Boer independence are passionately advocated on the plea of the abstract right of these 'nationalities' to separate existence. For the very reason that these races are assumed to have ends which differ from, and perhaps conflict with, those of the British Empire as a whole, it is asserted that they must, in justice, be allowed to pursue these ends at whatever cost to themselves and to their neighbours. What *vieux jeu* all this 'Early Victorian' nationalism now seems! What have we, the citizens of a commonwealth of four distinct races in these little islands alone (five if we include our Jews); of fellow citizens in our states over sea sprung from all European nations, conspicuously French, Italian, and Dutch; of countless tribes and castes of all human colours and nearly all human languages; what, in the name of common sense have we to do with obsolete hypocrisies about peoples 'rightly struggling to be free'?

11. From Herbert Samuel, *Liberalism* (Grant, Richards, 1902). Samuel (1870–1963) was elected to parliament as Liberal member for Cleveland in 1902 and served in the Asquith government from 1909 to 1916.

(*pp. 20–3*)

To many among the fathers of modern Liberalism, government action was anathema. They held, as we hold, that the first and final object of the State is to develop the capacities and raise the standard of living of its citizens; but they held also that the best means towards this object was the self-effacement of the State. Liberty is of supreme importance, and legal regulation is the opposite of liberty. Let governments abstain from war, let them practise economy, let them provide proper protection against violence and fraud, let them repeal restrictive laws, and then the free enterprise of commerce will bring prosperity to all classes, while their natural ambitions on the one hand, the pressure of need on the other, will stimulate the hindmost to seek and to attain their own well-being: such was their doctrine. The economics of Adam Smith and the philosophy of Bentham united to found a creed of non-interference which has inspired in large measure the politics of a century. Liberalism became a negative policy, opposing foreign enterprises and entanglements, attacking the laws regulating trade, opinion, combination, land tenure, which had been inherited from a previous generation; its positive proposals were constitutional, aiming at a democratic State structure, and they were constitutional only. If, especially, proposals were made for interfering with the conditions of employment, the Liberals of that generation heard them with suspicion and accepted them, if acceptance was forced by events, with reluctance.

Contrast this with the measures of social reform that were the distinctive work of the Liberal Government of 1892 to 1895. A striking departure from these principles will be seen. That Ministry passed a Local Government Act giving or confirming to local authorities power to acquire land, even without the consent of the owners, and to let it to labourers for cultivation; power, also, to cause any house they considered unhealthy to be repaired or closed; power to establish at the public expense a library, baths, a recreation-ground; power in a score of ways to intervene in the affairs of the inhabitants of the district. It passed a Railway Servants Act which enabled the Board of Trade to hear the complaints of men who were overworked by their employers and to compel those employers to grant whatever the Board considered to be a reasonable standard of hours. It passed an Act giving further facilities to local bodies for borrowing money in order to build houses for the working-classes; another forbidding parents to send their children to work before the age of eleven years; a Factory Act that dealt with the amount of air space for each worker in factories, the amount of steam that might be discharged into the atmosphere, the temperature to be maintained, the provision for escape from fire, the number of days in the week and in the year on which women and young persons might be employed overtime, the hours of work and of meals in laundries, the special conditions of dangerous trades and processes, the mode in which employers were to inform their work-people of the rate at which they would be paid, and other matters of even more minute detail. The Ministry introduced a Bill to cause landlords in Ireland to re-admit to their occupation certain tenants whom they had evicted; another to compel employers to compensate workmen who were injured in life, in limb, or in health during their employment, and to prohibit the parties from 'contracting out' of the law; another reducing the number of hours to be worked by young persons in shops. The majority of the members of the Government supported a Bill limiting the hours to be worked in mines to eight in the day. An Act was passed dealing with the rates of carriage charged by Railway Companies. A Commission was appointed to consider whether a scheme could be framed for giving State pensions to the aged poor. The ministers used their executive power to raise the wages and shorten the hours of large numbers of men employed by the State, beyond the point which the men would have been willing to accept rather than lose their employment. To secure the proper execution of previous laws, they made more stringent the inspection of factories. Finally they raised the standard of accommodation and of teaching in the public schools already existing. No more complete abandonment of the old theory of negation can be imagined than is shown by this governmental activity, so extensive and so minute.

(*pp. 28–9.*)

Three causes, then, combined to convert Liberalism from the principle of State abstention. Three causes made possible the adoption of a programme such as that of the recent Liberal Government. It was seen that the State had become more efficient and its legislation more competent, and laws of regulation were found by experiment neither to lessen prosperity nor to weaken self-reliance in the manner foretold. It was realized that the conditions of society were in many respects so bad that to tolerate them longer was impossible, and that the *laissez faire* policy was not likely to bring the cure. And it was realized that extensions of law need not imply diminutions of freedom, but on the contrary would often enlarge freedom.

Such are the facts and arguments which brought about this change. In them we find the answer to those who use the doctrine of the old Liberalism to attack the policy of the new. The State is not incompetent for the work of social reform. Self-reliance is a powerful force, but not powerful enough to cure unaided the diseases that afflict society. Liberty is of supreme importance, but State assistance, rightly directed, may extend the bounds of liberty.

12. From Leo Chiozza Money, *Riches and Poverty* (People's edition, 1909). Money (1870–1944) was later Liberal M.P. for North Paddington, 1906–10, and for East Northamptonshire, 1910–18. He joined the Labour Party in 1918.

(*pp. 41–3.*)

DISTRIBUTION OF THE NATIONAL INCOME AS BETWEEN THOSE WITH MORE AND THOSE WITH LESS THAN £160 PER ANNUM

	Number.	Income.
Persons with incomes of over £160 and their families (1,000,000 × 5) .	5,000,000	£830,000,000
Persons with incomes of less than £160 and their families (total population less 5,000,000)	38,000,000	880,000,000
	43,000,000	£1,710,000,000

Broadly speaking, it is shown that *nearly one-half of the entire income of the United Kingdom is enjoyed by but one-ninth of its population.*

But a still more extraordinary conclusion emerges from the facts we have examined. Of the 1,000,000 income tax payers 750,000 are persons with small incomes ranging from £160 to £700. The aggregate income of these 750,000 persons we estimated at £245,000,000, and the estimate is a liberal one. By subtraction from the total income of the income tax classes (£830,000,000) we see that the 250,000 rich persons with £700 and upwards per annum possess an aggregate income of £585,000,000 per annum. The facts are clearly shown in the following table:

RICHES, COMFORT AND POVERTY

Distribution of the National Income as between (1) those with £700 per annum and upwards; (2) those with £160 to £700 per annum; and (3) those with less than £160 per annum.

	Number.	Income.
RICHES		
Persons with Incomes of £700 per annum and upwards and their families 250,000 × 5 . . .	1,250,000	£585,000,000
COMFORT		
Persons with Incomes between £160 and £700 per annum and their families 750,000 × 5 . .	3,750,000	245,000,000
POVERTY		
Persons with Incomes of less than £160 per annum and their families	38,000,000	880,000,000
	43,000,000	£1,710,000,000

Thus, to the conclusion that nearly one-half of the entire income of the nation is enjoyed by but one-ninth of its population, we must add another even more remarkable, viz.: that *more than one-third of the entire income of the United Kingdom is enjoyed by less than one-thirtieth of its people.*

(pp. 318–21.)
If our national income had but increased at the same rate as our population since 1867 it would, in 1905, amount to but £1,200,000,000. As we have seen, it is now about £1,700,000,000. Yet the Error of

Distribution remains so great that while the total population in 1867 amounted to 30,000,000, we have to-day a nation of 30,000,000 poor people in our rich country, and many millions of these are living under conditions of degrading poverty. Of those above the line of primary poverty, millions are tied down by the conditions of their labour to live in surroundings which preclude the proper enjoyment of life or the rearing of healthy children. The comparatively high wages of London are accompanied by rents high in proportion and frequently by waste of income and time upon travelling expenses. In so far as the manual labourers have been reduced in proportion to population it has been to swell the ranks of black-coated working men, clerks, agents, travellers, canvassers, and others, whose tenure of employment is precarious, whose earnings are very low, and whose labour as we have already noted is largely waste.

We have won through the horrors of the birth and establishment of the factory system at the cost of physical deterioration. We have purchased a great commerce at the price of crowding our population into the cities and of robbing millions of strength and beauty. We have given our people what we grimly call elementary education and robbed them of the elements of a natural life. All this has been done that a few of us may enjoy a superfluity of goods and services. Out of the travail of millions we have added to a landed gentry an aristocracy of wealth. These, striding over the bodies of the fallen, proclaim in accents of conviction the prosperity of their country.

There leaps to the mind the mordant lines in which Ruskin, twenty-five years ago, wrote a 'modern version' of the Beatitudes:

Blessed are the Rich in Flesh, for theirs is the Kingdom of Earth.
Blessed are the Proud, in that they *have* inherited the Earth.
Blessed are the Merciless, for they shall obtain Money.

There is no whit of exaggeration in these lines. The passage of twenty-five years has but added to their sting. Twenty-five years of accumulation of the results of toil in hands other than those of the toilers have had for consummation the accusing series of facts which are examined in the early chapters of this book. Deprivation for the many and luxury for the few have degraded our national life at both ends of the scale. At the one end, 'thirteen millions on the verge of hunger', physically and morally deteriorated through poverty and unloveliness. At the other, the inheritors of the earth, 'senseless conduits through which the strength and riches of their native land are poured into the cup of the fornication of its capital'.

Blessed indeed are the Rich, for theirs is the governance of the realm, theirs is the Kingdom. Theirs is a power above the throne, for it has been a maxim of British politics that our government should be a poor government, and a poor government cannot contend in the direction of affairs with the imperium of wealth. This may be illustrated by our attempts to 'educate' the mass of the people. For a few brief years the government, with small funds raised with timorous hands, does a little to form the mind and character of the child. Even in those early years it consents that the future proud citizen of Empire shall be improperly fed and badly housed. These early moments passed, the mockery of 'education' ceases, and the child, taught by the State to read, to write, and to cipher, becomes a unit of industry. At this point begins the serious training of the citizen. Forthwith he is inducted into some more or less worthy employment, that employment, as we have seen, resulting from the great expenditure of the few and the poor expenditure of the many. Careers are thus chiefly shaped by the wealthy, for theirs is the greatest call. The demand for luxuries is too great; the demand for necessaries is too small; the unit of industry is fortunate, therefore, if he is inducted into useful service. The State washes its hands of his development. The educational sham over, the real education of life begins. So far as the State calls for privates of industry it is chiefly to make them soldiers, sailors, makers of guns, builders of battle-ships. The development of all things useful, of railways, of canals, of roads, of cities, of houses, is resigned to the blind call for commodities and the intelligence of individuals who, in search of private gain, seek, without regard to the national well-being, to profit by that blind call.

Yet the manner in which its people are employed matters everything to a nation. It is not sufficient to give the child a smattering of knowledge. We need to take a collective interest in the general education of our citizens, and that education is the result of expenditure. The consumer gives the order. Given a fairly equable distribution of income, the call will be as to the greater part for worthy things, as to the smaller part for luxuries. Given a grossly unequal distribution, and the call for luxuries will be so great as to divert a considerable part of the national labour into channels of waste and degradation.

To keep a government poor is to keep it weak. The poor government may resolve to educate, but it will have no means to carry out its resolve; its teachers will be underpaid; its schools inefficient. The poor government may pass Housing Acts; it will but call for better houses that will not come when it does call for them. The poor government may piously resolve to create small holdings; there will be no means to carry out the pious resolve. The poor government may, at periodic intervals, look the question of unemployment in the face; its legislation will but reflect its poverty, and be in its provisions an acknowledgment that the power to employ, the power to govern, is in other hands.

13. From R. J. Campbell, *The New Theology* (Chapman Hall, 1907), pp. 250–6. Campbell (1867–1956) was minister of the Congregationalist City Temple, 1903–15. He joined the Church of England in 1916, and later became chancellor of Chichester Cathedral.

Modern industrialism and the Church

Look for the spirit of Jesus at work and you have found the Church too.

Judged by this standard, where are the Churches to-day? We have seen that the only gospel which Jesus had to preach was the gospel of the Kingdom of God; everything He ever said can be included under that head. His Church, or Christian society, or whatever else we like to call it, has no meaning unless it exists for the realization of the kingdom of God. We cannot state this too strongly. The whole of the other-worldism of the Churches, the elaborate paraphernalia of doctrine and observance, is utterly useless, and worse than useless, unless it ministers to this end. Unless it can be shown that I am wrong in this supposition—and I think that will be pretty hard to do—a fairly good case could be made out for burning down most of the theological colleges in the land, and sending the bright young fellows in them to do some serious work for the common good. For it must be confessed, as I said at the beginning, that the Churches are to a large extent a failure. We cannot but recognize, for one thing, that our modern civilization, with all its boasted advance on the past, is still unchristian. It puts a premium upon selfishness. Modern industrialism is cruel and unjust, and directly incites men to self-seeking. The weak and unfortunate have to go to the wall. Little mercy is shown to the man who is not strong enough to fight his way and keep his footing in the struggle for existence. We are all the time making war upon one another, man against man, business against business, class against class, nation against nation. We talk of our freedom; but no man is really free, and the great majority of us are slaves to some corporation, or capitalist, or condition of things, which renders the greater part of life a continuous anxiety lest health or means should fail, and we should prove unequal to the demands made upon us. If a man goes under, his acquaintances will pity him for five minutes, and then forget all about him. There is no help for it; they cannot do anything else; they have their own living to get. They are like soldiers in the heat of battle; they must not pause to mourn over a fallen comrade, or they may soon be stretched beside him. I do not mean, of course, to make the foolish statement that present-day industrialism is unrestrainedly individualistic; thank God, it is not that. But the principle of competition still exercises a sway so potent as to stamp modern social organization as unchristian. We may just as well recognize that fact and state it plainly. The glaringly unequal ownership of material wealth is anti-social; it is good neither for the rich man nor for the poor, for it is to the interest of every man that the body politic should be healthy and happy. That so large a number of our total population should have to exist upon the very margin of subsistence is a moral wrong. We have no business to have any slums or sweating-dens, or able-bodied unemployed, or paupers. Poverty, dulness of brain, and coarseness of habit are often found in close association. Some amount of material endowment is required even for the development of the intelligence and the training of the moral faculties. Wealth possesses no value in itself; it only possesses value as a means to more abundant life. If there is one thing upon which Christianity insists more than another, it is the duty of caring for the weak and sinful; but at present this duty is only recognized to a very limited extent.

Christianity and Collectivism

In what I am now saying, I am well aware that I have come to a phase of my subject which thousands of my countrymen are stating so clearly and forcibly as to compel attention; but what I want to show is that the present unideal condition of the civilized world is an indictment of the Churches and their conventional doctrines. We seem to have forgotten our origin. I have long felt, as I suppose every Christian minister must feel, the antagonism between the Christian standard of conduct and that required in ordinary business life. There is no blinking the fact that the standard of Christ and the standard of the commercial world are not the same. Our work is to make them the same, and to that end we must destroy the social system which makes selfishness the rule, and compels a man to act upon his lower motives, and we must put a better in its place. We must establish a social order wherein a man can be free to be his best, and to give his best to the community without crushing or destroying any one else. In a word, we want Collectivism in the place of competition; we want the Kingdom of God. Charity is no remedy for our social ills and their moral outcome; the only remedy is a new social organization on a Christian basis. I do not believe that any form of Collectivism, as a mere system superposed from without, can ever really make the world happy; it must be the expression of the spirit of brotherhood working from within. Neither do I feel much faith in any sudden and cataclysmic reformation of society. The history of Christendom proves that no institution can be much in advance of human nature and survive. Covenanters and Puritans found that out when they tried to make men godly by Act of Parliament; Savonarola found it out when the wild passions of the Florentines, restrained for a brief hour, broke their chains and destroyed him; the Christians of New Testament times found it out when their beautiful experiment of social brotherhood came to an end in the horror and darkness of the break-up of Jewish national life. But at least we can recognize the presence of the guiding Spirit of God in all our social concerns, and work along with it for the realization of the ideal of universal brotherhood. We can show men what Jesus really came to do, and, as His servants, we can help Him to do it. We can definitely recognize that the movement towards social regeneration is really and truly a spiritual movement, and that it must never be captured by materialism. I deplore the fact that, for the moment, the main current of the great Labour movement which, perhaps more than any other, represents the social application of the Christian ideal, should appear to be out of touch with organized religion. This cannot continue, for I observe that the men who lead it are men of moral passion, and often men of simple religious faith. It could hardly be otherwise. It seems to me in the nature of things impossible to sustain a belief in a moral ideal without some kind of belief in God; and assuredly God is with these men in the work they are doing and have yet to do. In fact, the Labour Party is itself a Church, in the sense in which that word was originally used, for it represents the getting together of those who want to bring about the Kingdom of God.

The New Theology and Collectivism

The New Theology, as I understand it, is the theology of this movement, whether the movement knows it or not, for it is essentially the gospel of the Kingdom of God. No lesser theology can consistently claim to be this; systems of belief, which are weighted by dogmatic considerations, have not and cannot have the same power of appeal. This higher, wider truth, which sweeps away the mischievous accretions which have made religion distasteful to the masses, is the religious articulation of the movement towards an ideal social order. This fact ought to be realized and brought home to the consciousness of the earnest men who are labouring to redeem England and the world from the power of all that tortures and degrades humanity, and stifles or destroys its best life.

14. Memorandum by Herbert Gladstone, the Liberal Chief Whip, on his agreement with Ramsay MacDonald, secretary of the Labour Representation Committee: from Herbert Gladstone, Papers, B.M., Add. MSS., 46100.

Secret.

13 March 1903.

1. No compact alliance agreement or bargain.

2. There being no material points of difference in the main lines of Liberal policy we are ready to ascertain from qualified and responsible Labour leaders how far Labour candidates can be given an open field against a common enemy.

3. We are ready to do this as an act of friendship and without any stipulation of any kind, because we realize that an accession of strength to Labour representation in the House of Commons is not only required by the country in the interests of Labour but that it would increase progressive forces generally and the Liberal party as the best available instrument of progress.

4. The question then arises how and where can this open field be secured?
The Liberal Council is bound to act for and with recognized local Liberal Associations and this principle cannot be departed from *under any circumstances*. On the other hand, the Liberal Council can use its influence with the local associations to abstain from nominating a Liberal candidate, and to unite in support of any recognized and competent Labour candidate who supports the general objects of the Liberal party.

5. It is understood that the Labour Representation Committee propose to run about 30 candidates. This does not include (a) Scotland, (b) Miners' Federation, (c) Socialist bodies. It is not proposed to consider as a material question any action bodies like the S.D.F. and the N.S.F. may take. The Miners propose to run 15 or 18 candidates themselves.

6. This schedule sets forth available or possible seats for labour:

Where there is no difficulty

Blackburn (1)	Gorton	Croydon
Bolton (1)	Manchester S.W.	West Ham (1)
Bradford W.	Merthyr	Wolverhampton (1)
Clitheroe	Birmingham (1)	Woolwich
Darlington	Norwich	York (1)

Middlesborough	Oldham	S. Salford
Deptford	Preston	
Derby (1)	Stoke	
	Sunderland (1)	

Adjustable

Halifax	Wakefield	Southampton (1)
Newcastle (1)	Leicester (1)	

Claimed by L.R.C. and difficult

Durham Co. (1)	Sheffield (1)	Jarrow
Rochdale	Swansea District	

Available Alternatives

S. Nottingham	St. Helens
Wellington (Salop)	Barnard Castle
Wednesbury	Aston Manor

Labour seats not recognized by L.R.C.

Battersea	Middleton
Birkenhead	Hanley

7. The following represent seats occupied or claimed by Miners:

Morpeth	Normanton	Nuneaton
Wansbeck	E. Leeds	Ince
Durham Mid.	Newton	N.W. Staffs (?)
Rhondda	S. Glamorgan	Monmouth W.

In all at present 55.

8. At a friendly conference it is quite possible to arrange that Labour candidates should have an open field in 30 seats desired by the L.R.C.; that Miners' candidates should have 12.

9. It must however be distinctly understood that if in any agreed constituency the Liberal local association breaks away and runs a Liberal candidate, the Liberal Council must support that candidate.

10. But the Liberal Council will use every legitimate effort to secure this open field and to maintain it for authorized and responsible Labour candidates.

15. A speech by Sir Francis Channing at Ilchester, 13 September 1905: from F. A. Channing, *Memories of Midland Politics, 1885–*

1910 (Constable, 1918), pp. 308–10. Sir Francis Channing (1841–1926) was Liberal M.P. for East Northamptonshire, 1885–1910.

The corner-stone of Liberal policies should be the long-neglected group of Labour questions, which had been contemptuously pushed aside by this government. They had to assert the right to live, and to live happily, the right to combine, the right of the worker to share in determining the equitable distribution of gross profits between Capital and Labour. . . . They had heard it said that it was impossible for Liberalism and Labour to work together. He had been twenty years in the Commons, and had taken a fair share in the work of the House with regard to Land and Labour. On every issue he could remember, where the rights of Labour were concerned, he had found Liberals and Labour men fighting side by side. Where was the real difference of view between Socialists and thorough-going Liberals like himself? If it was Socialism for a State to insist that adult men should have reasonable hours of Labour, then they were all Socialists. He had his share on the very first occasion that Parliament ever determined the issue of interfering with excessive hours of adult labour, in the case of the railwaymen. That principle was asserted for the first time by a Liberal, in the motion as to Railway Hours he moved in 1891 and carried through the House by a Liberal Ministry, after a Liberal had fought that question for two years in a Select Committee of the House, and convinced that Committee of the justice of his proposals. That motion, which a Conservative majority had refused to accept before, was, as soon as the Liberal Ministry of Mr Gladstone came into power, made the law of the land.

Take 'Graduated Taxation'. Where was the difference on that? Liberals wanted a graduated Income Tax to relieve the poor man, absolutely fair adjustment of taxation as between one man and another. Then Liberals, just as Socialists, wanted taxation of land values. If Socialism meant that they should check physical deterioration by getting children fed properly before School, then they were all Socialists. In that wonderful session of 1891, first came that Liberal motion, moved by himself, to check excessive hours on railways, defeated by only seventeen votes, two years later made law. Then came Mr Robertson's amendment of the Conspiracy Laws which would have prevented the Taff Vale decision and established what nearly everybody supposed was the legal status of Trade Unions. Another Liberal motion to secure the rights of Labour. Then came third, Mr Sidney Buxton's resolution accepted in a modified form by the House of Commons, to secure the standard of 'Fair Wage' in Government contracts. That was a great Liberal contribution to the cause of Labour. . . .

He asked if it was generous or just, or whether there was a shadow of truth in any one saying that the Liberal Party, after such work was not in absolute sympathy with Labour, or fair to say to turn their backs on both of them? ... The Trades Disputes Bill, which had aroused intense interest, had been four times before the House of Commons, once in the hands of Mr Shackleton, who had worked with him loyally when they were pressing last winter for the settlement of the Raunds' dispute. ... John Burns was one of his best friends. On his 'Old Age Pensions Bill'—introduced again that year—to prove that question was a living issue—he had the name of Mr Keir Hardie. On all the three other occasions the Trades Disputes Bill was balloted for by many Liberals, and on those three other occasions the Bill was brought in by prominent Liberal Imperialists—last session by Mr Whittaker, who made the very best fight of all for the principle. So they had on the side of Labour not only men like himself, but strong representatives of the Imperialist wing also. Was it fair, then, to say that the one party was as bad as the other? ...

He cared not whether a man called himself Socialist, or Independent Labour, or Social Democrat, or any other name under heaven. If he was working for the benefit of his fellowmen, he was with him, and with him with all his heart.

16. Haldane to Knollys, 12 September 1905: from Roy Jenkins, *Asquith* (Collins, 1964), pp. 145–6. R. B. Haldane (1856–1928) was to be Secretary for War and then Lord Chancellor in the Liberal governments after 1905.

What is proposed is that Asquith should, in as friendly and tactful a way as possible, and without assuming that Sir H. C. B. is adverse, tell him of the resolution we have come to. We are none of us wedded to prospects of office .... But we are all ready to do our best cheerfully under Sir H. C. B. provided we have sufficient safeguards. What we would try to bring about is that, if the situation arises, and Sir H. C. B. is sent for, he should propose to the King the leadership in the House of Commons with the Exchequer for Asquith, either the Foreign or Colonial Office for Grey, and the Woolsack for myself.

17. Lord Rosebery's speech at Bodmin, 25 November 1905: from *The Times*, 26 November 1905.

The responsible leader of the Liberal Party ... has hoisted once more in its most pronounced form the flag of Irish Home Rule. I am not going even now to utter one jarring note which can conflict with the unity of the Free Trade party. To maintain that unity, even at the cost of personal effacement, must be the duty of every man who believes Free Trade to be the greatest practical issue before the country at the present moment. But I object to the raising of the banner of Home Rule, not merely because of high constitutional objections founded on the recent experience of foreign European countries, but also because of my belief as to what will really conduce to the welfare of the Irish people itself; but I object to it mainly on this occasion for this reason— that it impairs the unity of the Free Trade party, and that it indefinitely postpones discussion on social and educational reform, on which the country has set its heart. I will say no more on this subject except to say emphatically and explicitly and once for all that I cannot serve under that banner.

18. Asquith to Haldane, 6 December 1905: from Roy Jenkins, *Life of Asquith* (Collins, 1964), pp. 151-2.

The conditions are in one respect fundamentally different from those which we, or at any rate I, contemplated when we talked in the autumn. The election is before and not behind us, and a Free Trade majority, still more an independent majority, is not a fact but at most a probability.

I stand in a peculiar position which is not shared by either of you.

If I refuse to go in, one of two consequences follows: either (1) the attempt to form a Govt. is given up (which I don't believe in the least would now happen) or (2) a weak Govt. would be formed entirely or almost entirely of one colour.

In either event in my opinion the issue of the election would be put in the utmost peril. It would be said that we were at issue about Home Rule, the Colonies, the Empire etc., etc., and the defections of the whole of our group would be regarded as conclusive evidence. The *tertius gaudens* at Dalmeny [Rosebery] would look on with complacency. I cannot imagine more disastrous conditions under which to fight a Free Trade election.

And the whole responsibility, I repeat, would be mine. I could not say, after the offers made to Grey and you, that our group had been flouted, and the only ground I could take would be that I and not C-B must from the first lead the new H. of Commons. I could not to my own conscience or the world justify such a position.

If the election were over, and Free Trade secure, different considerations would arise.

B. The Liberals in Power (1905-15)

a. Welfare State and Political Crisis

19. Lloyd George's speech at the Guildhall, Caernarvon, 18 January 1906: from *The Times*, 19 January 1906. Lloyd George was the new President of the Board of Trade.

Mr Lloyd George then stated that he had received a number of questions containing the following—'Are you in favour of payment of Members of Parliament; of paying returning officers' fees out of Imperial taxes; of a Bill for the settling of trade union disputes; of amending the Compensation Act; of the taxation of ground rents; and old-age pensions?' Leaving out the last for the moment, he would say that he was absolutely in favour of all the others. With regard to the Trade Disputes Bill, he would just say that it was well known that the Government was prepared to introduce a Bill dealing with the question at the first opportunity, because they thought that the protection of trades unions was the best thing for capital as well as for labour.

As to old-age pensions. The money spent on the South African War would have been sufficient to give old-age pensions to every man over 65. They had reckoned it up at the time. They also discussed the question of 60 or 65 years of age, and they found that the difference between the two limits meant about 12 to 20 millions. At the present time it would be impossible to get the people of this country to face an expenditure of 20 million pounds on anything. Therefore the matter, when taken up, must be taken up gradually. They must, first of all, put the national finances in spick and span order, and then see that every man too old to pursue his ordinary avocation should be saved from the humiliation of the workhouse or parish charity.

20. From *The Nation*, 7 March 1908, pp. 812-13. Churchill was at this time Under-Secretary for the Colonies.

THE UNTRODDEN FIELD OF POLITICS.
To the Editor of The Nation.

SIR,—It is a year ago since your enterprise was launched. During the weeks that are gone, *The Nation* has maintained a position of sober but unflinching Radicalism, and has steadily acquired a true political significance. The period has been highly favourable to the discussion of large basic questions, and not unfavourable to the progress of social thought. When a Liberal and Radical administration is actually in being, when adventurous and extensive legislative proposals are being canvassed and debated in the country and in Parliament, when any proposal for reform, however utopian, is received with a measure of sympathy and interest, all parties and all persons are forced to turn their minds to these dominant domestic topics. Even the most conservative of mankind are compelled to address themselves to purely social issues. The more active, earnest, or embittered the opponents of Liberal and reconstructive ideas become, the more they are constrained to descend into an arena which *we* have smoothed and sanded, and engage with weapons and upon ground of which *we* have made the choice. The consequences of this concentration of many different and conflicting forces upon home questions, far reaching and to some extent incalculable, as they would in any case be, become all the more striking in contrast with the period of foreign and colonial activity to which they have succeeded. They comprise a complete change in political values, in the point of view from which public men judge and are themselves judged, and in the style and language of Parliamentary debate and party tactics.

This considerable revolution has been intimately connected with Mr Chamberlain's Fiscal propaganda. . . .

While these curious changes have been occupying the attention of the party world, a not less important modification has been consummated in the internal conception of the Liberal Party. It has not abandoned in any respect its historic championship of Liberty, in all its forms under every sky; but it has become acutely conscious of the fact that political freedom, however precious, is utterly incomplete without a measure at least of social and economic independence. This realization is not confined to our islands. It is taking hold of men's minds as it never has before, in every popularly governed State. All over the world the lines of cleavage are ceasing to be purely political, and are becoming social and economic. The present majority in the House of Commons is pervaded by a social spirit, which is all the more lively and earnest because it has yet to find clear-cut and logical formularies of articulate expression. A great body of opinion is slowly moving forward, conscious of possessing in its midst a vital truth, conscious, too, of the almost superhuman difficulty of affording to it any definition at once sufficiently comprehensive and precise. It is for this reason that no hard and fast line can be drawn between the varied elements which constitute the strength of the present Government upon any ground of political theory.

No true classification can be made in the abstract between Liberals and Radicals, or between Radicals and Labour representatives. It is only when confronted with some concrete fact that clear decisions can be taken. And hitherto most of the issues that have arisen have only served to demonstrate the general solidarity.

It is in such a situation, party and national, that the movement towards a Minimum Standard may well take conscious form. It is a mood rather than a policy; but it is a mood which makes it easy to perceive the correlation of many various sets of ideas, and to refer all sorts of isolated acts of legislation to one central and common test. Two clear lines of advance open before us: corrective, by asserting the just precedence of public interests over private interests; and constructive, by supplying the patent inadequacy of existing social machinery. It is this latter work which has lately attracted an increasing measure of attention throughout the country.

Science, physical and political alike, revolts at the disorganization which glares at us in so many aspects of modern life. We see the curse of unregulated casual employment steadily rotting the under side of the labour market. We see the riddles of unemployment and under-employment quite unsolved. There are mighty trades which openly assert the necessity of a labour surplus—'on hand' in the streets and round the dock gates—for the ordinary commercial convenience of their business. And they practise what they preach. There are political philosophers who complacently resign themselves to the doctrine of the *residuum*. There are other industries, which prey upon the future. Swarms of youths, snatched from school at the period in life when training should be most careful and discipline most exacting, are flung into a precocious manhood, and squander their most precious years in erratic occupations, which not only afford no career for them in after life, but sap and demoralize that character without which no career can be discovered or pursued. Thousands of children grow up not nourished sufficiently to make them effective citizens, or even to derive benefit from the existing educational arrangements. Thousands of boys are exploited in depressing men's wages, and are discharged when they demand such wages for themselves. The military obligations of foreign nations take two or three years from the life of every man, and ought thereby to give the dwellers in this island a mastery in peaceful crafts-manship over the whole world. All this inestimable advantage runs thriftlessly to waste. The army system is itself to a very large extent a pauperizing machine, nicely calculated to take the best years from the lives of its servants with the minimum obligation to the State.

It is false and base to say that these evils, and others like them, too many here to set forth, are inherent in the nature of things, that their remedy is beyond the wit of man, that experiment is foolhardy, that all is for the best in 'Merrie England'. No one will believe it any more. That incredulity is one of the most noteworthy features in the evolution of public opinion to-day. The nation, which is greater than either party, demands the application of drastic corrective and curative processes, and will crown with confidence and honour any party which has the strength and wisdom necessary for that noble crusade.

We are already in battle on more than one point in this large field. The Licensing Bill comes to grips not only with the excessive consumption of strong drink, but with the unwarranted assertions of private interest. The Trade Disputes Act is a charter to Trades Unionism, and to all the social insurance that Trades Unionism involves. The Land Acts, some passed, others on the anvil, open to the people a new sphere for enterprise and exertion and tend to afford a healthy stability to the Commonwealth.

But the future offers larger hopes and sterner labours. We have to contemplate the serious undertaking by the State of the elimination of casual employment through the agency of Labour Exchanges, and the scientific treatment, in every conceivable classification, of any unabsorbed *residuum* that may exist. The House of Commons has unanimously approved the institution of Wages Boards in certain notoriously 'sweated' industries, and this principle may be found capable of almost indefinite extension in those industries which employ parasitically underpaid labour. We have to seek, whether through the acquisition of the railways or canals, or by the development of certain national industries like Afforestation, the means of counterbalancing the natural fluctuations of world trade. We have by an altogether unprecedented expansion in technical colleges and continuation schools, to train our youth in the skill of the hand, as well as in arts and letters, and to give them a far greater degree of discipline in mind and body. We have to make that provision for the aged which compassion demands and policy approves.

It is certain that as we enter upon these untrodden fields of British politics we shall need the aid of every moral and religious force which is alive in England to-day. Sacrifices will be required from every class in the population; the rich must contribute in money and the poor in service, if their children are to tread a gentler path towards a fairer goal. A fiscal system which prudently but increasingly imposes the necessary burdens of the State upon unearned wealth will not only be found capable of providing the funds which will be needed, but will also stimulate enterprise and production. And thus from many quarters we may work towards the establishment of that Minimum Standard below which competition cannot be allowed, but above which it may continue healthy and free, to vivify and fertilize the world.

It is because the influence of *The Nation* may be powerful to aid and further these causes, that I send you my good wishes and congratulations to-day.—I am, Sir,

Yours faithfully,

Winston S. Churchill.

21. From *Beatrice Webb, Our Partnership,* B. Drake and M. I. Cole (ed.) (Longmans 1948), pp. 465–6, 473–4.

(*30 November 1910.*) ... The big thing that has happened in the last two years is that Lloyd George and Winston Churchill have practically taken the *limelight,* not merely from their own colleagues, but from the Labour Party. They stand out as the most advanced politicians. And, if we get a Liberal majority and payment of members, we shall have any number of young Fabians rushing from Parliament, fully equipped for the fray—better than the Labour men—and enrolling themselves behind the two Radical leaders.

(*13 May 1911.*) ... The splendid reception by all parties of Lloyd George's scheme of sickness insurance is a curious testimony to the heroic demagogy of the man. He has taken every item that could be popular with anyone, mixed them together and produced a Bill which takes some twenty millions from the property class to be handed over to the wage-earners *sans phrase* to be spent by them, as they think fit, in times of sickness or unemployment. If you add to this gigantic transfer of property from the haves to the have-nots the fact that the tax is to be collected in the most costly and extravagant fashion, and that the whole administration of the fund is to be put into the hands of the beneficiaries who are contributing only one-third, there is enough to make the moderate and constitutional Socialist aghast.

The first asset he started with was the word *insurance.* To the governing classes insurance has always meant the voluntary contributions of the persons benefited—a method of raising revenue which has saved the pockets of all other persons. During the controversy about old-age pensions, insurance gradually acquired a compulsory element, and the Conservative Party became pledged to raising money from wage-earners, employers and the general taxpayer, as an alternative to non-contributory pensions. Hence, by using this word Lloyd George secured the approval of the Conservative section of the community. Then there were the friendly societies who stood in the way. So he puts them into possession of the whole machinery of distribution: a fund that is mainly contributed by non-beneficiaries. This scheme has the adherence of the friendly society world and of the larger part of the working class.

J. R. MacDonald to the Master of Elibank, 4 October 1911: from Frank Owen, *Tempestuous Journey* (Hutchinson, 1954) pp. 207–8, The Master of Elibank was the Liberal Chief Whip; Ramsay MacDonald was now chairman of the parliamentary Labour Party.

I need not assure you that the statement I made to you about the attitude of the [Labour] Party on the Insurance Bill before we separated in the summer holds good.

The Party came to its decision and its decision will be carried out by the officers loyally and faithfully in spite of what two, or at the outside, three, Members may do to the contrary.

Master of Elibank to D. Lloyd George, 5 October 1911.

I have received the following letter from Ramsay MacDonald. The understanding—after the passage of Payment to Members—was that he and his friends should give general support to the Insurance Bill. . . .

22. Asquith's speech at the Royal Albert Hall, 10 December 1909: from *The Times*, 11 December 1909.

I tell you quite plainly and I tell my fellow countrymen outside that neither I nor any other Liberal Minister supported by a majority in the House of Commons is going to submit again to the rebuffs and the humiliations of the last four years. We shall not assume office and we shall not hold office unless we can secure the safeguards which experience shows us to be necessary for the legislative utility and honour of the party of progress. . . . We are not proposing the abolition of the House of Lords or setting up a single Chamber, but we do ask, and we are going to ask, the electors to say that the House of Lords shall be confined to the proper functions of a second Chamber. The absolute veto which it at present possesses must go. The power which it claims from time to time of, in effect, compelling us to choose between a dissolution and—so far as legislative projects are concerned—legislative sterility must go also. The people in future when they elect a new House of Commons, must be able to feel, what they cannot feel now, that they are sending to Westminster men who will have the power not merely of proposing and debating, but of making laws. The will of the people, as deliberately expressed by their elected representatives, must within the limits of the lifetime of a single Parliament, be made effective.

23. Mr Lloyd George's Memorandum on the Formation of a Coalition, 17 August 1910: from Sir Charles Petrie, *Life and Letters of Austen Chamberlain*, Vol. II (Cassell's, 1940), pp. 381–8.

Austen Chamberlain (1863–1937), was M.P. for East Worcestershire, 1892–1914, and for Birmingham West, 1914–37. His major government offices were Chancellor of the Exchequer, 1903–5 and 1919–21; Secretary for India, 1915–17; Lord Privy Seal, 1921–2; Foreign Secretary, 1924–9.

Mr LLOYD GEORGE'S MEMORANDUM ON THE FORMATION OF A COALITION, 17 AUGUST 1910. . . .

Some of the urgent problems awaiting settlement, problems which concern intimately the happiness and the efficiency of the inhabitants of these islands, their strength and influence, can only be successfully coped with by the active co-operation of both the great Parties in the State. Parties will always disagree on certain vital issues affecting the government of this country: their respective points of view are essentially different; but at the present moment the questions which are of the most vital importance to the well-being of the great community are all questions which are not only capable of being settled by the joint action of the two great Parties without involving any sacrifice of principle on the part of either, but which can be better settled by such co-operation than by the normal working of Party machinery. This country has gained a good deal from the conflict and rivalry of Parties, and it will gain a good deal more in the future from the same cause; but I cannot help thinking that the time has arrived for a truce, for bringing the resources of the two Parties into joint stock in order to liquidate arrears which, if much longer neglected, may end in national impoverishment, if not insolvency.

What are the questions which call for immediate attention and which could properly and effectively be dealt with by some combined effort as I indicate? There are first of all the questions which come under the category of Social Reform: they affect the health, the vitality, the efficiency, and the happiness of the individuals who constitute the races that dwell in these islands.

HOUSING

The putting an end to a system which houses millions of the people under conditions which devitalize their strength, depress their energies, and deprive them of all motive power for putting forth their best.

DRINK

The problem of excessive drinking has a most intimate relation to other questions of Social Reform. There is no doubt that a vast number of people in this country destroy their physical, mental, and moral powers owing to their addiction to alcohol. One Party has been for the moment completely captured by a rigid and sterile plan for effecting reform; the other Party's energies are concentrated upon resistance to this scheme. If both Parties put their heads together, they could discover some idea which, whilst treating vested interests fairly, and even generously, would advance the cause of national sobriety.

INSURANCE

Provision against the accidents of life which bring so much undeserved poverty to hundreds of thousands of homes, accidents which are quite inevitable, such as the death of the breadwinner or his premature breakdown in health. I have always thought that the poverty which was brought upon families owing to these causes presents a much more urgent demand upon the practical sympathy of the community than even old age pensions. With old age, the suffering is confined to the individual alone; but in these other cases it extends to the whole family of the victim of circumstances.

UNEMPLOYMENT

Unemployment might also be put in the same category. Whatever is done towards improving the trade conditions, we shall at any rate for some time to come have to face a percentage of unemployment, especially in certain precarious trades. No country has been able to avoid it, and, with fluctuations in trade, the constant improvements in machinery, the variations in public demands for commodities and many other reasons, men will be thrown out of employment temporarily, and great difficulty will be found in absorbing this surplus labour. Much misery will thereby be caused, misery often culminating in hunger and starvation. Every country ought to provide adequately against such disasters.

This question of insurance illustrates one of the difficulties that must necessarily be encountered by every Government that attempts to grapple with it without first of all securing the co-operation of its opponents. The hardest case of all is that of the man who dies in the prime of life leaving a widow and young children. She suddenly finds herself without any adequate means, very often with all her means exhausted by medical and funeral expenses, face to face with the task of having not merely to attend to her household duties and the bringing up of the children, but also with that of earning a livelihood for herself and for them. In Germany they contemplate adding provision for widows under these conditions to their ordinary invalidity insurance. It is comparatively easy to set up a system of that kind in Germany; but here one would have to encounter the bitter hostility of powerful organizations like the Prudential, the Liver, the Royal Victoria, the Pearl, and similar institutions, with an army numbering scores, if not hundreds of thousands, of agents and collectors who make a living out of collecting a few pence a week from millions of households in this country for the purpose of providing death allowances. The expenses of collection and administration come to something like 50 per cent of the total receipts, and these poor widows and children are by this extravagant system robbed of one half of the benefits which it has cost the workmen so much to provide for them. Sometimes these agents and collectors sell their books and sub-let them and make hundreds of pounds out of the transaction, all at the expense of the poorest and most helpless creatures in the land. This system ought to be terminated at the earliest possible moment. The benefits are small, costly, and precarious, for if a man is unable, owing to ill-health or lack of employment, to keep up his payments, his policy is forfeited. State insurance costs 10 per cent to administer, and, inasmuch as the State and the employer both contribute, either the premium is considerably less, or the benefits are substantially greater, than with the insurance companies. But, however desirable it may be to substitute State insurance, which does not involve collection and therefore is more economical, any Party that attempted it would instantly incur the relentless hostility of all these agents and collectors. They visit every house, they are indefatigable, they are often very intelligent, and a Government which attempted to take over their work without first of all securing the co-operation of the other Party would inevitably fail in its undertaking; so that, if a scheme of national insurance is taken in hand by any Party Government, it must be confined to invalidity, and the most urgent and pitiable case of all must be left out. I may add that compensation on an adequate scale is well-nigh impossible, inasmuch as it would cost something like twenty or thirty millions at the very least to buy off the interest of these collectors, and such a payment would crush the scheme and destroy its usefulness. On the other hand, the agents cannot be absorbed in the new system, there being no door-to-door collection contemplated.

This is an excellent illustration of the difficulty of dealing with some of these problems except by joint action.

THE POOR LAW

This requires overhauling and re-casting, and I can see nothing in the principles of either Party which are irreconcilable in this matter.

NATIONAL REORGANIZATION

There are several questions coming under this head which could be much better dealt with by a Coalition than by a Party administration.

There is education. Not merely could the denominational issue be thus much more satisfactorily disposed of, inasmuch as the Parties are committed to certain controversial solutions which may not be the very best, but there are questions like the raising of the age limit, which is quite essential if the youth of the country are to receive a training which will enable them to cope with the workmen of Germany and the United States of America.

The same observation applies to the development of technical instruction in this country. The raising of the age limit would excite a good deal of opposition in many quarters, and might gain for a Government great unpopularity, even amongst sections of its own supporters who benefit now largely by boy labour. The Unionist Government of 1886 discovered this, and it is only a Coalition that could, here again, have the strength to face the ignorant and selfish prejudices that will be aroused by any effort to keep the children at school instead of turning them out to make money for their parents.

NATIONAL DEFENCE

This ought to be thoroughly looked into from the point of view of both efficiency and economy.

There are undoubtedly directions in which money can be saved: there are others in which it is imperative that more money should be spent. The whole question of national defence ought to be boldly faced. I doubt whether we are getting our money's worth in any direction. I am strongly of opinion that even the question of compulsory training should not be shirked. No Party dare touch it, because of the violent prejudices which would be excited even if it were suspected that a Government contemplated the possibility of establishing anything of the kind. For that reason it has never really been looked into by statesmen in this country. The Swiss militia system might be considered and those liable to serve might be chosen by ballot. We have no such need as Continental countries labour under of organizing an Army of 3,000,000 or 4,000,000 for defence; but we might aim at raising 500,000 armed militia to supplement our Regular Army to provide against contingencies.

LOCAL GOVERNMENT

Our whole system of local government is on a very unsatisfactory basis. There are too many boards and there is no system of intelligent direction, such as is provided by the Burgomasters on the Continent. Whilst there are too many small boards and councils, there are too few large ones, and a good deal of work is cast upon the Imperial Parliament which could be much more efficiently discharged by local bodies on a large scale.

TRADE

The various problems connected with State assistance to trade and commerce could be enquired into with some approach to intelligent and judicial impartiality if Party rivalries were eliminated. We have not merely problems connected with tariffs, but we have the question of inland transport that ought to be thoroughly overhauled. In Germany, the railway is one of the most important weapons of the State for the purpose of promoting the foreign trade of that country.

THE LAND

There is no question which would gain more, by the elimination of Party strife and bitterness, than that of the land. It is admitted on all hands that the land of this country is capable of much more profitable use than is now given to it. Both Parties seem to imagine, for the moment, that the real solution lies in the direction of establishing a system of smallholdings. I think they have been rather too readily rushed by small, but well-organized, groups of their own supporters into an acceptance of this doctrine. These groups are inspired by men of no marked intelligence and with little knowledge of land cultivation. The smallholdings craze is of a very doubtful utility; and I do not think its devotees have sufficiently considered whether farming on a large scale by competent persons with adequate capital is not more likely to be profitable to the community than a system which divides the land amongst a large number of more or less incompetent smallholders. After all, farming is a business, and it requires just as much capacity to run successfully a 50-acre farm as it would to manage a 500-acre holding. There ought to be the same knowledge of the qualities of the soil, the same gift of buying and selling, the same skill in making the best of the soil in both cases. It is very rarely that men enjoy a combination of all these gifts; and it is far better that the majority of men should work under competent guidance, direction, and command than that they should undertake the responsibilities of management. Few are the men who can, if left to themselves, put their own labour to the more fruitful use. The alternatives are worthy of much more careful and thorough consideration than has hitherto been given to them. If a mistake is made, it will be irreparable for generations. Once a system of smallholdings is rooted in this country it will be almost impossible for a very long period to substitute for it a system of farming on a large scale with adequate capital, where the State might very well assist, and under intelligent management.

IMPERIAL PROBLEMS

Schemes for uniting together the Empire and utilizing and concentrating its resources for defence as for commerce might also to much better advantage be undertaken and put through by a Coalition. They are the most delicate and difficult questions that have to be settled by modern statesmanship. In many respects they are the most urgent. Now is undoubtedly the best time to approach them. After all, there are Parties in the Colonies as well as here; there are Parties in our Colonies whose sympathies are more naturally attracted to the Liberals, and some whose views perhaps bear an affinity to the Conservatives. In one section, Conservative statesmen are viewed with some suspicion; by others, the Liberal Party is regraded with much distrust; but a Government that represented both Parties would appeal to all sections and would carry infinitely greater weight. In this connection, the settlement of the Irish question would come up for consideration. The advantages of a non-Party treatment of this vexed problem are obvious. Parties might deal with it without being subject to the embarrassing dictation of extreme partisans, whether from Nationalists or Orangemen.

FOREIGN POLICY

Such a Government, representing as it would not a fragment but the whole nation, would undoubtedly enhance the prestige of this country abroad.

17 August 1910.

From David Lloyd George, *War Memoirs*, Volume I (Odhams, 1938 edition), pp. 21–3.

... I submitted to Mr Asquith a Memorandum urging that a truce should be declared between the Parties for the purpose of securing the co-operation of the leading party statesmen in a settlement of our national problems—Second Chamber, Home Rule, the development of our agricultural resources, National Training for Defence, the remedying of social evils, and a fair and judicial enquiry into the working of our fiscal system.

Mr Asquith regarded the proposal with considerable favour, and it was decided to submit it to four or five members of the Cabinet for their observations. So far as I can recollect, the only Cabinet Ministers who were called into consultation were Lord Crewe, Sir Edward Grey, Lord Haldane, and Mr Winston Churchill. I cannot recall any criticism in detail from any of them. They all approved of the idea in principle, and it was agreed that the proposal should be submitted to Mr Balfour, who was still the Leader of the Conservative Party. The only outsiders to whom I showed the document were Mr F. E. Smith (subsequently Lord Birkenhead) and Mr Garvin. They were very pleased with the whole conception.

Mr Balfour was by no means hostile; in fact he went a long way towards indicating that personally he regarded the proposal with a considerable measure of approval. He was not, however, certain of the reception which would be accorded to it by his party. Unfortunately, at that time he was not very firmly seated in the saddle. The Die-Hard cry against his leadership was getting audibly shriller each day. However, he consulted some of his leading colleagues, and he received from them replies which were by no means discouraging. I understood that Lord Lansdowne, Lord Cawdor, Lord Curzon, Mr Walter Long and Mr Austen Chamberlain favoured the plan. When he came to summon a more formal and general meeting of his colleagues, he again found that the ablest members of the Conservative Party were by no means antipathetic to the idea. So far as I can recollect, the only opposition came from the late Lord Londonderry. But when Mr Balfour proceeded later on to sound the opinion of less capable and therefore more narrowly partisan members of his party, he encountered difficulties which proved insurmountable. He called upon me one evening at 11 Downing Street to discuss the matter, and I found him then much more hesitant and reluctant. I gathered from him that the chief objection entertained by his colleagues was to my presence in such a combination. I was so completely associated in their minds with extreme radical proposals, I was so much in the front of the offence at that time, and I had said so many wounding things in the scrimmage, that they were more than doubtful whether they could secure the adhesion of their supporters to any Coalition of which I was a member. . . .

It very nearly came off. It was not rejected by the real leaders of the Party, but by men who, for some obscure reason best known to political organizations, have great influence inside the councils of a party without possessing any of the capabilities that excite general admiration and confidence outside.

24. From *The National Review*, January 1912, p. 712.

The Cabinet are pursuing their career of anarchy with a view to beating all previous records. In obedience to the orders of Mr Redmond, they are preparing to disrupt the United Kingdom and to provoke civil war in Ireland. They are following up the destruction of the Constitution by the destruction of the Church, to gratify the malignancy of Mr Silvester Horne and Dr Clifford. They seriously propose to flood the electorate with an indeterminate number of women—Mr Lloyd George thinks in millions—apparently in order to convert the greatest of Sea-powers into the smallest of she-powers. What can be done with such people except to send them about their business? That the constituencies already realize, and late in the day as it is, we entertain the hope that the Asquith anarchy may shortly collapse.

25. From Lucy Masterman, *C. F. G. Masterman, A Biography* (new edition, Frank Cass, 1968), pp. 233–5. Masterman (1873–1927) was Financial Secretary to the Treasury. This is an extract from his wife's diary, dated 26 June 1912, at a time of great labour unrest.

We were all barely through the Railway Strike and the Foreign complication when we were threatened with a Coal Strike. Neither side, at the beginning, I think, meant to go to extremes. But the South Wales wing in both parties practically stampeded the rest. There were scares and reassurances, ups and downs continually. At one moment, quite early in the proceedings, everybody was buying coal; at another, later on, people were assuring each other that there would be no strike. Taking it altogether when it finally came (in March), it was astonishing how little damage the strike seemed to do, at any rate to London itself. There were no extra necessitous children to be fed in the schools, and no one in the workhouses, although the prices of food and coal were both very high. But I rather fancy that another week of it would have produced a frightful amount of distress.

Lloyd George's personal sympathies are not really entirely Labour. Personalities count for a lot with him; and Hardie he did not particularly care for at that moment.

The time was one of pretty fair strain, with interviews and going between the parties. Luckily in this case there was no nonsense about employers and men not meeting.

....

Winston, who had been appointed to the Admiralty early in the session, under one influence and other, was becoming less and less

Radical in his sympathies, and was practically in a 'shoot-'em-down' attitude.

The Prime Minister is not fond of Labour at any time. George described one conference when I was there. 'There', he said, 'were the employers on the one hand, plump, full-fed men, well dressed—men who had never known what it was to go short in their lives. On the other side were the men, great, gaunt fellows, pale with working underground, their faces all torn (drawing his own nails down his cheeks) with anxiety and hard work.' He made a sort of gesture of dismissal. 'I know which side I am on when I see that sort of thing', he said.

....

... all this obscured the fact that there was very serious discontent brewing at the docks, where a strike broke out against the advice and judgment of the leaders, Gosling and Tillett. Part of the truth is that neither the Union nor the Employers Association is much accustomed to discipline in the Port of London, and consequently the infringement of agreements on both sides is a very common occurrence, which has set up a great soreness. Lord Devonport's action later on was the cause of frantic bitterness, and is being a heavy handicap to us in Bethnal Green.

The Cabinet's action on the subject irritated George very much. 'They make me wonder', was his comment, 'whether I am really a Liberal at all.' This irritation found vent in two furious speeches in Wales, foreshadowing a land policy which it is his intention to propound in the Autumn, and which was a great surprise to everyone who thought he was rather piano. The land, of course, is really the question he is keenest on of any next to Welsh Disestablishment.

b. *The Coming of War*

26. Speech by J. Allen Baker in Parliament on the Naval Estimates, 16 March 1910: from *Parliamentary Debates*, 5th series., Vol. XV, pp. 397–9. Baker (1852–1918) was a leading pacifist, prominent on the L.C.C.; he was Liberal M.P. for East Finsbury, 1905–18.

I cannot conceive how any Hon. or Right Hon. Member in this House can contemplate this new and, in my opinion, avoidable burden without a feeling of sadness, if not utter despair. At the last Hague Conference our chief representative, Sir Edward Fry, showed that, while in 1898 European countries spent £251,000,000 on armaments, in 1906 the amount was £320,000,000 or an increase of £69,000,000, or upwards of 27 per cent. 'This enormous growth', he added, 'represents the Christian peace of the civilized world in the twentieth century.' I wonder what our representative at the next Hague Conference will have to report if the same rate of expenditure continues during a further four years? There is more than £9,000,000 increase in our Navy Estimates this year over those of 1907–8. What will next year's be? This, we are not told, but only that there are five large armoured ships, five protected cruisers, and twenty destroyers; and submarines to cost £750,000. Are these five large armoured ships to be of the same construction as those that are now under construction, or are they to be like those which are proposed for the United States of America, costing probably £3,500,000 or £4,000,000 sterling each? It is not only the intolerable burden of the present year, but what we have to face in years to come, that should produce pause and hesitation on the part of the Committee before passing these Estimates. . . .

Where is all this mad competition to end? Surely we are approaching at express speed that cataclysm which, as the Foreign Minister said, will sooner or later submerge civilization. . . .

What is there to justify this expenditure? Certainly not the European situation. We are friendly with every European power. . . . It certainly is not acceleration on the part of Germany. That bubble, I think, has been burst, and we have proof to show that there has not been the alleged acceleration that was claimed by the Government last year. It is certainly not the 'Dreadnoughts' that Germany will have in April 1912. As pointed out by the *Navy League Annual*, the comparative figures are that we shall have at that date 101 battleships and armoured cruisers of 1,493,800 tons, and Germany will have 48 battleships and armoured cruisers of 578,210 tons. It is certainly not on account of the feeling of the German people towards this country. Of these feelings we have a thousand evidences; they are of a most friendly and cordial character. . . .

27. From Lloyd George's Mansion House speech, 21 July 1911: from *The Times*, 22 July 1911.

I am also bound to say this—that I believe it is essential in the highest interests, not merely of this country, but of the world, that Britain should at all hazards maintain her place and her prestige amongst the Great Powers of the world. Her potent influence has many a time been in the past, and may yet be in the future, invaluable to the cause of human liberty. It has more than once in the past redeemed Continental nations, who are sometimes too apt to forget that service, from overwhelming disaster and even from national extinction. I would make great sacrifices to preserve peace. I conceive that nothing would justify a disturbance of international good-will except questions of the gravest national moment. But if a situation were to be forced upon us in which peace could only be preserved by the surrenders of the great and beneficent position Britain has won by centuries of heroism and achievement, by allowing Britain to be treated where her interests were vitally affected as if she were of no account in the Cabinet of nations, then I say emphatically that peace at that price would be humiliation intolerable for a great country like ours to endure. National honour is no party question. The security of our great international trade is no party question; the peace of the world is more likely to be secured if all nations realize fairly what the conditions of peace must be.

28. From *The National Review*, January 1912, p. 708.

The great value of the speech delivered by the Chancellor of the Exchequer, was that it destroyed the dangerous delusion assiduously nursed in Berlin and Potsdam by international Jews and financiers, who believe that they stand to make more money by backing Germany against other Powers, and by sentimental Radical newspapers, which ostensibly in the interests of peace steadily support the enemies of their own country. Mr Lloyd George proved that the Cabinet was not divided, that 'Baptists' and 'Imperialists' were at one, and if the Ministers were not divided, certainly the country was not divided, as any Radical Government which has the gumption to uphold British interests can always count on the loyal support of a Unionist Opposition.

29. From David Lloyd George, *War Memoirs* (Odhams, Vol. 1, 1938), pp. 27-31.

During the eight years that preceded the war, the Cabinet devoted a ridiculously small percentage of its time to a consideration of foreign affairs. . . . Of course, certain aspects of foreign policy were familiar to those Ministers who attended the Committee of Imperial Defence, but apart from that the Cabinet as a whole were never called into genuine consultation upon the fundamental aspects of the foreign situation. There was a reticence and a secrecy which practically ruled out three-fourths of the Cabinet from the chance of making any genuine contribution to the momentous questions then fermenting on the continent of Europe, which ultimately ended in an explosion that almost shattered the civilization of the world. During the whole of those eight years, when I was a member of the Cabinet, I can recall no such review of the European situation being given to us as that which Sir Edward Grey delivered to the Colonial Conference in 1907, or to the Prime Ministers of the Dominions at the Committee of Imperial Defence in 1911. Even there the information that was withheld was more important than that which was imparted. For instance, nothing was said about our military commitments. There was in the Cabinet an air of 'hush hush' about every allusion to our relations with France, Russia and Germany. Direct questions were always answered with civility, but were not encouraged. We were made to feel that, in these matters, we were reaching our hands towards the mysteries, and that we were too young in the priest-hood to presume to enter into the sanctuary reserved for the elect. So we confined our inquisitiveness and our counsel to the more mundane affairs which we had taken part in Opposition during the whole of our political careers. Discussions, if they could be called discussions, on foreign affairs, were confined to the elder statesmen who had seen service in some previous ministerial experience. Apart from the Prime Minister and the Foreign Secretary, there were only two or three men such as Lord Loreburn, the Lord Chancellor, Lord Morley, Lord Crewe, and, for a short time, Lord Ripon, who were expected to make any contribution on the infrequent occasions when the Continental situation was brought to our awed attention. . . .

There is no more conspicuous example of this kind of suppression of vital information than the way in which the military arrangements we entered into with France were kept from the Cabinet for six years. They came to my knowledge, first of all, in 1911, during the Agadir crisis, but the Cabinet as a whole were not acquainted with them before the following year. There is abundant evidence that both the French and the Russians regarded these military arrangements as practically tantamount to a commitment on our part to come to the aid of France in the event of her being attacked by Germany. When the British Government was hesitating at the end of July 1914, as to whether it would support France in the event of a German attack, French statesmen almost reverted to the 'Perfidious Albion' mood, and even the meek M. Paul Cambon said that the only question was whether the word 'honour' was to be expunged from the British dictionary. On the whole, the view summarized in that pungent comment is the one I heard expressed by most supporters and opponents of our intervention in the Great War; and yet the Cabinet were never informed of these vital arrangements until we were so deeply involved in the details of military and naval plans that it was too late to repudiate the inference. . . .

Personally, I was prepared to accept the Foreign Secretary's assurances that we were not committed. I was strengthened in my conviction that there was no definite commitment to give military support to France in her quarrels with Germany by the meetings of the Committee of Imperial Defence during the Agadir crisis. . . .

30. A. Bonar Law to H. H. Asquith, 17 May 1915: from Lord Beaverbrook, *Politicians and the War* (Collins, 1960 edition), pp. 108-9.

Lord Lansdowne and I have learnt with dismay that Lord Fisher has resigned, and we have come to the conclusion that we cannot allow the House to adjourn until this fact has been made known and discussed.

We think the time has come when we ought to have a clear statement from you as to the policy which the Government intends to pursue. In our opinion things cannot go on as they are, and some change in the Constitution of the Government seems to us inevitable if it is to retain a sufficient measure of public confidence to conduct the war to a successful conclusion.

The situation in Italy makes it particularly undesirable to have anything in the nature of a controversial discussion in the House of Commons at present, and if you are prepared to take the necessary steps to secure the object which I have indicated, and if Lord Fisher's resignation is in the meantime postponed, we shall be ready to keep silence now. Otherwise, I must today ask you whether Lord Fisher has resigned, and press for a day to discuss the situation arising out of his resignation.

David Lloyd George to Mrs Lloyd George, 25 May 1915, National Library of Wales, MSS. 20,435C, No. 1584.

It was found impossible after all for the P.M. to hold Exchequer during the time I am occupied in organizing Munitions, so McKenna is to come here *temporarily*. I am to return as soon as I place the other business on a sound footing. I am glad of this. Exchequer & Munitions would have killed me—and that is not good enough. The Tories insisted that McK. should only hold this place temporarily—they would only agree on that condition. They were willing I should hold it but if I went altogether they claimed it for Bonar Law.

C. The Crisis of War, (1915-18)

a. The Liberal Party and the War, 1915–16

31. A 'Whip' issued by a 'ginger group' of eight back-bench Liberals led by Sir Frederick Cawley to their colleagues on the conscription issue: from *Cambria Daily Leader*, 28 July 1915.

On the adjournment of the House on Wednesday the question of national service will be raised.

It seems undesirable that the House should rise for six very important weeks without a statement from the Government of this country making it clear to both our troops and to the French people that we mean to submit ourselves without delay to any and every form of discipline in order to win the war.

We urge you to attend the debate and support this point of view.

32. From *Lord Riddell's War Diary* (London, Ivor Nicholson & Watson, 1933), pp. 136–7, 139. Riddell (1865–1934) was proprietor of the *News of the World* and other newspapers.

(*9 November 1915*.) . . . It is evident that L.G. is gradually shedding the Radical Party. None of the Radicals in the Cabinet is working with him. McKenna, Simon, Runciman, McKinnon Wood, Buckmaster, Harcourt etc. are opposed to him. He finds his supporters amongst the Conservatives. It looks as if he is going the same road as Chamberlain. L.G.'s attitude to the war makes his severance from the Radicals inevitable. The force of circumstances is leading him into the same position as that in which Chamberlain found himself. Bereft of his associates on the great question of the day, he is obliged to seek support elsewhere. L.G.'s future is interesting.

33. From Christopher Addison, *Four and a Half Years, 1914–19*, Vol. I. (Hutchinson, 1934), pp. 158–9.

Christopher Addison (1869–1951) Liberal, then Labour minister, was to serve in Lloyd George's governments from 1916 to 1921. In 1915–16 he was Lloyd George's parliamentary secretary at the Ministry of Munitions.

(Tuesday, 4 January 1916.) ... Simon has decided to resign on the question of compulsory military service, though concessions have been made to Runciman and McKenna sufficient to keep them in for the present: but there is a good deal moving under the surface. The *Manchester Guardian* is most emphatic in its opposition and unless some special case is shown, the conference of Labour Unions, which is to be held on Thursday, may go against the scheme. If so, Henderson and the other Labour members may have to resign and, if there is much determined opposition in the House by Irish Members, things will be very difficult.

From *Parliamentary Debates*, 6 January 1916. Sir John Simon (1873–1954) resigned as Home Secretary over the conscription issue.

Sir John Simon (Essex, Walthamstow): ... This Bill is still a Bill by which men will be compelled nevertheless. In other words, the condition that compulsion should only be adopted by general consent has been abandoned in favour of the condition that compulsion shall be adopted without any regard to the numbers to be compelled or the strength of the opposition. There are some of us who regard this principle of voluntary enlistment as a real heritage of the English people. If you are going to sell your birthright, at any rate make sure first that the mess of pottage you are likely to get will provide you with a square meal (cheers) ... Does anybody really suppose that, once the principle of compulsion is conceded, you are going to stop here? Is this principle of taking the unmarried man, even though he be 40 years old, and refusing to compel the married man, even though he be 21, a principle which has ever been known in this country or in any other? Was it the principle of the press-gang? Was it the principle of the law of the Militia ballot? Is it the principle of any conscriptionist country in the world? Is it not jeered at as an absurdity by conscriptionists? They have made it perfectly plain that the only value they attach to the Prime Minister's Bill is that it will commit him and the country to the principle of conscription.

34. From Christopher Addison, *Politics from Within, 1914–18* (Herbert Jenkins, 1924), Vol. I, pp. 246–7, 251.

(4 April 1916.) ... L.G. and I had a long talk over the political situation. Things are getting to a rather desperate pass in the Cabinet. The yield of the Derby's [*sic*] figures and under the Compulsion Bill is far short of the numbers required to keep up sixty-four divisions in France. The question of what is to be done about it has now been hanging fire for a

fortnight. There have been overtures made to L.G. on behalf of the Tories as to whether he would break on the subject. More or less informal offers were made to him that they would follow him. He says that he had told them frankly that he could only identify himself with the movement if he was going to have the support at the same time of a solid and sufficient body of Liberals. We decided to meet again and discuss the situation tomorrow.

(*Friday, 28 April 1916.*) ... This week has been accompanied by a strong movement against L.G. After the P.M. made the statement on Wednesday, the 19th, that unless something were agreed to the Government would break up, there was the meeting of Liberals. This was followed on Saturday by a long open article by 'A.G.G.'[1] in the *Daily News* against L.G., accusing him of intrigue, love of compulsion etc., etc. Some of it was sound enough, but Gardiner missed the point of what is necessary to beat the Germans.... Kellaway[2] on Sunday decided to write a reply on this, came up to the office on Monday and got it out. It was, on the whole, a vigorous and clever reply....

I have arranged for a few men to collect names and opinions and we have found, during the week, a good body of Members who are strongly supporting L.G., although saying nothing about it just now, and the proceedings of the week have undoubtedly strengthened his position in demanding a clear policy.

35. From Christopher Addison, *Four and a Half Years, 1914–19*, Vol. I (Hutchinson, 1934), pp. 202–3.

(*Monday, 8 May 1916.*) ... Last Monday (May 1) also David Davies M.P.[3] paid me a visit and was full of the subject of L.G. He is an out-and-out champion of drastic action and wanted L.G. to resign forthwith. In view of the fact that the Government is now certain to introduce a comprehensive Military Service Bill on the lines already indicated, I put it to Davies that I could not possibly see how L.G. could resign at the moment when he had got his way in the Cabinet. D.D. was, however, very vehement in his denunciation of the P.M., K[itchener] and others, and said that, in order to prosecute the war successfully, this was the only course for L.G. to take....

On Tuesday morning he came in again and had evidently had the matter out fairly and squarely with L.G. He procured, at my suggestion,

[1] A. G. Gardiner.
[2] F. G. Kellaway (1870–1933) was Liberal M.P. for Bedford, 1910–22.
[3] Member for Montgomeryshire (Liberal), 1906–29; created Baron Davies, 1932.

on Monday, a list of M.P.s which Kellaway and I had been getting together, who, we thought, might be relied upon to support an active policy. L.G. sent a message that he wanted to have dinner that evening with Astor,[1] D.D. and myself to talk things over.

On the same day I chanced to come across Reading at the Reform Club and lunched with him and we had a heart-to-heart talk over the situation. He had had a large share in inducing L.G. to remain and in promoting the compromise which has lasted so short a time. He is as keen on efficiency as any of us, but is strongly of opinion that L.G.'s proper policy is to remain in at present and he is using the whole of his influence in that direction. Happily he is *persona grata* both with the P.M. and L.G.

36. Esher to General Sir Douglas Haig, 29 September 1916: from *Journals and Letters of Reginald, Viscount Esher*, Vol. IV, 1915–30 (Ivor Nicholson, 1934), pp. 55–6. Reginald Brett, 2nd Viscount Esher (1852–1930), was a permanent member of the Committee of Imperial Defence.

Spender[2] has told me some curious things about L.G. and there is no sort of doubt that he means to take supreme power into his hands. He will leave no stone unturned.

However, you will be interested to see Spender, and I am anxious that he should see you. As you know, he has always been deep in the counsels of Asquith and Grey.

37. From H. A. Taylor, *Robert Donald* (Stanley Paul, 1934), p. 110. Donald (1861–1933) was editor of the *Daily Chronicle*, 1902–18.

(*Entry in diary, 24 November 1916.*) ... After lunch, Sir William [Robertson][3] asked me to walk with him to the War Office. He complained that there was far too much delay and no possibility of getting decisions out of the War Council. It was far too big and there was too much discussion. Something had to be done, in order to get a move on. He liked Mr Asquith, but he was indecisive and behaved more like a judge than a president who is leading a war policy. He heard discussions and generally decided by what appeared to be the opinion of the

[1] Waldorf, second Viscount Astor (1879–1952) was Unionist M.P. for Plymouth, 1910–19, and director of *The Observer*.

[2] J. A. Spender (1862–1942) was editor of the *Westminster Gazette*, 1896–1922, and a vehement partisan of Asquith.

[3] Robertson (1860–1933) was Chief of the Imperial General Staff, 1915–18.

majority, although it might be quite wrong, Sir William said that the only man who could decide quickly, say 'Yes' or 'No' without hesitation, was Lloyd George. He might say the wrong 'Yes' or the wrong 'No' sometimes, but he much preferred that to no decision at all. He was in favour of some arrangement which gave Mr Lloyd George greater power. He did not mean greater power to interfere with military operations, but greater power in the direction of war policy.

During the afternoon I called on Mr Bonar Law at the Colonial Office. He was rather despondent. He said that the more he saw of war the less confident he was to predict what would happen. He had made up his mind that some change must take place here. The War Council had grown too big and too clumsy in its methods. He was quite convinced from his point of view, and from his knowledge, that things could not go on as they were.

I told him that I had contemplated pointing out the need of more energetic methods, and the creation of a smaller and more businesslike War Council.

He suggested that I should see Mr Asquith on Monday, as soon as he returned to London.

b. *The Downfall of Asquith, December 1916*

---

38. Memorandum drawn up by Bonar Law, Carson, Aitken and Lloyd George, presented to Asquith 1 December 1916: from D. Lloyd George, *War Memoirs* (1938), Vol. I, p. 587.

1. That the War Committee consist of three members—two of whom must be the First Lord of the Admiralty and the Secretary of State for War, who should have in their offices deputies capable of attending to and deciding all departmental business, and a third Minister without portfolio. One of the three to be Chairman.
2. That the War Committee shall have full powers, subject to the supreme control of the Prime Minister, to direct all questions connected with the war.
3. The Prime Minister in his discretion to have the power to refer any question to the Cabinet.
4. Unless the Cabinet on reference by the Prime Minister reverses decision of the War Committee, that decision to be carried out by the Department concerned.
5. The War Committee to have the power to invite any Minister, and to summon the expert advisers and officers of any Department to its meetings.

([Lloyd George adds:] 'I showed it to Lord Derby who fully approved of its terms'.)

39. Asquith to Lloyd George, 1 December 1916: From Roy Jenkins, *Asquith* (Collins, 1964), pp. 429–30.

My dear Lloyd George,

I have now had time to reflect on our conversation this morning and to study your memorandum.

Though I do not altogether share your dark estimate and forecast of the situation, actual and prospective, I am in complete agreement that we have reached a critical situation in the War, and that our methods of procedure, with the experience that we have gained during the last three months, call for reconsideration and revision.

The two main defects of the War Committee, which has done excellent work, are (1) that its numbers are too large, and (2) that there is delay, evasion, and often obstruction on the part of the Departments in giving effect to its decisions.

I might with good reason add (3) that it is often kept in ignorance by the Departments of information, essential and even vital, of a technical kind, upon the problems that come before it; and (4) that it is over-charged with duties, many of which might well be delegated to sub-ordinate bodies.

The result is that I am clearly of opinion that the War Committee should be reconstituted, and its relations to and authority over the Departments be more clearly defined and more effectively asserted. I come now to your specific proposals.

In my opinion, whatever changes are made in the composition or functions of the War Committee the Prime Minister must be its Chair-man. He cannot be relegated to the position of an arbiter in the back-ground or a referee to the Cabinet.

In regard to its composition, I agree that the War Secretary and the First Lord of the Admiralty are necessary members. I am inclined to add to the same category the Minister of Munitions. There should be another member, either with or without portfolio, or charged only with comparatively light departmental duties. One of the members should be appointed Vice-Chairman.

I purposely in this letter do not discuss the delicate and difficult question of personnel.

The Committee should, as far as possible, sit *de die in diem*, and have full power to see that its decisions (subject to appeal to the Cabinet) are carried out promptly and effectively by the Departments.

The reconstruction of the War Committee should be accompanied by the setting up of a Committee of National Organization, to deal with the purely domestic side of our problems. It should have executive power within its own domain.

The Cabinet would in all cases have ultimate authority.

Yours always sincerely,

H. H. Asquith

From Lloyd George's *War Memoirs* (Odhams, 1938 edition), Vol. I, p. 589.

War Office,
Whitehall, S.W.1.

2nd December 1916.

My dear Bonar,

I enclose copy of the P.M.'s letter. The life of the country depends on resolute action by you now.

Yours ever,

D. Lloyd George

40. Edwin Montagu to H. H. Asquith, 2 December 1916: From S. D. Waley, *Edwin Montagu* (Asia Publishing House, 1964), pp. 104-6. Edwin Montagu (1879-1924) was Minister of Munitions, and a leading Liberal.

My dear Prime Minister,

The situation is probably irretrievably serious. I have just come from L. G., with whom I have spent an hour of hard fighting, but it seems to me to be of no avail and I fear he has committed himself. I have done everything in my power and you know that Rufus[1] has also done his best. Rufus has been with him throughout and I left him there. He says that he submitted proposals to you which are not acceptable to you, and that you have submitted proposals to him which are not acceptable to him. We then tried to arrange a compromise, but so far none is possible. ... He says that you as Prime Minister, with the House of Commons on your shoulders, with appointments to attend to and with the thousand and one duties of the Prime Minister, should be relieved of the day to day work of the War Committee, but should maintain the supreme control of the War, seeing the Chairman of the War Committee every morning before it met, receiving their reports and conferring with them when you thought fit. He says that your duties prevent sufficiently frequent sittings and that by this means quicker decisions would be arrived at. He does not for one moment regard it as possible for the War Committee without the Prime Minister to challenge the Prime Minister's supreme control of the War, but he regards it as essential that the small War Committee should sit so frequently and act with such rapidity that the Prime Minister, whoever he were, ought not to have a place upon it, but he is loud in his assertions that you are the right Prime Minister in the right place. He will not budge from this position and I cannot do anything more.

Audacious as I am of advice, I am at a loss to give any. I receive very bitter letters from Margot, but I have not had time or courage to answer them. She, like McKenna, attributes everything that has appeared in the Press to L. G., notwithstanding the fact that the views in the Press are nearly all inconsistent with L. G.'s scheme.

I remain of opinion, unshakeable and based not only on affection, but on conviction, that there is no conceivable Prime Minister but you. I remain of opinion that Lloyd George is an invaluable asset to any War Government. His brain is the most fertile we possess. The speeches that he will make will, in my opinion, not only make it impossible for

[1] I.e. Rufus Isaacs, 1st Marquess of Reading (1860–1935), Attorney-General, 1910–13, and Lord Chief Justice, 1913–31.

the Government to carry on, but will plunge this country into recrimination and public debate in the face of the enemy which will hearten them up and shake to its foundations the Alliance. Added to this, I think it would be quite impossible, if Lloyd George and Lord Derby go—and they are going together—for Bonar Law to remain.

You may entertain your own opinion. I have expressed mine of the vital mistake that Lloyd George is making in plunging the country into this condition, but it is for you as Prime Minister, I assume, to try and prevent this. I cannot believe that this can be done by the mere publication of two formal letters, and I think it ought to be attempted by prolonged conversation rather than risk the events which I foresee.

It is all a nightmare to me. So far as I can discover, in matters of policy you and Lloyd George are in complete agreement. In matters of mutual confidence there is not much which I desire. The Government will break up on matters of machinery, but the argument will be that through this very machinery the situation in Roumania, Serbia etc. has resulted, and even the financial situation, and it will be said that the Government was broken up deliberately by L. G. and his friends because they saw no prospect of improvement—and curiously enough on this side of the question he will be supported by the soldiers who have been suborning the Press.

I am willing to do anything you suggest, but I can do nothing more without your orders.

E. S. M.

The Right Hon. H. H. Asquith, K.C., M.P.

41. Bonar Law's account of the subsequent meeting with Asquith: from Robert Blake, *The Unknown Prime Minister* (Eyre and Spottiswoode, 1955), p. 320.

I told him [Asquith] of the decision we had come to, but, though I had the resolution in my pocket, as I had not begun by handing it to him but had simply communicated its contents, I forgot to hand him the actual document. The Prime Minister was not only greatly shocked but greatly surprised by our communication, and asked me to treat it as if it had not been made, until he had an opportunity of discussing the matter with Lloyd George.

From H. A. Taylor, *Robert Donald* (Stanley Paul, 1934), p. 116.

(*Diary, 3 December 1916*.) ... On Sunday, December 3rd, 1916, the Unionist members of the Cabinet, with the exception of Mr Balfour, met at Mr Bonar Law's house. They passed a resolution suggesting that the Prime Minister should resign, which meant, of course, that the whole Government should resign, and if he did not do so, they would.

Mr Bonar Law was deputed to take the resolution to the Prime Minister and to explain that the object in view was not to embarrass him, but to help him. The Prime Minister, apparently, did not see how their action could help him, and it was thought that the matter was not quite clearly explained to him. Lord Curzon and some other Unionist members also saw Mr Asquith and pointed out to him the advantages of the policy which they suggested. It was quite evident that the purpose of the Unionist was to give the Prime Minister a free hand in reconstructing his Government.

42. Asquith to Lloyd George, 4 December 1916: from D. Lloyd George, *War Memoirs* (1938 edition), Vol. I, pp. 590–1.

My dear Lloyd George,

Such productions as the first leading article in today's *Times*, showing the infinite possibilities for misunderstanding and misrepresentation of such an arrangement as we considered yesterday, make me at least doubtful as to its feasibility. Unless the impression is at once corrected that I am being relegated to the position of an irresponsible spectator of the War, I cannot go on.

The suggested arrangement was to the following effect: The Prime Minister to have supreme and effective control of the war policy.

The agenda of the War Committee will be submitted to him; its chairman will report to him daily; he can direct it to consider particular topics or proposals; and all its conclusions will be subject to his approval or veto. He can, of course, at his own discretion attend meetings of the Committee.

Yours sincerely,

H. H. Asquith.

Lloyd George to Asquith, 4 December 1916.

My dear Prime Minister,

I have not seen *The Times* article. But I hope you will not attach undue importance to these effusions. I have had these misrepresentations to put up with for months. Northcliffe frankly wants a smash. Derby and I do not. Northcliffe would like to make this and any other rearrangement under your Premiership impossible. Derby and I attach great importance to your retaining your present position—effectively.

I cannot restrain or, I fear, influence Northcliffe. I fully accept in letter and in spirit your summary of the suggested arrangement—subject, of course, to personnel.

Ever sincerely,

D. Lloyd George.

Asquith to Lloyd George, 4 December 1916: from J. A. Spender and Cyril Asquith, *Life of Lord Oxford and Asquith*, Vol. II (Hutchinson, 1932), p. 266.

My dear Lloyd George,

Thank you for your letter of this morning. The King gave me today authority to ask and accept the resignation of all my colleagues, and to form a new Government on such lines as I should submit to him.

I start therefore with a clean slate.

The first question I have to consider is the constitution of the new War Committee.

After full consideration of this matter in all its aspects, I have come decidedly to the conclusion that it is not possible that such a Committee could be made workable and effective without the Prime Minister as its Chairman. I quite agree that it will be necessary for him, in view of the other calls upon his time and energy, to delegate from time to time the chairmanship to another Minister as his representative and *locum tenens*; but (if he is to retain the authority which corresponds to his responsibility as Prime Minister) he must continue to be, as he has always been, its permanent President. I am satisfied on reflection that any other arrangement (such for instance as the one I indicated to you in my letter of today) would be in experience impracticable and incompatible with the Prime Minister's final and supreme control. The other question which you have raised relates to the personnel of the Committee. Here again after deliberate consideration I find myself unable to agree with some of your suggestions.

I think we both agree that the First Lord of the Admiralty must, of necessity, be a member of the Committee.

I cannot (as I told you yesterday) be a party to any suggestion that Mr Balfour should be displaced. The technical side of the Admiralty has been re-constituted with Sir John Jellicoe as First Sea Lord. I believe Mr Balfour to be, under existing conditions, the necessary head of the Board.

I must add that Sir E. Carson (for whom personally and in every other way, I have the greatest regard) is not, from the only point of view which is significant to me (namely the most effective prosecution of the

War) the man best qualified among my colleagues, present and past, to be a member of the War Committee. I have only to say, in conclusion, that I am strongly of opinion that the War Committee (without any disparagement of the existing Committee, which in my judgment is a most efficient body and has done, and is doing, invaluable work) ought to be reduced in number, so that it can sit more frequently and overtake more easily the daily problems with which it has to deal. But in any reconstruction of the Committee, such as I have, and have for some time past had in view, the governing consideration to my mind is the special capacity of the men who are to sit on it for the work which it has to do.

That is a question which I must reserve for myself to decide.

Yours very sincerely,

H. H. Asquith.

43. Edwin Montagu to Asquith, 5 December 1916: from S. D. Waley, *Edwin Montagu* (Asia Publishing House, 1964), pp. 108–9.

... What has caused your withdrawal of your own proposals? I see three causes:

(1) Northcliffe's article in *The Times*. It is lamentable to think that you should let him achieve the victory that he has long sought. He wanted to drive you out; he alone is fool enough not to believe in you. His efforts were resisted by Lloyd George, by Bonar Law, by Lord Derby, by Carson, by Robertson. Using information that he had no right to obtain, he sees a chance of success, takes it and is successful. He published that article in order to wreck the arrangement and you have let him do it. I do not say that this was avoidable, but I say that his personal victory in this matter is a matter of the deepest possible chagrin to me.

(2) The advice given you by McKenna, Runciman and Grey. That advice could have been foreseen. It came in my opinion rather late, when you had already made your offer to Lloyd George. Grey always wants to resign when there are complications. It is his pretty little way of assisting matters. Runciman is merely a reflection of McKenna, and McKenna's loyalty to you is above suspicion but always unwise, because he hates Lloyd George, whom you deliberately chose as your colleague and kept as your colleague, as much, if not more than he likes you. He can only see one object to be achieved, to drive Lloyd George out of the Government, and he takes no view but that. Far be it from me to under-rate McKenna's abilities or the importance of his position, but he has irritated the Allies and the City and quarrelled with his best advisers,

and if you have to choose between Lloyd George and McKenna, there is little doubt as to whom you could best do without, whichever is the best character.

(3) The question of personnel. Lloyd George wanted Carson in. I think his main object was loyalty to Bonar Law, who had been working with him and who feels acutely the position in which his Party is being split by Carson's rival leadership. Carson is leader of the Opposition, and at a time when you are reconstructing your Government, surely to make a new Coalition in order to help Bonar Law and the Parliamentary situation, it is not a very unknown thing to take in the most conspicuous Opposition leader. But Lloyd George, I know now, would have been more accommodating than I imagined on personnel and would have given way certainly about Balfour.

However all this is over, and I am confronted with a position in which I see no help for it but your resignation and a Government which must split the country in the face of the enemy from top to bottom. Both these facts are horrible to contemplate. A government which you do not lead means disaster. A split country means victory for the enemy.

I therefore feel it my duty to tell you, because I want to do nothing behind your back, what I have done. Lloyd George sent for me this afternoon and I spent some time with him. I found him in almost as great a condition of misery and unhappiness as I am myself. Believe me or not as you will, he wanted to work with you. He did not want a victory for Northcliffe. He was completely satisfied with the arrangements you had come to and meant to work them loyally. He does not want, I am confident, to be Prime Minister. I told him that I could do nothing more, that I had done everything I could and that my feeling of despair was such that I wished most devoutly that I had never entered public life.

I have worked persistently since 1906 with the sole idea, according to my own views, of helping to preserve, extend and make successful your control of British politics. I have failed and I know nothing left for me to do.

Montagu's account, 5 December 1916: from S. D. Waley, *Edwin Montagu*.

(*p 110.*)

At a meeting of the Liberal members of the Cabinet it was agreed that the Prime Minister should resign. I urged him not to resign, but to suggest to the King that he should send for Asquith, George, Bonar Law and Henderson, to try and agree a National Government under the leadership of Asquith. My suggestion was derided, and McKenna most helpfully asked me if I wanted four Prime Ministers, or, if not, which one I wanted. (I had already suggested to Derby that he should urge the King to send for George and Asquith together, but I added the other two at the meeting of the Liberal members of the Government because I thought he ought to see the leaders of the four parties.)

(*pp. 110–11.*)

On Wednesday, December 6th I went to breakfast with George, who was still anxious to go back to the Sunday arrangement. He was even willing, on representations from Masterton, to keep Balfour at the Admiralty for a short time. He was quite willing to go into conference, and willing to suggest it to the King if he were sent for, but he was quite confident that he could form a Government if he had to. He still preferred not to have to, but to serve under Asquith. (There was never any doubt expressed by the Liberal members of the Cabinet that if he tried he could form a Government.) He asked me what had occurred at the meeting yesterday, and said he had heard that we all resolved not to serve in a Government of which he was the head. I replied that there was no such resolution, but I thought it would be very difficult for any of us to come in.

He went to see Balfour and Bonar Law about the suggested Conference, and sent for me to come and see him at the War Office at about twenty minutes to twelve, where I met Bonar Law just off to see the King. Apparently Bonar Law had objected to any Conference to put Asquith back, saying that the country would never stand it after Asquith had broken up his Government and resigned because he refused to accept the Lloyd George formula. It would look like vacillation on Asquith's part and on their part, and he said that Balfour was in agreement with him on this. But he was going to see the King to recommend a Conference at which Asquith should be implored to serve under George or Bonar, whichever he preferred.

I then asked George whether he wanted any of his Liberal colleagues. He said he did, and I told him that if he would keep Grey at the Foreign Office, I thought he could have any others that he wanted. He said that he would not.

44. Notes of an interview of Donald with Bonar Law, 29 December 1916: from H. A. Taylor, *Robert Donald* (Stanley Paul, 1934), pp. 131–2.

I still thought that, in spite of this most unfortunate disturbance of the negotiations, the situation could be saved. I called on Monday afternoon at 10 Downing Street. Lord Crewe, Mr Runciman and Mr Harcourt were waiting to see the Prime Minister. When I went in I found

McKenna with him. I told him that, whatever he did, not to fall between two stools, and indicated that I thought there was still a chance for him to keep the Government together, if he acted promptly. On Tuesday morning, Mr Lloyd George telephoned to me to go to the War Office to show me the letter which he had received from the Prime Minister. I thought it was better that I should not be seen about the War Office, and asked Mr Lloyd George to send the letter completely turning down the whole scheme and leaving Mr Lloyd George no option but to resign.

45. From Christopher Addison, *Politics from Within*, *1914–19*, pp. 270–2.

The fact was that on the Monday (4 December) Kellaway, Glyn Jones[1] and I had gone through the list of Members of Parliament which had been made in the summertime when a crisis was threatened. We divided them into 'doubtfuls' and those whom we thought to be 'for' L.G., and I arranged for a small band of men to canvass round and report through Kellaway. By Wednesday evening it was certain that L.G. was going to get a good deal of support, and that a large number of Members would support him if he succeeded in forming a Government. . . . They realized that our first duty was to fight the Germans. I had a preliminary list of them in my pocket all the time that I was being sympathized with at the Club as the only Liberal follower L.G. had.

The five of us (i.e. L.G., Bonar Law, Carson, Talbot and Addison) reassembled at the War Office at ten o'clock, and made great progress. Whatever may be the sequel, I shall always be proud to think that I was able to contribute a good many suggestions of men that were accepted. . . . We got a long way with the chief offices in a provisional form, and it was agreed that the first effort on Thursday morning should be to secure the concurrence of the Conservatives and to try and obtain the support of Labour. . . .

(*9 December*.) . . . During Wednesday, Kellaway had had a long talk with J. H. Thomas,[2] who has considerable influence in the country, and I, too, had a talk with Thomas and some others. Kellaway was to dine in the evening with Hodge. Late on Wednesday night I was able to report that L.G.'s following amounted to 49 out-and-out supporters, whatever happened, and 126 others amongst the Liberal Party who

[1] Sir William S. Glyn-Jones (1869–1927), Liberal M.P. for Stepney, 1911–1918.
[2] J. H. Thomas (1874–1949) was at this time assistant secretary of the National Union of Railwaymen and Labour (later National Labour) M.P. for Derby (1910–36).

would support him if he could form a Government. On Tuesday night Bonar Law had been rather disposed to look upon me as very sanguine when I told him that there would be a good list and a stampede in a day or two. However, the reports which came in on Wednesday evening cheered him up mightily. We arranged that Thomas should come to breakfast with L.G. and me at 8.15 the following morning at David Davies's flat, where I was to spend the night. The excitement in the Ministry of Munitions during this day and at home may well be imagined. . . .

46. Notes on a conversation between Donald and Asquith: from H. A. Taylor, *Robert Donald* (Stanley Paul, 1934), pp. 118–23.

(*7 December 1916.*) . . . I called on Mr Asquith at 10 Downing Street, at 4 o'clock. He was sitting at the large table in the Cabinet room, his back to the fire. He looked a very lonely figure and a tired man. Lying in front of him were a few letters, just received from political friends. He had a quiet and severe expression.

I asked him for his version of the negotiations which had been going on. We began talking of Mr Lloyd George, and I asked if he thought, as it seemed on the surface, that Mr Lloyd George, or somebody in his interest, had been preparing for the failure in the negotiations which had occurred and for the removal of himself as Prime Minister.

He said that Mr Lloyd George had always professed to be most friendly with him and no rift had occurred in their personal relations. He had the greatest admiration for him. Lloyd George possessed unique gifts, a real flair for politics, foresight, inspiration etc. He would not say that Lloyd George owed everything to him, but he certainly owed a great deal. He saved him during the Budget of 1909, when all the Cabinet turned against him, and he came to his rescue and risked his own fate with Lloyd George's (see Lloyd George's reference to this remark). There was another occasion, better known, upon which he prevented Lloyd George from having to disappear for a time from public life. (Mr Asquith was no doubt referring to the Marconi incident.)[1]

Mr Asquith had been convinced for some time that the War Council had become too cumbersome and that a more workmanlike body was necessary. Representations had been made to him, both by Mr Bonar Law and Mr Lloyd George. He had discussed the subject with both of them, but nothing definite had been arrived at and no workable plan had been produced.

[1] See above, pp. 50–1.

Mr Asquith went to Walmer for the week-end. Hearing that developments were taking place the Prime Minister motored to Downing Street from Walmer on Sunday, and sent for Mr Bonar Law and for Mr Lloyd George. (Bonar Law had seen him earlier, to convey to him the resolution of the Unionist members, but the Prime Minister asked him to think that the resolution had not been delivered.) They then discussed the scheme for the smaller War Council. Most of the suggestions came from Mr Asquith and subsequently were referred to in a letter which he sent to Mr Lloyd George. There was practically no difference of opinion as to the general scheme. The Prime Minister, of course, was to be a member of the Council and to attend as often as he could. As a matter of course he could not attend all the meetings, because the idea was that the Council should meet daily; in his absence Mr Lloyd George was to be chairman. A strong difference of opinion developed on the suggested personnel of the Council, and that matter was left over for adjustment on Monday.

On Monday the Prime Minister saw an article in *The Times*, stating that the proposal was to exclude him from the War Council altogether; the personnel was suggested, and other information given which could only have emanated directly or indirectly from Mr Lloyd George. This revelation led to the suggestion that the one purpose in view was to humiliate the Prime Minister and to place him in a position which could only have led to more embittered attacks and increasing insults. His position would have been made untenable. He wrote to Mr Lloyd George saying that he feared that the statement in *The Times* would make any rearrangement difficult, if not impossible. He then recounted in writing, for the first time, what 'the suggested arrangement' was, writing in the past tense, and using the word 'suggested' as no agreement had been arrived at and no definite arrangement settled. Mr Lloyd George replied during the morning that he had not read *The Times* and asked the Prime Minister not to close the negotiations because of what had happened.

Later in the day, the Prime Minister saw Lord Grey, Mr McKenna, Mr Runciman and some other friends. He gave the subject further thought, and on Monday night sent a letter to Mr Lloyd George closing the negotiations, and leaving the Minister for War no option but to resign.

Mr Asquith explained why he objected to the personnel of the Council, as proposed by Mr Lloyd George. The whole proposal of creating a smaller War Council was, he said, to make it more efficient for running the war. Mr Lloyd George was the most eminently qualified person to be on the board and the best fitted to take the chair in the absence of the Prime Minister. He was entitled to do so because of the position he occupied and because of the great part which he played in the war previously as Chancellor of the Exchequer and as Minister of Munitions.

As regards Mr Bonar Law, Mr Asquith said he was on the War Council, not in virtue of any office he held, or of any ability which he possessed, or for his knowledge about the war, but because he was the leader of the Conservative Party. He had nothing to say against him; he had accepted him because of the position he held, but he did not consider that he had shown any great qualities in helping them to run the war. He was afraid to take decisive action, was very timid, and always showed up better in the House of Commons than he did in Council. Mr Asquith said he had a very great personal regard for Mr Bonar Law, who had been most loyal and friendly to him, and he appreciated his high character and personal qualities more the longer he knew him. Mr Asquith believed that he had been a very good iron-master who had come into political life late, and had shown no qualities which entitled him to occupy a commanding position.

As regards Sir Edward Carson, Mr Asquith would not have him at any price. He ruled him out at once. He said that his would be purely a political appointment, less justified than Mr Bonar Law's. Sir Edward Carson had been in the Cabinet for six months, during which time he had shown no initiative, had made no helpful suggestions, and really was a disappointment to his friends. He had been a personal friend of Mr Asquith for many years, but judging the War Council purely from the point of view of efficiency he considered that Sir Edward Carson's presence would be a drag, and could not be justified.

The inclusion of a Labour member was also purely political, with no reference to the knowledge which the member possessed, or his capacity to help them in running the war. Mr Henderson had been mentioned, but he failed entirely to pass any test which could be applied to a member of a War Council, except as a delegate of Labour. The body which Mr Lloyd George proposed was, then, acceptable as regards the number, but, with the exception of the Prime Minister and himself, it was far less efficient than the existing War Council. Mr Asquith said that the personnel of the new Council was a body *pour rire*. In regard to himself, every personal consideration would induce him to retire. He had had two-and-a-half years of very strenuous work in a difficult position and he said he was almost *au bout de mes forces*. If he had accepted the part in the new War Council which was evidently destined for him, his life would have been intolerable. The attacks upon him would have been renewed, and, after a gradual process of humiliation, he would have had to retire.

The personnel of the proposed Council had not been seriously discussed, except with regard to Mr Balfour. Mr Asquith said that he insisted that Mr Balfour, as head of the Admiralty, should be a member. He objected strongly to his removal. Mr Balfour had just carried through a most difficult scheme of reorganization.

Mr Asquith, for many months, had been very anxious to get Jellicoe to the Admiralty as First Sea Lord. After the Battle of Jutland the relations between Jellicoe and Beatty became so strained, each with their strong partisans, that it was extremely difficult to make a change. Mr Balfour went to Edinburgh, and it was due to his tact and skill that he succeeded in getting Jellicoe to come to the Admiralty as First Sea Lord; which was not so difficult, it appeared, as to get Jellicoe to consent to placing Beatty in command of the Grand Fleet. Mr Asquith considered that Beatty had his limitations, but, granted that Jellicoe had to go to the Admiralty, he believed that Beatty was the next best man to command the Grand Fleet. To have removed Mr Balfour from the Admiralty after he had accomplished this work would have been most unjust and would have had a bad effect on the Service. Mr Asquith considered that the Navy liked Mr Balfour. They did not like Mr Churchill, and were not too fond of Mr McKenna, although he worked loyally with them. Mr Asquith felt that it would be disastrous if Lord Fisher were brought back to the Admiralty.

Mr Asquith spoke with great bitterness with regard to the calumnious and unscrupulous campaign which had been directed against him and his colleagues. He seemed to be more concerned for his colleagues than for himself.

....

Although it seemed then that Mr Lloyd George would succeed in forming his government, it was very doubtful whether it would last long, and in that case I presumed that he, Mr Asquith, would be sent for again. I asked him what his attitude would then be towards Mr Lloyd George and others.

He said, with a good deal of animation and firmness, 'then Mr Lloyd George would have to come in on *my* terms'. My impression was that Mr Asquith was quite convinced that Mr Lloyd George could not form a stable government.

Mr Asquith was evidently not in touch with public opinion, and had only prejudiced sources of information. He complained of the Press attacks, but he never took any account of the Press himself. He maintained a curious aloofness and regarded newspapers as not being of much account. He took no pains, either personally or through his secretaries, to keep in touch with newspapers which were his supporters. They had to support him in the dark.

c. *Lloyd George as Prime Minister*

47. From Christopher Addison, *Four and a Half Years* (Hutchinson, 1934), Vol. II, p. 315. (11 January 1917.)

Dinner in the evening at Primrose's with the P.M., Mond,[1] Cornwall.[2] We discussed the prospect so far as it concerns L.G. and the Liberal Party. There is a disposition not to rush things which I think is wise. At the same time, we ought to get together the nucleus of an organization, especially in those constituencies where the men are definitely against him. As time goes on, however, the number of men who come over to his side will materially increase. We discussed the establishment of Liberal War Committees up and down the country and arranged for L.G. to make a speech in his constituency before the opening of Parliament.

48. Lord Derby to Sir Philip Sassoon, 22 July 1917; from Randolph Churchill, *Lord Derby*, '*King of Lancashire*' (Heinemann, 1959), pp. 281–2.

Now, as to things political. Strictly between ourselves, Lloyd George made a *coup de main* when he appointed Geddes, Winston Churchill and Montagu. I never knew a word about it until I saw it in the paper and was furious at being kept in ignorance, but you can judge of my surprise when I found the War Cabinet had never been told! Lloyd George had acted on a prerogative which is undoubtedly his, to make any appointment he likes without consulting his colleagues, though I believe they did know about Carson leaving the Admiralty. The latter, however, did not know that Geddes was going to succeed till he was informed the evening before.

   Myself I do not think the appointments are so very bad. Winston Churchill is the great danger, because I cannot believe in his being content to simply run his own show and I am sure he will have a try to have a finger in the Admiralty and War Office pies. We have an assurance that he will not do so, and I do not think that Geddes or I would

[1] Sir Alfred Mond, 1st Baron Melchett (1868–1930), was Liberal M.P. for Chester (1906–10), Swansea (1910–23) and Carmarthen (1924–8): he joined the Conservatives in 1926. He was first Commissioner of Works, 1916–21, and Minister of Health, 1921–2.

[2] Sir Edwin Cornwall (1863–1953) was Liberal M.P. for N.E. Bethnal Green, 1910–22.

stand for it for one moment, but I feel convinced he will try it on. The appointment of Montagu, a Jew, to the India Office has made, as far as I can judge, an uneasy feeling both in India and here, but I, personally, have a very high opinion of his capability and I expect he will do well. There is no doubt that the appointment of Winston and Montagu is a very clever move on Lloyd George's part. He has removed from Asquith his two most powerful lieutenants and he has provided for himself two first-class platform speakers and it is platform speakers we shall require to steady the country which is at present very much rattled by that distinguished body the House of Commons. . . .

49. From Sir Maurice Hankey, *The Supreme Command, 1914–18* (Allen & Unwin, 1961), Vol. II, p. 728. Hankey was secretary to the Cabinet from December 1916.

(*Entry from diary, 15 November 1917.*) . . . War Cabinet at 11.30. I lunched with the Asquiths, having Ll.G.'s consent; . . . Asquith, while talking of the Italian situation, let the cat slip out of the bag, mentioning that he had seen Robertson that morning. I have no doubt that Robertson is intriguing like the deuce. Last night House let slip that Robertson was coming to see him this morning. His private secretary, thinking I was on Robertson's staff, came in to say that Bliss particularly wanted Robertson to repeat to House what he had said to him. Why does Robertson cut the War Cabinet and see House and the Leader of the Opposition? Was it in order to intrigue against the Council? Carson told me this afternoon that he was very sick with Lloyd George's speech and opposed to the Supreme War Council but meant to stick to him because he was the only man to win the war. Had a long talk with Strachey of the *Spectator* who had written a violent article against L.G. I put L.G.'s point of view and he said he was glad he had not seen me before because he would not have written his article.

50. From Lord Riddell, *War Diary* (Ivor Nicholson and Watson, 1933), pp. 309–12.

(*27 January 1918.*) . . . We discussed the political situation. L.G. thinks that the Liberal Party in its old form is a thing of the past and cannot be galvanized into life. He doubts the success of the great efforts now being made by the Liberal organization, who are very busy indeed in all directions. He thinks that it may come to a fight between him and Henderson,[1] and that all Parties, including

[1] Arthur Henderson (1863–1935), Labour M.P. for Barnard Castle (1903–1918), who had resigned from the War Cabinet, August 1917.

Labour, will be split and reconstituted. I said, 'But you must have candidates. You cannot vote without having someone to vote for.' L.G. agreed and said that he had some men coming to see him about the matter tomorrow morning, with the object of forming an organization. He said that he proposed to appoint Beaverbrook to succeed Carson as head of the Department of Information. He asked my opinion. I replied that I thought he would do the work well.

51. Captain F. Guest to Lloyd George, 26 February 1918. 'Secret': from Lloyd George Papers, F/21/2/13.

Notes on the Resolution forwarded by the Unionist War Committee to the Prime Minister.

If you intend to act in the spirit of the above Resolution it will be necessary for you to dismiss Rothermere, Beaverbrook and Northcliffe, as none of them will resign. Beaverbrook would continue to support you and your Government up to, and through, the next General Election. I think Rothermere would feel inclined to do the same. Northcliffe may do anything.

My advice is to stand to your guns, for the following reasons:

1. It is essential that you should stand by your friends and appointments.
2. That out of the eighty members of the Unionist War Group I do not think more than thirty-five would vote against the Government on this question.
3. The other Conservatives will stand by their leaders.
4. I am almost sure that within two or three months at the latest both Rothermere and Beaverbrook will resign; Rothermere on account of ill-health, and Beaverbrook because he will, by that time, have set up for you a perfectly organized Propaganda Department and will want to regain his liberty.

I, however, believe that the agitators have very inconvenient proofs of Sutherland's activities and that, at times, our Press opponents have got the better of him and have given him away. There is also some evidence available to the effect that he has subordinated the interests of your colleagues in his intense loyalty to yourself. An atmosphere has thereby been created which, I fear, cannot fail to accumulate to your disadvantage.

I do not recommend that so loyal a friend should be thrown to the wolves, but I do recommend that he should be instructed to curtail his activities.

When I first took over, last May, I agreed to leave all connection with the London Press entirely in his hands and have, therefore, no responsibility for any of the so-called 'inspirations', but I believe it would be wise that the Whips' Office should resume its traditional function of being the chief repository of information suitable for the Press. Of course I exclude the issue of Government announcements, appointments etc. which bear the official stamp of No. 10.

I have sounded the following Ministers on the general situation and report as follows:

Talbot is anxious to find a way out. He thinks the movement serious, but does not think it will be forced to extremes.

Hewart and *Illingworth* entirely agree with the advice which I submit.

F. E. Smith and *W. S. C.* [Churchill] think that you should stand by your guns.

[Guest goes on to suggest that a Commission might be set up to inquire into the question of newspaper proprietors holding office.]

52. Conversation of Repington with Arthur Henderson, 22 April 1918: from C. à C. Repington, *The First World War, 1914–18. The Personal Experiences of Lieutenant-Colonel C. à C. Repington* (Constable, 1920), p. 278. Repington (1858–1925) was military correspondent to *The Times* and then (from January 1918) the *Morning Post.*

H.'s account of the War Cabinet in his time very illuminating. L.G. was the War Cabinet and nobody else really counted. L.G. threatened to resign like a spoilt child, whenever he was opposed, and as his resignation would have brought the whole Cabinet down the rest always gave way. H. said that L.G. had made Hankey ask Austen Chamberlain and himself for all their Cabinet papers when they left the Cabinet. The course was unusual, but as Chamberlain has assented H. could not do less.

53. From Lord Riddell, *War Diary* (Ivor Nicholson & Watson, 1933), p. 324.

(*Sunday, April 1918.*) ... L.G.: I should describe myself, incongruous as it may appear, as a Nationalist-Socialist. I was and am a strong believer in nationality, and I believe in the intervention of the State to secure that everyone has a fair chance and that there is no unnecessary want and poverty. Of course, there are wasters who must suffer the penalty of their own misconduct; but every member of the community who behaves properly and does his best should be secured a fair chance. That has always been my creed. I don't know that I have altered much.

I have grown more tolerant; I have come to see that usually there is something to be said for the other side. For instance, I have grown to recognize that Dissenters are not always in the right and Anglicans always in the wrong, and that all landlords are not scoundrels of the deepest dye.

R.: But you started with a sympathetic policy for the underdog, and that is still your policy. You may have changed your opinions regarding methods, but the object is still the same.

L.G.: Yes, that is quite true. I have not changed. My policy is still the same.

54. From *The Times*, 7 May 1918. Maurice (1871–1951) had been director of military operations for the Imperial General Staff until April 1918.

To the Editor of The Times

Sir,—My attention has been called to answers given in the House of Commons on April 23 by Mr Bonar Law to questions put by Mr G. Lambert, Colonel Burn, and Mr Pringle as to the extension of the British front in France (Hansard, Vol. 105, No. 34, page 815). These answers contain certain mis-statements which in sum give a totally misleading impression of what occurred. This is not the place to enter into a discussion as to all the facts, but Hansard's report of the incident concludes:

Mr Pringle: Was this matter entered into at the Versailles War Council at any time?

Mr Bonar Law: This particular matter was not dealt with at all by the Versailles War Council.

I was at Versailles when the question was decided by the Supreme War Council, to whom it had been referred. This is the latest of a series of mis-statements which have been made recently in the House of Commons by the present Government. On April 9 the Prime Minister said:

'What was the position at the beginning of the battle? Notwithstanding the heavy casualties in 1917, the Army in France was considerably stronger on the 1st January 1918, than on 1st January 1917.' (Hansard, Vol. 104, No. 24, page 1328.)

That statement implies that Sir Douglas Haig's fighting strength on the eve of the great battle which began on March 21 had not been diminished.

This is not correct.

Again, in the same speech the Prime Minister said:

'In Mesopotamia there is only one white division at all, in Egypt and in Palestine there are only three white divisions, the rest are Indians or mixed with a very, very small proportion of British troops in those divisions—I am referring to the infantry divisions.'

This is not correct.

Now, Sir, this letter is not the result of a military conspiracy. It has been seen by no soldier. I am by descent and conviction as sincere a democrat as the Prime Minister and the last thing I want is to see the Government of our country in the hands of soldiers. My reasons for taking the very grave step of writing this letter are that the statements quoted above are known to be incorrect, and this knowledge is breeding such a distrust of the Government as can only end in impairing the splendid *morale* of our troops at a time when everything possible should be done to raise it.

I have therefore decided, fully realizing the consequences to myself, that my duty as a citizen must override my duty as a soldier, and I ask you to publish this letter in the hope that Parliament may see fit to order an investigation into the statements I have made.

I am yours faithfully,

F. Maurice, Major-General.

20 Kensington Park Gardens, 6 May.

55. Captain Guest to Lloyd George, 20 July 1918. 'Private': from Lloyd George Papers, F/21/2/28. This letter refers to the negotiation of the so-called 'coupon'.

Dear Prime Minister,

I herewith enclose draft of the agreement to be signed by Bonar Law on behalf of the Conservative Party.

You will note that this gives us 98 old seats.

In the new seats in England and Wales we have placed 7 new candidates, in Scotland none, but we have reason to believe that 9 new candidates, who have been placed in the new seats there, will be friendly.

The new candidates have been placed without any rupture with the official Liberal Party, but of course we are prepared to fill up a good many of the claims, which are unpegged out, with your candidates, as soon as:

(1) The Alliance
(2) The Programme

are announced.

This will give you the following Party:

Liberal Ministers	..	..	..	25
Supporters	..	..	..	73
Candidates:				
(a) England & Wales		..	..	7
(b) Scotland	..	..	..	9
				114

In addition to this there are:

Labour Ministers	..	..	8
Labour Supporters, probably		..	7
Victor Fisher candidates			
(For whom you may think it advisable and possible to obtain immunity from the Conservatives)		.. ..	17 (12 already placed)
			146

Yours sincerely,
Frederick Guest.

56. H. A. L. Fisher's *Diary* (Bodleian Library). Fisher (1865–1940), an eminent historian, was a Liberal and President of the Board of Education, 1916–22.

(*6 November 1918.*) ... We talk of Election prospects. L.G. says Asquith has definitely decided not to join. He is too proud. The Coalition must go on. We discuss the programme. He says We must give the Tories something. If they accept Home Rule we must give them something on Fiscals [*sic*]. He suggests saying 'We will not go beyond the Paris resolutions', which were drafted by Runciman. L.G. had criticized these resolutions at the time. The points on which he lays stress are (i) some anti-dumping legislation, (ii) key industries. Churchill says he cannot consent to abnegate his economic creed, though he is willing to acquiesce in temporary measures to meet an emergency. As to H.R., L.G. will offer the exclusion of 6 counties. I raise the question of Carson. L.G. gives satisfactory guarantee about India. He has a sketchy programme of social reform. Nothing said about conscription or League of Nations. Winston raises question of Constitution of Cabinet. Will the War Cabinet continue? L.G. thinks not beyond the War: his idea is a cabinet of about 12. The big body too unwieldy. We point out that L.G.'s strength in bargaining with the Tories is that the Tories can't do without him as P.M.

Drive home with Winston who sees that here is a great split.

From S. D. Waley, *Edwin Montagu* (Asia Publishing House, 1964), pp. 187–90.

Private and Secret

(*Dictated Thursday*, 7 *November*.) . . . The great dinner is over. The guests were Gordon Hewart, Fisher, Addison, Munro, Winston, Freddie Guest and myself, Rufus and Megan [Lloyd George], who left after dinner. Rufus was taken ill at the end of dinner and left after we had gone some little way with the discussion.

....

As to business, he told us that there would be no difficulty at all with the Conservatives about a very advanced social programme, Housing, Land, something far better than had ever been done before in this country, transportation, and so forth. That was all right.

We then came to Tariffs, and he said his policy was Key Industries, Imperial Preference on existing or future taxes and anti-dumping, and he said it was all covered by the Paris Resolutions. Winston, Fisher and I here interposed that the Paris Resolutions went too far and that dumping was good for a country. We all said that we were quite prepared for the sake of the Coalition to sacrifice our principles for the Reconstruction period and as a temporary expedient, and that as a matter of fact it would never be necessary to apply them during that period. The Prime Minister agreed, but pointed out that we must make some sacrifices for the Coalition. I reminded him that we had one asset that the Conservatives have not got, namely, the Prime Minister, who belonged to us, and that they could not get on without him. He liked this and said that he had already told them that they could not poll one-third of the people without him. This, mark you, was the second indication in the course of the evening, his remarks on social reform being the first, that he had already negotiated with the Conservatives, and as he continually read from documents prepared by Philip Kerr, I cannot help being confirmed in my opinion that the whole thing was arranged by him and Bonar Law with Kerr's assistance during their time in Paris. How much could it be otherwise?

He said at one moment rather sharply to Winston, but intending it for us all, that in the course of a few days he was entitled to know who were going on with him and who were not.

We then went to Home Rule, on which he remarked that the only possible Home Rule was Home Rule excluding the six Counties. Fisher urged that he should do a Home Rule Bill on the lines of his letter to the Convention. No; he would not have it. In fact, he really does not want to modify anything in Kerr's notes. We did not get on to a League of Nations or conscription.

Addison asked about War Pledges. He said they must be honoured, but he did not take that view at this morning's Cabinet so far as honouring them now was concerned.

I then said that there was a small country called India about which I was bound to speak. Did he propose to go on with my policy? 'Yes, certainly', he said, 'there was only one man against it.' 'Well', I said, 'you must choose between my policy and the policy of Lord Sydenham.' He said he didn't mean Sydenham, there was only one man in the Government against it. 'Yes', I said, 'but is that one man in the Government going to be coerced?' 'Certainly', he replied. 'Then he does not share Ulster's privilege of never being coerced', I said. 'No', said Lloyd George, with a laugh, 'I shall take pleasure in coercing him.'

That is very satisfactory. I don't know how it will turn out.

Finally it was agreed that a manifesto ought to be issued and Fisher was entrusted with the task of writing such a manifesto.

(*Friday, 8 November.*) . . . Last night I saw Max Beaverbrook. He had got the Lloyd George programme at the end of his tongue and he described it as a complete victory for the Conservatives, the capture of Lloyd George and the abandonment of Free Trade.

He seems to have seen Winston whom he describes as certain to accept anything. He thinks Winston is making a great mistake and it always pays to stick to one's principles. He seems strangely anxious that Winston and I should leave. But, mark the significance, in a moment of indiscretion he disclosed to me the fact which all these notes show that I have long suspected, that a letter was written to Mr Bonar Law by the Prime Minister in Paris embodying the terms and that he, Max, had seen the letter. It does not matter, it is a mere fleabite, it doesn't alter the merits of the question, but every illustration of how we work is food for reflection and for amusement.

57. *To the Electors of Great Britain and Ireland.* The election manifesto of the Coalition government, drafted by Lloyd George and Bonar Law: from *The Times*, 22 November 1918.

Our first task must be to conclude a just and lasting peace and so to establish the foundations of a new Europe that occasions for further war may be for ever averted. . . . To avert a repetition of the horrors of war, which are aggravated by the onward march of science, it will be the earnest endeavour of the Coalition Government to promote the formation of a League of Nations, which may serve, not only to ensure society against the calamitous results of militarism, but to further a fruitful mutual understanding between the associated peoples. . . . The care of the soldiers and sailors, officers and men, whose heroism has won for us this great deliverance, and who return to civil life, is a primary obligation of patriotism. . . . Plans have been prepared, and will be put into execution as soon as the new Parliament assembles, whereby it will be the duty of public authorities and, if necessary, of the State itself to acquire land on simple and economical bases for men who have served in the war. . . .

One of the first tasks of the Government will be to deal on broad and comprehensive lines with the housing of the people which during the war has fallen so sadly into arrears and upon which the well-being of the nation so largely depends.

Larger opportunities for education, improved material conditions, and the prevention of degrading standards of employment; a proper adaptation to peace conditions of the experience which during the war we have gained with regard to the traffic in drink—these are among the conditions of social harmony which we shall earnestly endeavour to promote. It will be the fundamental object of the Coalition to promote the unity and development of our Empire and of the nations of which it is composed. . . . Until the country has returned to normal industrial conditions, it would be premature to prescribe a fiscal policy intended for permanence. We must endeavour to reduce the war debt in such a manner as may inflict the least injury to industry and credit. . . . Fresh taxes ought not to be imposed upon food or upon the raw materials of our industries. At the same time a preference will be given to our Colonies upon existing duties and upon any duties which, for our own purposes, may be subsequently imposed. . . . If production is to be maintained at the highest limit at home, security must be given against the unfair competition to which our industries may be subjected by the dumping of goods produced abroad and sold on our market below the actual cost of production. . . .

It has been recognized by all parties that reform is urgently required in the constitution of the House of Lords, and it will be one of the objects of the Government to create a Second Chamber which will be based upon direct contact with the people, and will, therefore, be representative enough adequately to perform its functions.

The people of this country are not unmindful of the conspicuous services rendered by the Princes and peoples of India to the common cause of civilization during the war. The Cabinet has already defined in unmistakable language the goal of British policy in India to be the development of responsible government by gradual states. To the general terms of that declaration we adhere and propose to give effect.

Ireland is unhappily rent by contending forces, and the main body of Irish opinion has seldom been more inflamed or less disposed to compromise than it is at the present moment. So long as the Irish question remains unsettled there can be no political peace in the United Kingdom or in the Empire, and we regard it as one of the first obligations of British statesmanship to explore all political paths towards the settlement of this grave and difficult question, on the basis of self-government. But there are two paths which are closed—the one leading to a complete severance of Ireland from the British Empire, and the other to the forcible submission of Ulster to a Home Rule Parliament against their will. . . .

D. Lloyd George
A. Bonar Law

58. From J. M. Keynes, *The Economic Consequences of the Peace* (Macmillan, 1919), pp. 127-33. (New edition in 1971.)

On December 6, the Prime Minister issued a statement of policy and aims in which he stated, with significant emphasis on the word *European*, that 'All the European Allies have accepted the principle that the Central Powers must pay the cost of the war up to the limit of their capacity'.

But it was now little more than a week to Polling Day, and still he had not said enough to satisfy the appetites of the moment. On December 8, *The Times*, providing as usual a cloak of ostensible decorum for the lesser restraint of its associates, declared in a leader entitled 'Making Germany Pay', that 'the public mind was still bewildered by the Prime Minister's various statements'. 'There is too much suspicion', they added, 'of influences concerned to let the Germans off lightly, whereas the only possible motive in determining their capacity to pay must be the interests of the Allies.' 'It is the candidate who deals with the issues of to-day', wrote their Political Correspondent, 'who adopts Mr Barnes's phrase about "hanging the Kaiser" and plumps for the payment of the cost of the war by Germany, who rouses his audience and strikes the notes to which they are most responsive.'

On December 9, at the Queen's Hall, the Prime Minister avoided the subject. But from now on, the debauchery of thought and speech progressed hour by hour. The grossest spectacle was provided by Sir Eric Geddes in the Guildhall at Cambridge. An earlier speech in which, in a moment of injudicious candour, he had cast doubts on the possibility of extracting from Germany the whole cost of the war had been the object of serious suspicion, and he had therefore a reputation to regain. 'We will get out of her all you can squeeze out of a lemon and a bit more,' the penitent shouted. 'I will squeeze her until you can hear the pips squeak'; his policy was to take every bit of property belonging to Germans in neutral and Allied countries, and all her gold and silver and her jewels, and the contents of her picture-galleries and libraries, to sell the proceeds for the Allies' benefit. 'I would strip Germany', he cried, 'as she has stripped Belgium.'

By December 11 the Prime Minister had capitulated. His Final Manifesto of Six Points issued on that day to the electorate furnishes a melancholy comparison with his programme of three weeks earlier. I quote it in full:

1. Trial of the Kaiser.
2. Punishment of those responsible for atrocities.
3. Fullest Indemnities from Germany.
4. Britain for the British, socially and industrially.
5. Rehabilitation of those broken in the war.
6. A happier country for all.

Here is food for the cynic. To this concoction of greed and sentiment, prejudice and deception, three weeks of the platform had reduced the powerful governors of England, who but a little while before had spoken not ignobly of Disarmament and a League of Nations and of a just and lasting peace which should establish the foundations of a new Europe.

On the same evening the Prime Minister at Bristol withdrew in effect his previous reservations and laid down four principles to govern his Indemnity Policy, of which the chief were: First, we have an absolute right to demand the whole cost of the war; second, we propose to demand the whole cost of the war; and third, a Committee appointed by direction of the Cabinet believe that it can be done. Four days later he went to the polls.

The Prime Minister never said that he himself believed that Germany could pay the whole cost of the war. But the programme became in the mouths of his supporters on the hustings a great deal more concrete. The ordinary voter was led to believe that Germany could certainly be made to pay the greater part, if not the whole cost of the war. Those whose practical and selfish fears for the future the expenses of the war had aroused, and those whose emotions its horrors had disordered, were both provided for. A vote for a Coalition candidate meant the Crucifixion of Anti-Christ and the assumption by Germany of the British National Debt.

It proved an irresistible combination, and once more Mr George's political instinct was not at fault. No candidate could safely denounce this programme, and none did so. The old Liberal Party, having nothing comparable to offer to the electorate, was swept out of existence. A new House of Commons came into being, a majority of whose members had pledged themselves to a great deal more than the Prime Minister's guarded promises. Shortly after their arrival at Westminster I asked a Conservative friend, who had known previous Houses, what he thought of them. 'They are a lot of hard-faced men', he said, 'who look as if they had done very well out of the war.'

This was the atmosphere in which the Prime Minister left for Paris, and these the entanglements he had made for himself.

59. Edwin Montagu to Lloyd George, 16 December 1918: from Lloyd George Papers, F/40/2/24.

You can now, I think, snap your fingers at all Party hacks and all questions of reward for political services. There has never been an election like this in its one man nature. Somebody said to me the other day that the only speeches in the papers were your speeches, that the thing the country listened to was what you said. That is true.

D. The Lloyd George Coalition (1918-22)

a. The Coalition and Party Politics

60. Montagu to George Lloyd, 25 June 1919: from S. D. Waley, *Edwin Montagu* (Asia Publishing House, 1964), p. 216. Montagu was now Secretary of State for India.

I am glad you don't know this Parliament. You were never very fond of the House of Commons—you would not be fond of this one. It looks in part like a Trades Union Congress, and in other parts like a meeting of a Provincial Chamber of Commerce. All the best of the old men have gone, and as far as the new men—I have not yet seen the Prime Minister of the future. But of course it has not found itself. Its Government has been non-existent.

61. From H. A. L. Fisher's *Diaries*.

(*28 January 1920.*) ... L.G. agitated about a new party. Thinks we can't go on losing by-elections. He has a good programme—Home Rule, Temperance, Purchase of Holdings, Security to Agricultural Tenant. After these measures are passed there will have to be a period of administration.

(*4 February 1920.*) ... [Meeting of Lloyd George at Cobham with Liberal ministers—Macnamara, Kellaway, Shortt, Munro, Addison, Thompson, Sutherland, Hewart, Fisher and Lewis present. Lloyd George sums up.] Liberal labels lead nowhere; we must be prepared to burn them. No one will take the Coalition brew.... Unity of command in France, so here. Impossible to reunite Liberals. Liberalism not enough anyhow to govern the country with etc.

62. From an article by Lord Birkenhead, the Lord Chancellor: from *The Weekly Dispatch*, 1 February 1920.

In the forefront of the programme of the National Party I would put a sane foreign policy, the support of the League of Nations as the security for peace, the strengthening of good relations with all our neighbours—and especially with our Allies in the late war—and, last but not least, the maintenance of a Navy and Army which will secure the Empire, should the League of Nations fail, against the possibility of successful attack from without.

In the second place, I would put the consolidation and development of the Empire.

Next there is the question of Ireland. Of all problems there is none which it is more urgent to settle than the Irish question. It makes difficulties at home, in America, and in the Dominions. In dealing with it I would abide firmly by the three principles laid down by the Prime Minister in his recent speech on Ireland. First, that Southern Ireland must no longer be denied self-government; second, that the solid anti-Home Rule population of Ulster must not be forced under a Dublin Parliament against its will; and third, that the secession of Ireland or any part of Ireland from the British Empire must be resisted to the end. I believe that these principles will be accepted by all those who I think are likely to become members of the National Party.

Finally, there are all the questions which come within the compass of the phrase 'domestic affairs'. Broadly speaking, I would say that the watchword of the National Party should be 'reform', not 'revolution', and 'individual liberty' rather than 'governmental control'. There is no doubt that with good will and good organization and hard work, we can give everybody a better time than they had before the war, and can mitigate the inequalities in wealth and power which lie at the root of so many of our industrial and social problems today.

63. Bonar Law to Balfour, 24 March 1920, from Bonar Law Papers, 96/4/11.

You probably have not taken the trouble to see what has happened in the papers in regard to closer union. What happened was this—L.G. first of all met his Liberal Ministers and he found that they were much more frightened at the idea of losing their identity as Liberals and giving up the name than he had expected. In consequence when he met the Coalition Liberals as a whole he spoke only of the need of closer co-operation. The result of this is that any further step has in the meantime been postponed. What we are thinking of now is getting Resolutions passed by both sections approving of closer co-operation and suggesting that a Committee representative of both sides should be appointed to make proposals for this purpose. The result of this will probably be not to attempt any real fusion of the Parties but get co-operation something on the lines of the Liberal Unionists and Conservatives in the early days. This will be very difficult to arrange effectively and will certainly not be so efficient, but personally I am not sorry at the turn events have taken. I do not like the idea of complete fusion if it can be avoided but I had to come to think, as I think you had also, that it was really inevitable if the Coalition were to continue, but it has always seemed to me more important from L.G.'s point of view than from ours. As a Party we were losing nothing and since the necessity of going slowly in the matter has come from L.G.'s own friends and not from ours I do not regret it.

64. From *Lord Riddell's Intimate Diary of the Peace Conference, and After, 1918–23* (Gollancz, 1933), p. 179.

(*27 March 1920.*) . . . I notice that L.G. has steadily veered over to the Tory point of view. He constantly refers to the great services rendered by captains of industry and defends the propriety of the large share of the profits they have taken. He says one Leverhulme or Ellerman is worth more to the world than say 10,000 sea captains or 20,000 engine drivers, and should be remunerated accordingly. He wants to improve the world and the condition of the people, but wants to do it in his own way.

He seems convinced that Socialism is a mistaken policy. I have observed this conviction growing upon him during the past four years. His point of view has entirely changed.

65. Walter Long to Bonar Law, 8 May 1920; from Bonar Law Papers, 102/5/16. Walter Long, first Viscount Wraxall (1854–1924) was First Lord of the Admiralty.

I hope that the Leamington Meeting[1] will lead to some very different action in the future. If it does not, then I am sure that the break-up of the Coalition is imminent. I want to say two things: first, this result was inevitable. The Coalition Liberals have been content in many cases to retain as their Agents, Chairmen, etc. men who are entirely out of touch with their constituencies and are old-fashioned Asquithian Liberals. These are the men who formed the Leamington Gathering. You could not have a better proof of this than in the return of Hamar Greenwood simultaneously with the affair at Leamington. . . .

[1] Of the National Liberal Federation.

Second, this is our business. We have been patient, self-sacrificing, loyal and what do we find ? Our Liberal colleagues go down to Leamington and ask the audience to believe that they are just as Liberal as ever they were. In other words, that there has been no Coalition, no mutual concessions, but that they have swallowed us.

I hope most sincerely that you will put this very plainly to Lloyd George, because I assure you that if this is to be taken as the real declaration of the policy of the Liberal section of the Coalition it means ruin, not merely for the Coalition but for the country, as a break-up of the Coalition means the triumph of the Labour Party, and in their disorganized condition this means a triumph for the extremists.

66. Memorandum by Sir William Sutherland, 2 January 1922: from Lloyd George Papers, F/35/1/1. Sutherland, Chancellor of the Duchy of Lancaster, was intimately involved in the amassing of the 'Lloyd George Fund'.

I think that, speaking generally, our routine Liberal politicians, especially of the elderly school, over-rate the importance of many of our old party war cries in the modern electorate. All Liberals do a lip service in appropriate areas, to free trade, temperance legislation, education, Home Rule (or Free States) all round etc.; but the things that really matter at the present time are the earnings that can keep a home together, and it is also the question which touches the woman voter—and her enormous importance must be kept in mind in every appeal. It is not suggested that these traditional questions should be ignored, but too much must not be expected of them. They are old horses who have run a lot of races in their time but have hardly got the pace needed today. They mean much to the elderly pundits in Liberal politics, but less to the legions of the new voters, who take these things on their merits as applied to the circumstances they know. The average voters are grim realists today; in only too many cases unfortunately casting about for life lines in their sea of troubles. It is the Asquithian party's failure to realize that so much limits the possible audiences to whom they appeal to people over fifty years of age.

67. H. A. L. Fisher to Lloyd George, 20 March 1922: from Lloyd George Papers, F/16/7/84.

It seems to me to be quite clear that the rank-and-file of the Tory party will never be content until they have tried the experiment of a pure Tory administration. They want to get rid of you and they want to get rid of your Liberal ministers. . . .

Meanwhile the position is disagreeable and humiliating for the Liberals in the Government. The loyalty of our Conservative colleagues in the government is perfect but our colleagues do not command their following and their following wishes us away. I am, therefore, of the opinion that we ought to allow this experiment of a pure Tory government to be tried. It will last for a few months and then when our friends are faced with an Election, they will find that they need our support once more.

My strong view is that your own reputation in the country would gain by resignation and that in a few months' time you would come back again stronger than ever.

I think, however, that the Government is bound to see the present Irish Bills through Parliament and I also attach great importance to Genoa,[1] as furnishing the first substantial opportunity of pacifying Eastern Europe and of bringing Russia into the comity of nations. I am therefore anxious that you should go to Genoa and that you should then resign and take your Liberal ministers with you. I know that some of my Liberal colleagues think differently on this point but I am sure they are wrong and that the fundamental fact of the situation is that the Cabin boy and his following will not have us, until they have been taught by adversity that they cannot float without our support.

68. Hilton Young to Edward Grigg, 23 March 1922: from Lloyd George Papers, F/86/1/35. Hilton Young (1879–1960), Coalition Liberal M.P. for Norwich, was financial secretary to the Treasury, 1921–2. He joined the Conservatives in 1929 and was made Baron Kennet in 1935.

We Liberal coalitionists who follow the P.M. have had no doubt or hesitation about our right course. Our aim was to consolidate the party of the right under his leadership, and under the shadow of his wing, to do what we could to make that party a liberal and not a reactionary party. Hitherto we have not doubted that that could be done in office, and under the form of a coalition.

Recent events have made me, at any rate, doubt whether it can. What happened in the last month?—the most reactionary elements in the Conservative party have pushed the moderate elements, with whom we were working for a common ideal, right off the stage. The moderate are outcrowded and outfaced, and have lost heart. I hear that that is so in the country; I see that it is so in the House. . . .

[1] I.e. the forthcoming international conference in Genoa, to be held in April.

Were the P.M. to come out, the Conservative party would feel at once the dangers of the isolation into which it had been led by yielding to the reactionaries. Many of the guns of the Wee Frees would be spiked in the constituencies. After the Election, he would be free to reform the group of the right on a footing equal to that of its other constituent element.

I feel the strongest impression that this course is now the best possible in order to secure a united coalition, and one that will have a liberal and not a reactionary complexion. . . . I dream of a constitutional union of the Liberal and Conservative parties, within which those parties would work for a common policy, and with a common plan of campaign, as the British and French armies worked in the last year of the war, the P.M. our Foch.

b. The Decline and Fall of Lloyd George

69. From H. A. L. Fisher's *Diary*.

(*2 August 1921*.) . . . P.M. proposes a business Cttee. under E. Geddes to recommend economies. I oppose; so does Churchill, very vehemently; Baldwin also. However the thing is carried. The P.M. writes a note to Mond to tell him to support it. The point is the P.M. is dead tired & wants to throw a sop to Anti-Waste before the recess.

70. From *The Times*, 11 February 1922.

The first and second sections of the report of the Geddes Economy Committee were issued yesterday in two Blue Books. A third report has yet to come. . . . The members of the Committee are Sir Eric Geddes (chairman), Lord Inchcape, Lord Farringdon, Sir J. P. Maclay and Sir W. Guy Granet.

The savings recommended so far total £75,061,875 towards the £100,000,000 which the Chancellor asked the Committee to find, in addition to the savings of £75,000,000 suggested by the Departments. The report shows that the Committee has gone with great thoroughness into the expenditure of the Departments, but the report reiterates again and again that the detailed economies suggested are not exhaustive, and that the recommendations give the 'minimum economies' which should be made. . . .

It is from that standpoint that the Committee recommends savings to the following amounts:

	£
Navy	21,000,000
Army	20,000,000
Air	5,500,000
Education	18,000,000
Health	2,500,000
War Pensions	3,300,000
Trade Group	538,000
Export Credits	500,000
Agricultural Group	855,000
Police and Prisons	1,595,000

£

| Minor Services | 102,000 |
| Net Additional Savings | 1,171,875 |

Total reductions in 1st and
2nd reports   £75,061,875

No account has been taken of economies made possible by the decisions of the Washington Conference.

The principal recommendations and conclusions of the Committee are as follows:

....

EDUCATION

(11) Children under 6 to be excluded from school.

(12) Cost of teaching to be brought down. Alteration of grant system, substituting block payments for percentages.

(13) State-aided or free secondary education for a class that can afford to pay to be reviewed. Free secondary education not to be seriously reduced, but confined to children whose mental calibre justifies it and whose parents cannot afford to pay for it.

(14) Superannuation of teachers to be put on a contributory basis.

HEALTH AND HOUSING

(15) A vigorous policy of sale of subsidized housing.

(16) Revision of burdens of National Health Insurance scheme to reduce the liability of the State.

(17) Tuberculosis, maternity, and child welfare expenditure not to exceed that of the current year. State contributions to be on lump sum and not percentage basis.

UNEMPLOYMENT INSURANCE

(18) Appointment of committee of experts with a view to simplifying unemployment insurance scheme, amalgamating unemployment and health insurance cards, records, and, as far as possible, administration, and exploring possibility of developing unemployment insurance by industry.

(19) Industrial Relations Department and Trade Boards Division to be considered after receipt of report of Lord Cave's Committee; also possibility of transfer to Board of Trade.

(20) Subject to the foregoing, abolition of Unemployment Exchanges and Ministry of Labour should be considered. . . .

71. From *Thomas Jones: Whitehall Diary*, Vol. I, 1916–25 (Oxford, 1969), p. 203.

(*11 July 1922.*) ... Luncheon with the P.M. and Hankey after the Cabinet Meeting. The Cabinet had been discussing the forthcoming debate on Honours and the P.M. was obviously perplexed as to the best line to take and asked my opinion on the Cabinet discussion. I replied that I thought it most difficult to decide what course to take but on the whole I was for his making a statement in the House of Commons on Monday in which he would state that he had continued the practice of his predecessors and in which he should state frankly that the present system is based on rewarding party services and that any alternative would land us in the worst abuses of the States and the Dominions. I should refuse to stand in a white sheet and refuse to go even so far as some of his colleagues desire and appoint a couple of advisers to be interposed between the Whips and the P.M. as an admission of default in the past. He might admit that he had not given that close care to the matter which perhaps he should have done owing to the great pressure of other duties.

... I also referred to the tales current about the way in which Sir William Sutherland used to hawk baronetcies at the Clubs. The P.M. at once remarked that Sutherland had had nothing to do with the recent Honours. He went on to say that the root of the agitation lay in the dislike of the Tories to his (the P.M.) having a party fund of his own. The matter had been raised immediately after he became Prime Minister for that reason. ...

72. Montagu to Lord Reading, 30 November 1921: from S. D. Waley, *Edwin Montagu* (Asia Publishing House, 1964), p. 261.

Politics here at home are in an awful state. We are governed by the Prime Minister who has confidence only in Chamberlain, F.E. and Horne and carries with him Winston because of the necessity of doing so. F.E. has become a very much larger figure of recent months and is really the Prime Minister's right hand man. The Cabinet is hardly ever called together and then only to register decisions. Everything that wants doing is given to one of these people to do; and if you want evidence as to my partiality for your subjects, I am told I care for no political question except Turkey! I have not seen a single one of my colleagues this week and in all probability I shall not. ...

73. From Sir Charles Petrie, *Life and Letters of Austen Chamberlain*, Vol. II (Cassell, 1940), pp. 170–1. Chamberlain was now Lord Privy Seal and leader of the Unionists. (January 1922.)

I am opposed to a dissolution at the present time—
(1) *Because our work is not done.*
    (*a*) Ireland. It would in my opinion be taking grave and unjustifiable risks to leave the new Irish policy incomplete and exposed to all the accidents of the weeks in which every member of the Government would have to be stumping the country instead of governing it.
    (*b*) House of Lords. We are doubly and trebly pledged to reform the House of Lords before a dissolution. It would be discreditable as well as unsafe to dissolve without attempting to deal with this question, and indeed without any agreement among ourselves as to the scope of the reform.
(2) *The time is inopportune.*
    (*a*) Revival of trade is all important. A dissolution with its turmoil and expense would be the worst thing possible for trade.
    (*b*) With such extensive unemployment *that* must be the dominant issue, and the immediate result would be an auction for votes at the taxpayer's expense.
(3) *Party grounds.*
    (*a*) My object has been to lead the Unionist Party to accept merger in a new Party under the lead of the present Prime Minister and including the great bulk of the old Unionists and old Liberals so as to secure the widest and closest possible union of all men and women of constitutional and progressive views. This requires time and careful preparation. No one except myself has ever begun to touch it. An early dissolution would at best find us still a Coalition—which is both unsatisfactory and unpopular—and quite likely two independent and, not improbably, two hostile Parties. I am not sure that the mere talk of dissolution has not made my policy impossible.
    (*b*) The feeling of my Party is almost universally against it.
    (*c*) It would be a gamble in which the only things certain are that the Coalition would lose many seats and that many Unionists would refuse to stand as Coalitionists.

74. Lord Salisbury to Bonar Law, 4 March 1922: from Bonar Law Papers, 107/2/21.

The Prime Minister now is entirely unfitted for his task. Everything to do with Genoa is deplorable: the disorganization of the Foreign Office;

the neglect of America; the estrangement of Great Britain from Great Power after Great Power; the growth of the German-Russian understanding. The Prime Minister's policy in Ireland seems to be almost irretrievable. . . . ['The "Diehard" movement' is one of] honest men who have risked their political reputation.

75. From *Thomas Jones: Whitehall Diary*, Vol. I, 1916–25 (Oxford, 1969), p. 197. Thomas Jones was Deputy-Secretary to the Cabinet; Sir Edward Grigg was Lloyd George's private secretary.

(*28 March 1922*.) . . . Grigg and I went off to luncheon at Gatti's, Grigg full of trouble both about the P.M.'s future and his own. He had written to Criccieth urging the P.M. to resign. I told him it was a month too late and that the P.M. would not be willing to appear to resign as a man defeated by Northcliffe and Rothermere. We both agreed that the P.M. seemed to be losing his punch and grip. Grigg said that three-quarters of the Cabinet were now disloyal to him and that the rot had spread ever since he had made them dance attendance on him at Inverness. Churchill had that morning received messages from Northcliffe and Rothermere urging him to come out as the leader of the Tory Party. Grigg himself had agreed to stay with the P.M. for a year or till the Election, whichever came first. He would carry on till Genoa was over but was anxious to get out. Sometimes one and sometimes another acted without proper co-ordination. Complaints had repeatedly reached him about the treatment of the Court under the present regime. The P.M. went off to Criccieth for three weeks as originally proposed and the King first heard of his departure in the newspapers and sent a hot message to Chamberlain on the morning of his departure to ask, 'Have I a Prime Minister or not?' Grigg very much feared that the P.M. would come back from Genoa with lots of 'Resolutions' and try to run another election on false hopes like that of December 1918.

76. From *The Times*, 7 October 1922. (To the Editor.)

It would serve no useful purpose to criticize or even to consider the circumstances which have led to the present situation. . . . When the Greek forces were annihilated in Asia Minor and driven into the sea at Smyrna, it seems to me certain that, unless a decisive warning had been issued, the Turkish forces flushed with victory would have attempted to enter Constantinople and cross into Thrace. . . .

It would certainly have involved Thrace in horrors similar to those that have occurred in Anatolia, and the probability—indeed I think it is a certainty—of the renewal of war throughout the Balkans.

It was therefore undoubtedly right that the British Government should endeavour to prevent these misfortunes. It is not, however, right that the burden of taking action should fall on the British Empire alone. The prevention of war and massacre in Constantinople and the Balkans is not specially a British interest. It is the interest of humanity. The retention also of the freedom of the Straits is not specially a British interest; it is the interest of the world. We are at the Straits and in Constantinople not by our action alone, but by the will of the Allied Powers which won the war, and America is one of those Powers.

What, then, in such circumstances ought we to do? Clearly the British Empire, which includes the largest body of Mohammedans in any State, ought not to show any hostility or unfairness to the Turks. In the agreement arranged with the Allies in Paris by Lord Curzon, proposals were made to the Turks which are certainly fair to them, and beyond these terms, in my opinion, the Allies ought not to go.

I see rumours in different newspapers, which I do not credit, that the French representations with the Kemalist forces have encouraged them to make impossible demands. The course of action for our Government seems to me clear. We cannot alone act as the policeman of the world. The financial and social condition of this country makes that impossible. It seems to me, therefore, that our duty is to say plainly to our French Allies that the position in Constantinople and the Straits is as essential a part of the Peace settlement as the arrangement with Germany, and that if they are not prepared to support us there, we shall not be able to bear the burden alone, but shall have no alternative except to imitate the Government of the United States and to restrict our attention to the safeguarding of the more immediate interests of the Empire.

Yours truly,
A. Bonar Law.

77. Baldwin's speech to the meeting of Conservative M.P.'s at the Carlton Club, 19 October 1922; from G. M. Young, *Stanley Baldwin* (Rupert Hart-Davis, 1952), pp. 41–2. At this meeting the vote to terminate the Coalition was carried; Lloyd George resigned the same day. Baldwin had been President of the Board of Trade, 1921–2.

As I am only going to speak for a very short time, I will not beat about the bush, but will come right to the root of the whole difficulty, which is the position of the Prime Minister. The Prime Minister was described this morning in *The Times*, in the words of a distinguished aristocrat, as a live wire. He was described to me, and to others, in more stately language, by the Lord Chancellor (Lord Birkenhead) as a dynamic force, and I accept those words. He is a dynamic force, and it is from that very fact that our troubles, in our opinion, arise. A dynamic force is a very terrible thing; it may crush you, but it is not necessarily right.

It is owing to that dynamic force, and that remarkable personality, that the Liberal Party, to which he formerly belonged, has been smashed to pieces; and it is my firm conviction that, in time, the same thing will happen to our party. . . . I think that if the present association is continued, and if this meeting agrees that it should be continued, you will see some more breaking up, and I believe the process must go on inevitably until the old Conservative Party is smashed to atoms and lost in ruins.

78. From C. F. G. Masterman, *The New Liberalism* (Leonard Parsons, 1920), pp. 163–4.

In 1909, in a famous Land Campaign, Liberalism advanced to the attack all along the line. It was this iniquitous system in the towns, far more than any general resentment against the land monopoly of rural England, which gave that campaign its passion and its triumph. And it was the towns which responded to Mr Lloyd George's appeals, and in two successive elections broke the power of the landlords and the House of Lords. The actual and immediate results of that campaign were small. A small tax on increment, a small tax on reversions, a tax on undeveloped land of a halfpenny in the pound, represented perhaps a too scanty harvest for so vigorous a sowing. But the valuation of unused site apart from building was recognized by all as being the centre of the whole matter. Landlords or reformers feared or hoped that the valuation would prove the starting-point of a larger policy. 'This Bill is a beginning', said Mr Lloyd George triumphantly, 'and with God's help it is but a beginning.'

Ten years after, with or without God's help, this Bill was proved to be an end. Liberalism looked on, saddened and amazed, while the new Parliament destroyed all the results of the vigorous campaign. The Coalition dug the grave wide and deep. They flung into it the Land Taxes of Mr Lloyd George, the Land Valuation of Mr Lloyd George, and the Land Policy of Mr Lloyd George. They dumped earth upon it. They stamped down the ground over the grave. They set up a stone to commemorate their victory for testimony to the passing stranger. 'Here, buried for ever, lies the Land Crusade.' And finally—so that there could be no doubt at all as to their triumph—they extorted from the taxpayer of the present every penny which had been paid by the landlords as Land Taxes in the past, and returned two millions of money, as an unexpected windfall to the landlord owners of the increment of the urban lands of Britain. Never, it would seem, was a cause so sensationally and utterly destroyed.

79. C. P. Scott's Diary, 6 December 1922: from C. P. Scott Papers (B.M., Add. MSS., 50906, f. 207–8).

[Lloyd George says] I cannot accept the part often proposed to me of a traitor to Liberalism who can only be taken back as penitent. As a matter of fact the record of Liberal measures passed by the Coaln. Govt. is a fine one—the greatest measure of Irish self-govnt. ever proposed or thought of, a very great measure of franchise extension, a remarkable temperance measure, a not insignificant measure of land reform, which accepts my land valuatn. survey as its basis, an important international agreemt. as to disarmament.

The real ground of attack is the *Land*.

E. The Liberal Decline
(1923-9)

a. Liberal Reunion

80. From Baldwin's speech to the National Unionist Association at Plymouth, 25 October 1923: from *The Times*, 26 October 1923.

Mr Bonar Law's pledge, given a year ago, was that there should be no fundamental change in the fiscal arrangements of the country. That pledge binds me, and in this Parliament there will be no fundamental change, and I take those words strictly. I am not a man to play with a pledge.... Now from what I have said I think you will realize that to me, at least, this unemployment problem is the most crucial problem of our country. I regard it as such. I can fight it. I am willing to fight it. I cannot fight it without weapons. I have for myself come to the conclusion that—owing to the conditions that exist today in the world, having regard to the economic environment, having regard to the situation of our country—if we go pottering along as we are we shall have grave unemployment with us to the end of time. And I have come to the conclusion myself that the only way of fighting this subject is by protecting the home market (loud and continued cheering). I am not a clever man. I know nothing of political tactics, but I will say this: having come to that conclusion myself, I felt the only honest and right thing as a leader of a democratic party was to tell them at the first opportunity I had, what I thought, and submit it to their judgements (cheers).

81. Liberal Party conference communiqué: from *The Times*, 14 November 1923.

Arrangements are now completed for all Liberals to fight the coming election as a united party, both in the constituencies and at headquarters. All candidates will be adopted and described as Liberals, and will be supported by the whole strength of the party, without regard to any past differences.

Mr Asquith and Mr Lloyd George at their meeting this morning settled plans for a campaign in common, and it is already certain that

Liberal candidates will go to the poll in such numbers as to make united Liberalism a practical alternative to the present Government.

The Liberal campaign will open immediately, and there will be a common output of election literature from 42 Parliament St., S.W., and a common list of speakers allocated from Abingdon St., where numbers 21 and 18 are being occupied by the Liberal election organization.

Mr Asquith has invited Mr Lloyd George to speak at the Queen's Hall meeting already arranged for Thursday afternoon, but, in view of the House of Commons debate on the vote of censure, that proves to be impracticable. It is, however, hoped that Mr Fisher will take part.

The early meetings of the campaign will demonstrate to the country the reality of the unity now achieved, and the effectiveness of the united Liberal appeal. A manifesto will be issued dealing with the Protectionist plunge of the Government, with the failure and inefficiency of their foreign policy, and with the Liberal policy for unemployment and other problems of the time.

82. From *The Liberal Party Election Manifesto, 1923 General Election.*

Trade restriction cannot cure unemployment. Post-war conditions do not justify such restriction; they merely render it more disastrous. High prices and scarcity can only lower the standard of living, reduce the purchasing power of the country, and thereby curtail production. An examination of the figures shows that the suggested tariff cannot possibly assist those trades in which unemployment is most rife. The last thing which taxation on imports can achieve is to provide more work for those engaged in manufacture for exports.

Mr Baldwin asks for a blank cheque, and if he is wrong the country must take the risk. He offers no evidence. He formulates no scheme. In the face of declarations made last year by prominent Tariff Reformers, like Mr Bonar Law and Mr Austen Chamberlain, that afterwar conditions make proposals for tariff reform inopportune and injurious, he asks for power to tax an undefined number of commodities, without any disclosure of the scale or range of the duties or the industries to be disturbed.

The Liberal Party is equally convinced that the remedies recommended for unemployment by the Labour Party—Socialism and the Capital Levy—would prove disastrous. What is needed is not the destruction of enterprise, but its encouragement; not the frightening away of capital, but its fruitful use. . . .

Mr Baldwin's sudden plunge has thrown his own supporters into confusion and has firmly united the Liberal forces. The country has now the opportunity of overthrowing a Government whose record is one of unrelieved futility, and of calling for an alternative Administration, which will pursue peace and reconciliation abroad, social and industrial improvement at home, and which is definitely committed to the defence of Free Trade as the best basis upon which to rebuild the life of the nation.

(*signed*) H. H. Asquith
(*signed*) D. Lloyd George.

b. *The Failure of the Last Crusade*

83. Viscount Gladstone to Asquith, 1 August 1924: from Asquith Papers, 147 (Bodleian Library). Herbert, Viscount Gladstone had been party organizer for the Independent Liberals since January 1922.

. . . . Only one thing is possible—to get a business guarantee of sufficient help from L.G.

If we take a firm stand he cannot refuse to give what we reasonably ask. With power to raise a million in cash—given him presumably for political purposes—it is impossible for him to justify refusal in the open. He does refuse so far as we at Abingdon St. are concerned.[1] He cannot refuse you & the party. I suggest to you 2 possible courses. You could send my official letter (enclosed) to L.G. & see him on the subject. I have drawn the letter with that in view. It is just a statement of fact.

Donald [Maclean][2] finally asked if he would guarantee £100,000. Now that figure is too limited & will make finance anxious. We might get through but it would leave us penniless & still at L.G.'s feet. I don't say that I would not accept it. This is the less difficult because my responsibility ends in any case with the Gen. El. But I don't like it to end under such conditions. Therefore I put the figure at £130,000 & we ought to get that. . . .

After all we are not asking for much of an advance for he did in a sort of way agree to contribute. He can afford £130,000 easily. . . .

I detest bothering you but it is sheer necessity.

84. From 'The New Parliament' by 'a Correspondent': from *The Nation*, 13 December 1924, p. 404.

The new House of Commons represents the appearance of a company overwhelmed by an earthquake. . . . As one gazes at these dense masses of desirable citizens one suddenly asks, where is the Liberal Party? For the first time for some two hundred years they have disappeared from the Front Bench altogether. Only after microscopic examination

---

[1] The Independent Liberal headquarters were at 21 Abingdon Street: Lloyd George's 'National Liberal' headquarters were at No. 18.

[2] Donald Maclean (1864–1932) was Liberal M.P. for Bath (1906–10), Peebles & Selkirk (1910–18), Peebles & S. Midlothian (1918–22) and North Cornwall (1929–32). He was parliamentary leader of the Independent Liberals, 1919–22.

could one discover, last Tuesday, in a remote corner of a back bench, Mr Lloyd George's good grey head, flanked by Captain Wedgwood Benn on one side and Sir John Simon on the other. Then other fragments appeared literally lost in a sea of irrelevant Tories and Socialists encompassing them on the right hand and on the left, in front of them and behind. Mr Lloyd George's speech, although a very effective one ... was not well heard and would have been far more effective if delivered down on the floor. One cannot help regretting that a party which inherits the tradition of all our past, hopes for a future and even today represents three million votes, should have scuttled to these remote upper benches from which it can hardly be heard in the galleries. . . .

Mr Lloyd George, speaking from the seat which he occupied twenty-five years ago, and seeing the serried hundreds which he once commanded in utter subservience to his will, now reduced to a tiny party themselves disunited, presented almost a tragic figure. From his first sentence the back benches of the Labour Party commenced to 'barrack' him, and for some time it appeared that they might succeed. . . . But he carried the debate on to a high and unchallengeable level. On the questions of Egypt, of the Protocol, of the League of Nations, of the Inter-Allied debts, of the restoration of British prosperity, he found approval and interest from all quarters. And when he boldly declared enthusiasm for Mr Baldwin's Albert Hall speech, and a promise that the little band of Liberals would give every support to the suggestion of the breaking down of all vested interests in order to improve the condition of the people, he exercised something of the old skill and magic which made him unequalled in the House in former days.

85. David Lloyd George, *Land and the Nation* (Hodder and Stoughton, 1925), pp. 299–300.

CULTIVATING TENURE

THE POLICY.

Division I.

Transfer to New Tenure.

RESUMPTION OF LAND BY STATE

235. On and from an appointed date the State shall be deemed to have resumed possession of all land in the United Kingdom which at that date is used for or capable of use for the production of foodstuffs, timber or other natural products.

This definition shall be regarded as excluding all land which is used as a site for buildings, for the curtilage of buildings, or for gardens attached to or belonging to dwelling houses, and all land in public ownership or dedicated to public use, and all land legitimately used by any individual or company or corporation for the purposes of a business other than agricultural. All land included by the definition is hereafter to be referred to as 'Cultivable Land'.

TRANSFERENCE TO CULTIVATING TENANTS

236. On and from a date to be appointed the State shall have the right to transfer any cultivable land to any person competent to use it to the advantage of the community as a whole.

Every farm holding shall be transferred forthwith to its then tenant, subject to a decision by the competent authority, hereafter to be defined, that the tenant is a person competent to use it for its full productive purpose. The land shall henceforth be held in Cultivating Tenure, as hereafter to be defined, and its holders shall be known as Cultivating Tenants.

This transference shall not be carried out until arrangements are made for a payment of just compensation to the present landowner in the form of an annuity equivalent to the present fair net rent of the land. On and from the appointed date all sales of cultivable land shall be prohibited.

OPTION TO LANDLORD

237. The landlord may, subject to the payment of proper compensation and to any relevant conditions in his lease or agreement with the tenant, take over and himself farm any land which has customarily been occupied as a home farm, or any land which the competent authority considers should in the interests of good cultivation be cultivated by him, and he shall henceforth be the Occupying Owner of that land, provided that proper compensation as defined in the Agricultural Holdings Acts shall be paid to the tenant of such land.

OCCUPIER-OWNED LAND

238. All cultivable land which, at the appointed date, is held in freehold and occupied by a *bona fide* agriculturist, shall be left in the hands of its holder.

The right of the State to secure the proper use of the land for productive purposes shall apply to this as to all other cultivable land, and, accordingly, the competent authority, already referred to, shall have the right to purchase any occupier-owned holding which is found to be

badly farmed in order to transfer it in Cultivating Tenure to a person
or persons able to farm it well.

An occupying owner shall have a right to transfer his holding to
Cultivating Tenure by selling his interests in it to the State on the
terms described in Section 241 of this Report. The terms there described
shall apply to the purchase of occupier-owned holdings taken over as
badly farmed.

An occupying owner shall have the same right of bequest as a Cultivating Tenant (see Paragraph 247) and shall be eligible to benefit by
the system of Credit established and by other schemes undertaken by
the State on the basis of Cultivating Tenure.

86. From J. M. Keynes, 'Liberalism and Industry', in H. L.
Nathan & H. Heathcote Williams, *Liberal Points of View* (Benn,
1927), pp. 205–6, 218–9.

... the subject matter of Liberalism is changing. The destruction of
private monopoly, the fight against Landlordism and Protection, the
development of personal and religious liberty, the evolution of democratic government at home and throughout the Empire—on all these
issues the battle has been largely won.

Today and in the years to come the battle is going to be fought on
new issues. The problems of today are different, and, in the main, these
new problems are industrial or, if you like, economic. Now, this change,
which will be a disturbing thing for all the historic parties, is partly a
result of the victory of democracy, and of the new self-consciousness
and the new organization of the wage-earning classes. But it is not
entirely psychological in its origins. It is due also, I believe, to the
arrival of a new industrial revolution, a new economic transition which
we have to meet with new expedients and new solutions.

The main political problem of today is the safe guidance of the
country through this transition and towards the establishment of an
economically efficient and economically just society in the changed
conditions.

[He goes on to outline the bases of a new industrial policy—the
government to collect and disseminate industrial knowledge; new forms
of industrial partnership between the state and private enterprise;
new roles for the state in the regulation of capital, in promoting social
welfare, and in dealing with the education and mobility of labour.]

Many of those who, without disrespect, I may call the Old Liberals,
are blind to this new problem, are suspicious of and hostile to any
policy directed towards solving it, and they are not ready to co-operate

with Labour on any likely terms. If that is true, it means that on the economic issue they are Conservatives. This is compatible with regaining good Liberals on the old issues—Free Traders, supporters of self-government in democracy, moderation in armaments, the liberty of the subject, and so on—all the great good old causes—it means that they remain good Liberals in respect of the things which mattered most twenty-five years ago, but that they are Conservatives in respect of the new problems which are now in the centre of the picture. . . . In my judgement, that is no sufficient purpose for a Liberal Party, no reason why it should continue to exist, except to contribute, firstly, to international peace in all its aspects, and, secondly, to the gradual evolution of a reformed economic society which shall be acceptable, just and efficient in the changed conditions of the age. The test of a man's Liberalism today must be not his attitude towards the questions which were important a generation ago, but to those which are most important to the generation coming.

87. David Lloyd George, *We Can Conquer Unemployment* (Cassell, 1929). This was actually written by William Wallace.

(*pp. 51–3.*)

IX

WORK FOR THE WORKLESS, NOW

We have felt it advisable to refer thus briefly to these numerous directions in which work of national development is called for outside of the six groups upon which attention is here mainly concentrated; and to point out that whilst we consider this policy of national development to be of paramount immediate importance, it forms only part of a larger whole. Having done this, we return to our main theme, namely, the provision of work for the workless, now.

Adopting a reasoned and balanced view throughout, and stating the details for consideration, we have outlined proposals which we believe will provide a great volume of useful employment over a period of years. In particular, we have shown how by work of necessary development in six chosen spheres alone, work can be directly provided in the following estimated proportions, the figures summarizing the effect of the proposals given in detail above.

Estimated additional work for a year in Great Britain for the number of men below, directly provided as a result of our detailed proposals under six specific heads, and apart from indirect results:

	Within the First Year from the Schemes Starting Work.	Within the Second Year.
Roads and Bridges	350,000	375,000
Housing	60,000	60,000
Telephone Development ..	60,000	60,000
Electrical Development ..	62,000	62,000
Land Drainage	30,000	30,000
London Passenger Transport	24,000	24,000

EMPLOYMENT UNDER OTHER HEADS

This, as we have said, is the additional employment estimated only under these six heads where proposals have been worked out in detail. Other directions in which employment will be directly provided under the policy we put forward include—

(1) work on arterial drainage on which, on the conditions mentioned, there might be employed, within six months, 50,000 men, this rising within a limited period to a much higher figure;
(2) the re-conditioning of houses;
(3) the improvement of canals;
(4) afforestation;
(5) reclamation;
(6) land settlement;
(7) increased employment upon the land when the cultivator is secure in his position and assured of his market;
(8) work resulting from re-opening of trade relations with Russia.

INDIRECT EFFECTS ON EMPLOYMENT

In all this, so far, we have taken no account of the large increase in employment everywhere resulting indirectly from the addition to the national purchasing power represented by the wages of those workers directly employed in this way. The income of every one of these will have increased twice or thrice; and this will be reflected at once in a corresponding increase in expenditure on food, clothing, boots, housing, travelling, entertainment, and other amenities. As a result, a stimulus will be given to the whole of the industry and commerce of the country, reflected, in turn, in increased employment.

Again, we have included in our figures those employed in industries directly supplying the materials to be used in our national development schemes, but not those less directly affected. Thus, while we have included those working on roads, we have not included those making the additional vehicles which in consequence will come upon those roads; those building houses, but not those making the furniture and carpets for those houses; those installing electric generating plant and cables, but not those manufacturing the lamps and fittings which will be used at the ends of those cables.

After taking all these things into account, we have every confidence that **within three months of a Liberal Government being in power, large numbers of men at present unemployed could be engaged on useful work of national development; and that within twelve months the numbers unemployed would be brought down to normal proportions.**

Statistical evidence shows the normal pre-war percentage of unemployment to have been some 4.7 per cent. Applied to the present insured population this represents about 570,000.

We should not, of course, rest satisfied with that, but should resume that policy which Liberalism was pursuing up to the outbreak of war, designed to reduce and mitigate still further the burden of normal unemployment.

To summarize: **Unemployment is industrial disorganization. It is brought to an end by new enterprise, using capital to employ labour. In the present stagnation the Government must supply that initiative which will help to set going a great progressive movement.**

(*pp. 60–2.*)

A SUMMARY OF THE FINANCIAL EFFECT

This, then, is the situation. We have certain expenditure on telephone, electrical and transport development which, over a due period, can be justified as an ordinary commercial proposition. Some slight assistance in the way of reduced interest may be required in the first two or three years but this can be recouped later. We have certain road expenditure offering no direct financial return, though a large indirect return in savings to the nation in cost of transport and otherwise. But to meet the interest and sinking fund on the loan to finance this, we have a steady increase in receipts from motor vehicle taxation year by year, which increase alone at the present level of taxation, together with receipts from betterment, **is likely to be sufficient to meet interest and repay the whole State expenditure within a comparatively short period of years. All this work therefore, makes no drain on the Exchequer.** In the housing work there is an increased annual charge for subsidy; but this is well within the limits envisaged by

Parliament in 1924 as a proper charge from a housing as distinct from an unemployment point of view. Finally there is the cost of land drainage. This will be contributed to by the landowner to the extent to which benefit has accrued to specific land, but a large part of the cost must fall upon the State, particularly in the case of schemes of arterial drainage. This last is the only new new additional charge upon the Exchequer.

Against this is to be set:

(1) **a direct saving to the Unemployment Benefit Fund of many millions of pounds. Taking, again, for the purpose of our illustration, the same figure of a reduction of 750,000 in numbers unemployed, the saving to the Fund would be from £25,000,000 to £30,000,000 during each of the first two years in which the scheme operates, resulting in the repayment to the Treasury well within these two years of the full debt owing, which at present is over £31,000,000.** This is quite apart from any future saving resulting from the general stimulus given to industry;

(2) **an increase in receipts from existing taxation of some £10,000,000 to £12,000,000 per annum.**

This takes no account of indirect increases in tax receipts resulting from the general stimulus to industry, such as increased profits of shopkeepers and others as a result of the substantial increase in purchasing power; and no account of reduction in poor law relief, nor in cost of health and similar services resulting from the increased well-being of the worker.

Leaving out of account, for the moment, the great contribution to human welfare resulting from the provision of work, does this policy look as if it would 'pay' as a mere business proposition, or does it not?

It is obvious that it must. **So, by a longer argument, we have come back to our first, and not very surprising, conclusion, that it pays a community better to have its citizens working than to have them idle!**

XII

THE ALTERNATIVES

We have shown that reliance upon long-period remedies alone is a cruel and wasteful process and we have outlined a bold programme, which we are confident will reduce unemployment to normal proportions, and give a stimulus to industry which will set it on the high road to prosperity. What are the alternatives?

WAGE REDUCTION

The first is an all-round cut in wages brought about by increased financial restriction. That we condemn.

INFLATION

The second is inflation. Inflation, whilst it would temporarily solve our problem, would mean the departure from the gold standard, a reduction in the real standard of life of those at present employed, and the grave risk of economic collapse in the long run. It can be entirely ruled out.

PROTECTION

The third is Protection. But (apart from all other objections) Protection cannot give assistance where assistance is needed, namely, to the export industries. Moreover, any assistance which might be given could only be at the expense of a reduction in the general standard of life. All-round Protection means an all-round increase in the cost of living, which is only a roundabout way of reducing real wages. **Safeguarding is the protection of inefficiency at the expense of the rest of the community.** Standard of life must depend ultimately on efficiency, because there is nothing else upon which it can depend.

NATIONALIZATION

The last is Nationalization. Nationalization means running an industry by the State either as an independent and self-supporting concern, or as one subsidized by the taxpayer. In the former case, the question of whether in consequence it will be able to absorb more labour depends upon whether it is likely to be run more efficiently than by private enterprise; and all judgment and experience is against that hypothesis, at any rate, so far as concerns the industries which are suffering to-day. If it is to be subsidized, then, of course, the only limit to its capacity to absorb labour is the taxpayer's purse; but this again is just making possible uneconomic operation in one industry at the expense of others elsewhere.

THE PRESENT GOVERNMENT'S POLICY

There are no other alternatives. The fundamental choice is between the great Liberal Programme of National Development and another five years of Trade Depression under a Tory Government.

88. Memorandum by Donald Maclean, 30 July 1929: from Herbert Gladstone Papers (B.M., Add. MSS., 46474, ff. 218–22). Donald Maclean was now Liberal M.P. for North Cornwall.

My first impression as to the rank-and-file of the Liberal Party in the House has been amply confirmed. The quality is excellent, and it is clear that although over 80 per cent of them must have received assistance, in part or in whole, from the Ll.G. Fund for the Election, very few of them regard themselves as being in any way tied by any special obligation to the holder of the Fund.... There is enough material there to form an effective Opposition not far short of the Irish Party—I will not say in its best days, but certainly well up to the normal effectiveness of that famous fighting body, and anyhow vastly superior to anything that the Labour Party could turn out. Our Front Bench has intervened with unvarying success—Walter Runciman particularly good on Free Trade, Tudor Walters on Housing and Samuel at the top of his form. Norman Birkett deeply impressed the House by his handling late at night of a minor incident connected with a boy at Election time by some Labour bullies. Lloyd George has been, for him, very quiet, but effective—notably his cross-examination of Jim Thomas was a work of art. No dissension of any kind is yet apparent....

The Party meetings are very well attended, the discussion free, and suggestions put forward by the leaders freely but respectfully criticized. More than once, Ll.G.'s first proposal has been so modified as to be almost reversed. I must say that his chairmanship has been tactful, conciliatory and, thus far at any rate, open and above board.

Memorandum by Maclean, 22 December 1929 (f. 229).

The most interesting feature is the undoubted revival of the power and prestige in the House as a debater of Lloyd George.

89. Special Mission to Europe of Sumner Welles, Under-Secretary of State: from *Foreign Relations of the United States*, Diplomatic Papers, 1940 (U.S. Department of State), pp. 85–6.

LONDON, March 13, 1940.
With the Ambassador I called upon Mr Lloyd George at his apartment at 10.30 A.M.

I had not seen Mr Lloyd George for 17 years, but he has changed very little in the intervening period, although he has now reached the age of 77 years. He is alert, mentally very keen, and minutely familiar with every detail of both British domestic affairs and British Foreign Relations. The only sign of his increasing years is shown by his tendency to talk of earlier years, and his extreme loquacity.

I was with him for nearly two hours.

Mr Lloyd George immediately referred to the present war as the most unnecessary war, the most insanely stupid war, that had ever been forced upon England....

He said that Great Britain had blundered into this war because of the egregious mistakes in policy of her recent Governments. He stated that there was no reason, from the standpoint of either Great Britain or France, why Germany should not unite under one Government the Germanic peoples of Central Europe, or why Germany should not obtain and enjoy a special economic position in Central Europe, and, at least in part, in Southeastern Europe. If the German people were thus granted the recognition of their racial unity and of their economic security, such problems as disarmament, a possible European regional federation, and colonies, would automatically settle themselves. What was the key to the problem was the need to convince the German people that they had an equality of opportunity with the other great nations, that justice had been done them, and that they could look ahead with 'confident hope' to the future. The policy of Great Britain and of France during the past years had achieved exactly the reverse.

Forgetting, apparently, his own direct responsibility for the terms of the Versailles Treaty, Mr Lloyd George inveighed bitterly against the terms which had to do with German frontiers. He referred to the separation of East Prussia from Greater Germany by the Polish Corridor as 'damnable', and spoke of the arrangement covering the institution of the Free City of Danzig—which he referred to as a completely German city—as a 'criminal farce'.

He spoke with particular bitterness of French policy towards Germany since 1921. All in all, it was his opinion that no policy could have been more criminally stupid than that pursued by the present Allies towards Germany during recent years.

He felt that it was not too late to remedy the mistakes, and repair the irreparable disasters which would result from a long-drawn out war of attrition, or a war of devastation. The territorial and political questions should present no real obstacles; the economic postulates for a sane world commercial and financial relationship could be established with the aid of the United States; the problem of security could then be determined through disarmament and international control of armament. If the opportunity were offered the British people now for a peace built upon these terms, the overwhelming majority of them would enthusiastically support such a peace, and he himself would publicly support it up and down the length and breadth of the land.

'Do not believe them', he said, 'when they tell you that the British people want this war. I know them, and I know they do not—they want security, and if they can obtain it on the terms I have mentioned, they will demand peace.'

Mr Lloyd George spent most of the time talking of the last war, and of his Prime Ministership. He spoke of President Wilson with respect, but with no particular enthusiasm, and of French statesmen with neither respect nor enthusiasm.

Mr Lloyd George expressed the conviction that if peace were restored as the result of an understanding of the kind he had mentioned, between Great Britain, France, Germany and Italy, Russia would once more withdraw from active participation in Western European affairs, and afford no problem of any real gravity.

A NOTE ON FURTHER READING

There is, as yet, no wholly satisfactory full-length biography of Lloyd George. The best at present are Malcolm Thomson, *David Lloyd George* (London, 1949), and Thomas Jones, *Lloyd George* (London, 1951). There is much valuable raw material in Frank Owen, *Tempestuous Journey* (London, 1954), though the book as a whole is disappointing. For Lloyd George's early career, see W. Watkin Davies, *Lloyd George, 1863–1914* (London, 1939). There is some useful personal information in William George, *My Brother and I* (London, 1958) and Frances Lloyd-George, *The Years that are Past* (London, 1967). Short studies of Lloyd George include A. J. P. Taylor, *Lloyd George: Rise and Fall* (London, 1961); Kenneth O. Morgan, *David Lloyd George: Welsh Radical as World Statesman*, Cardiff, 2nd edition, 1964; and C. L. Mowat, *Lloyd George* (Oxford, 1964). Some major aspects of his career are dealt with in A. J. P. Taylor (ed.), *Lloyd George: Twelve Essays* (London, 1971).

Among the studies of some other leading Liberals in this period are Robert Rhodes James, *Rosebery* (London, 1963); José F. Harris and Cameron Hazlehurst, 'Campbell-Bannerman as Prime Minister', *History* (October, 1970); Roy Jenkins, *Asquith* (London, 1964); Cameron Hazlehurst, 'Asquith as Prime Minister, 1908–1916', *Eng. Hist. Rev.* (July, 1970); D. A. Hamer, *John Morley* (London, 1968); Randolph S. Churchill, *Winston S. Churchill* Vols. I & II (London, 1966 and 1967: subsequent volumes by Martin Gilbert); Lucy Masterman, *C. F. G. Masterman* (London, new edition 1968); L. Ó'Broin, *The Chief Secretary: Augustine Birrell in Ireland* (London, 1969); S. D. Waley, *Edwin Montagu* (Bombay, 1964); Trevor Wilson (ed.), *The Political Diaries of C. P. Scott* (London, 1970).

For aspects of Liberalism in the constituencies, see Henry Pelling, *Social Geography of British Elections, 1885–1910* (London, 1967); Paul Thompson, *Socialists, Liberals and Labour* (London, 1967); P. F. Clarke, *Lancashire and the New Liberalism* (Cambridge, 1971); Janet Howarth, 'The Liberal Revival in Northamptonshire, 1880–95', *Hist. Jnl.*, XII, I (1969); Kenneth O. Morgan, *Wales in British Politics, 1868–1922* (Cardiff, 2nd edition, 1970); idem., 'Cardiganshire Politics: the Liberal Ascendancy, 1885–1923', *Ceredigion* (1967); James G. Kellas, 'The Liberal Party and the Scottish Church Disestablishment Crisis', *Eng. Hist. Rev.* (January 1964); idem., 'The Liberal Party in Scotland, 1876–1895', *Scottish Hist. Rev.* (April, 1965).

For aspects of the period 1890–1915, see Peter Stansky, *Ambitions and Strategies* (Oxford, 1964); D. A. Hamer, 'The Irish Question and Liberal Politics, 1886–1894', *Hist. Jnl.*, XII, III (1969); H. W. McCready, 'Home Rule and the Liberal Party', *Irish Hist. Stud.* (September, 1963); Bernard Semmel, *Imperialism and Social Reform* (London, 1960); Bernard Porter, *Critics of Empire* (London, 1968); Asa Briggs, *Seebohm Rowntree*, (London, 1961); Henry Pelling, *The Origins of the Labour Party, 1880–1900* (London, 1954); Frank Bealey and Henry Pelling, *Labour and*

Politics, 1900–1906 (London, 1958); Philip Poirier, *The Advent of the Labour Party* (London, 1958); Henry Pelling, *Popular Politics and Society in Late Victorian Britain* (London, 1968). For social reform, see Bentley Gilbert, *The Evolution of National Insurance in Great Britain* (London, 1967); and Sir Henry Bunbury (ed.), *Lloyd George's Ambulance Wagon* (London, 1957). For Liberal views of foreign affairs, see A. J. P. Taylor, *The Trouble Makers* (London, 1957). An important study is Cameron Hazlehurst, *Politicians at War, July 1914 to May 1915* (London, 1971).

For the period after 1915, a work of immense value is Trevor Wilson, *The Downfall of the Liberal Party, 1914–35* (London, 1966), which is, however, somewhat marred by persistent animus against Lloyd George throughout. The works of an eye-witness but to be used with caution are Lord Beaverbrook's three volumes, *Politicians and the War, 1914–16* (London, new edition, 1960); *Men and Power, 1917–18* (London, 1956); and *The Decline and Fall of Lloyd George* (London, 1963). For the war years, see J. P. Mackintosh, *The British Cabinet* (1962); A. J. P. Taylor, *Politics in Wartime* (London, 1964); Cameron Hazlehurst, 'The Conspiracy Myth', in M. Gilbert (ed.), *Lloyd George* (London, 1968); Robert Blake, *The Unknown Prime Minister* (London, 1955); A. M. Gollin, *Proconsul in Politics* (London, 1964); Randolph S. Churchill, *Lord Derby, King of Lancashire* (London, 1959); K. Middlemas (ed.), *Thomas Jones: Whitehall Diary, Vol. I, 1916–25* (Oxford, 1969); S. K. Roskill, *Hankey: Man of Secrets, Vol. I* (London, 1970). For the post-war period, see Kenneth O. Morgan, 'Lloyd George's Premiership', *Hist Jnl.*, XIII, I (1970); Susan Armitage, *The Politics of Decontrol in Industry* (London, 1969); *The History of the Times, IV* (London, 1952); K. Middlemas and John Barnes, *Baldwin* (London, 1969); K. Middlemas (ed.), *Thomas Jones: Whitehall Diary, Vol. II, 1926–30* (Oxford, 1969); R. Rhodes James, *Memoirs of a Conservative* (London, 1969); Roy Harrod, *Life of John Maynard Keynes* (London, 1951); Robert Skidelsky, *Politicians and the Slump* (London, 1968); and Thomas Jones, *A Diary with Letters, 1931–50* (Oxford, 1954).

Among the major works that have appeared since this book was completed are Robert Blake, *The Conservative Party from Peel to Churchill* (Oxford, 1970); Keith Robbins, *Sir Edward Grey* (London, 1971); Maurice Cowling, *The Impact of Labour, 1920–1924* (Cambridge, 1971); and A. J. P. Taylor (ed.), *Lloyd George: a Diary by Frances Stevenson* (London, 1971). An edition of *Lloyd George's Family Letters*, edited by Kenneth O. Morgan, will appear in 1972. Two major biographies of Lloyd George, by Cameron Hazlehurst and John Grigg respectively, are currently being prepared.